THE WORLD ALMANAC OF PRESIDENTIAL FACTS

THE WORLD ALMANAC® OF
PRESIDENTIAL
FACTS

LU ANN PALETTA
AND FRED L. WORTH

WORLD ALMANAC

AN IMPRINT OF PHAROS BOOKS • A SCRIPPS HOWARD COMPANY

NEW YORK

Cover design: Nancy Eato
Interior design: C. Linda Dingler
Cover illustration: John Lane

First published in 1988.

Distributed in the United States by Ballantine Books, a division of Random House, Inc., and in Canada by Random House of Canada, Ltd.

Library of Congress Cataloging-in-Publication Data:

Paletta, Lu Ann
    The world almanac of presidential facts/Lu Ann Paletta and Fred L. Worth.
        p.   cm.
    Includes index.
    Pharos Books ISBN 0-88687-310-X; ISBN 0-88687-326-6 (pbk.)
    Ballantine Books ISBN 0-345-34888-5; ISBN 0-345-34977-6 (pbk.)
        1. Presidents—United States—Miscellanea. 2. United States—Politics and government—
    Miscellanea. I. Worth, Fred L. II. Title.
E176.1.P34 1988
973'.09'92—dc19
[B]   87-17771
                                                                                                  CIP

Printed in the United States of America

World Almanac
An Imprint of Pharos Books
A Scripps Howard Company
200 Park Avenue
New York, NY 10166

10 9 8 7 6 5 4 3 2 1

Dedication

Lu Ann Paletta:

For M & D
L.F.U.O.D.

Fred L. Worth:

To my friend Steve Tamerius

CONTENTS

EDITOR'S NOTE

In compiling THE WORLD ALMANAC OF PRESIDENTIAL FACTS the authors have done a fine job finding facts that will entertain and inform at the same time. This volume is not intended as a totally comprehensive study of the presidents, however. For instance, in the presidential profiles, under the heading Home (or Homes), you will find listed the primary residence and perhaps another if it tells an interesting story, but the listing by no means covers all the homes in which that president lived. Others volumes must be consulted for such details. We do believe, however, that this volume will bring the nation's presidents to life in a way that other books do not.

ACKNOWLEDGMENTS

Special thanks to Denise Adams, Marion Boos, Eleanor Ozbolt, Christine Vrabel and Michael Granito. Research assistance was provided by the Porter (Westlake), Cuyahoga County, and Cleveland Public Libraries and the American Political Item Collectors. Special recognition also goes to the Doctors Three.

THE WORLD ALMANAC OF PRESIDENTIAL FACTS

PRESIDENTIAL PROFILES

GEORGE WASHINGTON

First president

1789-97

The Straight Facts

Born: February 22, 1732
Birthplace: Westmoreland County, Virginia
Ancestry: English
Physical Characteristics; 6'2" tall, blue eyes, brown hair, 200 lbs.
Religion: Episcopalian
Occupation: Surveyor, planter

Wife: Martha Dandridge Custis Washington (1731-1802)
Date of Marriage: January 6, 1759
Children: None; wife had two children by first marriage
College: None
Military History: General, Continental Army
Political Party: Federalist
Previous Political Offices: Member, Virginia House of Burgesses (1758-74); Justice of the peace, Fairfax County (1770); Delegate, First Continental Congress (1774); Delegate, Second Continental Congress (1775); Delegate, Constitutional Convention (1787)
Vice-President: John Adams
Died: December 14, 1799, at Mount Vernon, Virginia
Burial Place: Family vault, Mount Vernon, Virginia
Firsts: First president to be born in Virginia
First general to serve as president
First president to take oath of office in two different cities
First president to be younger than his wife
First Federalist president
Biography in Brief: George Washington, first president, was the son of Augustine Washington and Mary Ball. His father died when George was 11. He studied mathematics and surveying and when 16 went to live with his half brother Lawrence, who built and named Mount Vernon. He accompanied Lawrence to Barbados, West Indies, contracted smallpox, and was deeply scarred. Lawrence died in 1752 and George acquired his property by inheritance. He valued land, and when he died owned 70,000 acres in Virginia and 40,000 acres in what is now West Virginia.

Washington's military service began in 1753 when Governor Robert Dinwiddie of Virginia sent him on missions deep into Ohio country. He clashed with the French and had to surrender Fort Necessity July 3, 1754. He was an aide to Gen. Edward Braddock and at his side when the army was ambushed and defeated on a march to Fort Duquesne, July 9, 1755. He helped take Fort Duquesne from the French in 1758.

After his marriage to Martha Dandridge Custis, a widow, in 1759, Washington managed his family estate at Mount Vernon. Although not at first for independence, he opposed British exactions and took charge of the Virginia troops before war broke out. He was made commander-in-chief by the Continental Congress June 15, 1775.

The successful issue of a war filled with hardships was due to his leadership. He was resourceful, a stern disciplinarian, and the one strong, dependable force for unity. He favored a federal government and became chairman of the Constitutional Convention of 1787. He worked for the ratification of the Constitution and was inaugurated as president of the United States, April 30, 1789, on the balcony of New York's Federal Hall.

He was reelected 1792, but refused to consider a third term and retired to Mount Vernon.

This Federalist cartoon shows Washington and his federal chariot heading off an invasion by French Republican "cannibals." At the right, Jefferson and friends try to block the wheels and a dog lifts his leg on a Republican newspaper.

The More Colorful Facts

Astrological Sign: Pisces

Nicknames: Atlas of America, Deliverer of America, Farmer President, Father of His Country*, Flower of the Forest, Freedom's Favorite Son, The Hero Who Defended the Mothers Will Protect the Daughters, Hero of American Independence, Old Fox, Old Muttonhead†, Sage of Mount Vernon, Stallion of the Potomac, Surveyor President, Sword of the Revolution.

Original Family Name: De Wessyngton. The roots of his ancestors can be traced to Crinian, Hereditary Lay Abbot of Dunkenfeld, ca.1000 A.D.

Family Motto: *Exitus Acta Proba* (the end justifies the means)

Presidential Notes: GW's neighbor in Alexandria, Virginia, Richard Conway, lent him $600 to attend his own inaugural as the first president of the U.S.

The first president to be depicted on a postage stamp, a ten-cent stamp issued in 1847.

The first U.S. anthem, "God Save Great Washington," was set to the tune of "God Save the King."

---

*The first reference to GW as "Father of His Country" was as *Des Landes Vader* in a 1779 German almanac.

†Given to him by Vice-president John Adams.

GW's second inaugural address, only 133 words long, is the shortest on record. It took only two minutes to deliver.

Family Notes: GW's nickname for wife Martha was "Patsy."

GW always wore a miniature of Martha around his neck.

Namesakes: George Washington Bridge, which spans the Hudson River between Manhattan, New York, and Fort Lee, New Jersey.

Washington Monument, a 555-foot, 5⅛-inch obelisk. Designed by Robert Mills, it is the tallest masonry structure in the world. Built from 1848 to 1885, the monument was dedicated on February 21, 1885, and opened to the public on October 9, 1888.

Washington College (now Washington and Lee College), located in Lexington, Virginia.

Washington, D.C., the capital of the U.S.

Washington, the state, is the only one in the U.S. named after a president.

Washington, Georgia, the first town to be named at its origin after a U.S. president, received its charter on January 23, 1780.

Washington, North Carolina, originally Fork's of Tar River, was the first city named after George Washington, changing its name on November 5, 1775.

Washington Pie, a cake with layers put together with jam or jelly filling, custard or the like.

U.S.S. *George Washington,* the first U.S. ballistic missile submarine, launched at Groton, Connecticut, on June 9, 1959.

Also named after Washington are 33 counties, 120 villages or towns, 7 mountains, 8 streams, 10 lakes, and 9 colleges.

Stamp: Washington Bicentennial Issue: 12 postage stamps issued in honor of GW's 200th birthday, 1932.

Washington Birthday Issue, a five-cent stamp issued in honor of GW's 240th birthday, February 22, 1962.

Homes: Mount Vernon, 2,500-acre estate located 15 miles south of Washington, D.C., which GW inherited in 1761 upon the death of his brother's wife. By the time of his death in 1799, the landholdings had increased to 8,000 acres, making him one of the largest landholders in the young United States.

Other Positions: GW's first job was as a surveyor, at the age of 16. He was employed by Lord Thomas Fairfax, a wealthy landowner.

Surveyor of Culpepper County, Virginia, appointed July 20, 1749.

Patron of the Friendship Fire Company in Alexandria, Virginia. In 1799, the year of his death, GW helped put out a fire with the volunteers, using the small four-wheeled pumper which he had purchased for them.

Early Love Life: Sally Carey Fairfax, the wife of his neighbor and friend, (George) Will(iam) Fairfax, was supposedly the most passionate love of his life.

Boot Size: 13

Favorite Foods: Crabmeat soup, egg nog

Favorite Sport: Fox hunting

Favorite Christmas Carol: "While Shepherds Watched Their Flock by Night"

False Teeth: GW's first pair was made of hippopotamus ivory.

Cherry Tree Legend: This, plus many other fictitious accounts, originated from *The Life of George Washington; With Curious Anecdotes, Equally Honorable to Himself and Exemplary to His Young Countrymen,* the best-selling book by a clergymen, Mason Locke Weems, first published in 1800.

Last Hours: When James Craik, his personal physician and chief surgeon of the Continental Army, was called to GW's deathbed, he had already bled himself and was regularly checking his pulse. Craik diagnosed the illness as "inflamatory quinsy" (inflamed sore throat). GW died about 14 hours after Craik arrived.

Last Words: "Doctor, I die hard, but I am not afraid to go."

Eulogy: Delivered by Light Horse Harry Lee, a Revolutionary War patriot and governor of Virginia, and father of Robert E. Lee. In it he coined the phrase describing GW as "First in war, first in peace, and first in the hearts of his countrymen."

Burial Rite: According to family history, GW insisted that he be embalmed in whiskey for three days after his death, just to be sure he was really gone, before they buried him.

JOHN ADAMS
Second president
1797-1801

The Straight Facts

Born: October 30, 1735
Birthplace: Braintree (now Quincy), Massachusetts
Ancestry: English
Physical Characteristics: 5'7" tall, brown eyes, brown hair, 190 lbs.
Religion: Unitarian
Occupation: Schoolteacher, lawyer
Wife: Abigail Smith Adams (1744-1818)
Date of Marriage: October 25, 1764
Children: Two daughters, three sons
College: Harvard University, class of 1755
Military History: None
Political Party: Federalist
Previous Political Offices: Member, Massachusetts legislature (1768); Member, Revolutionary Provincial Congress of Massachusetts (1774); Delegate, First Continental Congress (1774); Delegate, Second Continental Congress (1775); Member, Massachusetts Constitutional Convention (1779); U.S. minister to France (1779); U.S. minister to Netherlands (1780-1785); U.S. minister to Great Britain (1785-1788); Vice-president of the United States (1789-97).
Vice-President: Thomas Jefferson
Died: July 4, 1826, in Quincy, Massachusetts
Burial Place: First Unitarian Church, Quincy, Massachusetts
Firsts: First vice-president to be elected to presidency
First president born in Massachusetts
First president to live in the White House
First president to serve only one term
First president to be defeated for reelection
First and only president whose son would later become president
Biography in Brief: John Adams was the son of John Adams, a farmer, and Susanna Boylston. He was a great-grandson of Henry Adams who came from England in 1636. After graduation from Harvard, he taught school, and studied law. In 1765 he argued against taxation without representation before the royal governor. In 1770 he defended the British soldiers who fired on civilians in the "Boston Massacre." He was a delegate to the first Continental Congress, and signed the Declaration of Independence. He was a commissioner to France, 1778, with Benjamin Franklin and Arthur Lee; won

recognition of the U.S. by The Hague, 1782; was first American minister to England, 1785-88, and was elected vice-president, 1788 and 1792.

In 1796 Adams was chosen president by the electors. Intense antagonism to America by France caused agitation for war, led by Alexander Hamilton. Adams, breaking with Hamilton, opposed war.

To fight alien influence and muzzle criticism Adams supported the Alien and Sedition laws of 1798, which led to his defeat for reelection.

The More Colorful Facts

Astrological Sign: Scorpio

Nicknames: Apostle of Independence, Architect of the Revolution, Colossus of Debate, Colossus of Independence, Father of America's Navy, Father of American Independence, Old Rotundity, Old Sink or Swim, Your Superfluous Excellency*.

Presidential Notes: JA was the only two-termed vice-president to be directly elected to the presidency. Richard Nixon was also a two-termed vice-president, but lost his direct election to John F. Kennedy in 1960.

At 90 years, 247 days, JA's life was the longest of all the presidents to date.

Family Notes: "Mrs. President" was the uncomplimentary nickname given to Abigail Adams because of her influence on JA.

Homes: 141 Franklin Street, Quincy, Massachusetts, JA's birthplace where the newly wed Adamses lived, and where their son John Quincy Adams was born.

Peacefield, farm in Quincy, Massachusetts, that JA purchased in 1787.

Other Positions: Surveyor of highways, in Braintree, Massachusetts, appointed in 1761.

Favorite Christmas Carol: "Joy to the World"

Memberships: Sons of Liberty, from 1770.

Sodality, Boston law society, joined in 1765.

Pen Names: Humphrey Ploughjogger, for an essay on agriculture that appeared in both Boston newspapers on July 18, 1763.

Claradon, used in writing articles for the Boston *Gazette* on American constitutional rights in January of 1766.

Novanglus, for articles in the Boston *Gazette* on the legal position of the American patriot in the conflict with England.

Quote: "The most insignificant office that ever the inventions of man contrived"—on the vice-presidency.

Famous Descendants: Hollywood actor Wendell Corey

News commentator Chet Huntley

Books: *Thought on Government,* 1776

*So-called by Benjamin Franklin when JA was vice-president.

Essays: "Braintree Instructions," opposing the Stamp Act, 1765.
"Discourses on Davilia," a series of articles written while vice president discussing the advantages of the American form of government over that set up in France after the revolution, 1790-91.

Last Words: "Thomas Jefferson survives." JA did not know that Jefferson had predeceased him by three hours.

THOMAS JEFFERSON
Third president
1801-09

The Straight Facts

Born: April 13, 1743
Birthplace: Albermarle County, Virginia
Ancestry: Welsh
Physical Characteristics: 6'2½" tall, hazel eyes, red hair
Religion: No specific denomination
Occupation: Writer, inventor, lawyer
Wife: Martha Wayles Skelton Jefferson (1748-82)
Date of Marriage: January 1, 1772

Children: Five daughters, one son
College: College of William and Mary, class of 1762
Military History: None
Political Party: Democrat-Republican
Previous Political Offices: Member, Virginia House of Burgesses (1769-74); Deputy delegate, Second Continental Congress (1775); Delegate, Second Continental Congress (1775); Delegate, Virginia House of Delegates (1776-79); Delegate, Virginia General Assembly (1776); Governor, state of Virginia (1779-81); U.S. minister to France (1784-89); Secretary of state (1790-93); Vice-president of the United States (1797-1801)
Vice-President: Aaron Burr (1756-1836), first term; George Clinton (1739-1812), second term
Died: July 4, 1826, at Monticello, in Virginia.
Burial Place: Monticello Estate, Charlottesville, Virginia
Firsts: First president inaugurated in Washington, D.C.
First president to walk to his inaugural
First to have been a state governor
First to have served as a cabinet officer (secretary of state)
First Democratic-Republican president
Biography in Brief: Thomas Jefferson was the son of Peter Jefferson, a civil engineer of Welsh descent who raised tobacco, and Jane Randolph. His father died when he was 14, leaving him 2,750 acres and his slaves. Jefferson attended the College of William and Mary, 1760-62, read classics in Greek and Latin and played the violin. In 1769 he was elected to the House of Burgesses. In 1770 he began building Monticello, near Charlottesville. He was a member of the Virginia Committee of Correspondence and the Continental Congress.

Named a member of the committee to draw up a Declaration of Independence, he wrote the basic draft. He was a member of the Virginia House of Delegates, 1776-79, elected governor to succeed Patrick Henry, 1779, reelected 1780, resigned June 1781 amid charges of ineffectual military preparation. During his term he wrote the statute on religious freedom. In the Continental Congress, 1783, he drew up an ordinance for the Northwest Territory, forbidding slavery after 1800; its terms were put into the Ordinance of 1787. He was sent to Paris with Benjamin Franklin and John Adams to negotiate commercial treaties, 1784; made minister to France, 1785.

Washington appointed him secretary of state, 1789. Jefferson's strong faith in the consent of the governed, as opposed to executive control favored by Hamilton, secretary of the treasury, often led to conflict: December 31, 1793, he resigned. He was the Democrat-Republican candidate for president in 1796; beaten by John Adams, he became vice-president. In 1800, Jefferson and Aaron Burr received equal electoral college votes for president. The House of Representatives elected Jefferson. Major events of his administration were the Louisiana Purchase, 1803, and the Lewis and Clark Expedition. He established the University of Virginia and designed its buildings.

The More Colorful Facts

Astrological Sign: Aries

Nicknames: Apostle of Democracy, Father of the Declaration of Independence, Friend of the People, Moonshine Philosopher of Monticello, Noble Agrarian, Old Sachem, Pen of Revolution, Red Fox, Sage of Monticello, Scribe of the Revolution.

Original Family Name: Jeaffreson. The name can be traced back to around 1590 A.D.

Presidential Notes: The first president to take the oath of office in Washington, D.C. He had to walk the one block to the Capitol for his inauguration because his son-in-law Jack Epsfield didn't arrive in time with the carriage.

TJ's personal wine bill during his eight years in the Executive Mansion was $10,835.

TJ paid $15 million for the Louisiana Territory, or about three cents an acre for the 600 million-acre tract.

Grandson, James Madison Randolph, was the first child born in the White House, on January 17, 1806.

"Mad Tom in a Rage." An 1801 anti-Jefferson etching depicts him as a madman and a drunkard.

Family Notes: TJ had a brother and sister who were twins, Randolph and Anna. He was the only president to have twinned siblings.

Campaign Notes: "Fair and Free Elections" was his campaign song.

Namesakes: Jefferson Memorial Monument, located on the banks of the Potomac, designed by John Russell Pope, was built from 1938 to 1943. Inscribed in it are TJ's words: "I have sworn on the altar of God eternal hostility against every form of tyranny of the mind of man." President Franklin D. Roosevelt dedicated the memorial on April 13, 1943, the 200th anniversary of TJ's birth.

Jefferson, as the original name of the state of Colorado.

Jeffersonia, a genus of American perennial herbs with lobed leafs, capsular fruit, and white flowers.

Jeffersonite, a mineral Ca (Mn, Zn, Fe) SI_2O_6, consisting of a dark green or greenish black pyroxene.

Homes: Monticello, near Charlottesville, Virginia, which TJ designed himself. It was built from 1769 to 1802.

Early Love Life: His first love was Rebecca Burwell. When he didn't propose early enough, he lost her to Jacquelin Amber.

Mistress: TJ supposedly had a 38-year affair with Sally Hemings, one of his black slaves. Historians now believe that he was the father of her seven children. She was nicknamed "Black Sal" by the Federalists.

IQ: 145 (projected)

Memberships: TJ was elected president of the American Philosophical Society on March 14, 1797, and served until his death nearly 30 years later.

Quotes: "Life of splendid misery"—on his life in the White House.

Anonymous Name: A.Z. was the name TJ used to submit a design for the Executive Mansion. The judges believed that A.Z. was the Alexandria, Virginia, builder Abraham Faws. Irishman James Hoban submitted the winning design and received the $500 prize.

Inventions: Baked Alaska, a cake and ice cream concoction. TJ also introduced ice cream to America.

Chicken a la king, a dish consisting of chicken, peas, and carrots in white sauce. It was a favorite dish of George Washington.

Dumbwaiter.

Folding chair.

Lazy susan, a revolving tray placed on a dining table for serving food.

Pedometer, a device to measure how far he walked.

Swivel chair.

Folk Remedies: TJ would bathe his feet in a bucket of cold water daily as he believed this would prevent colds.

Last words: "Is it the Earth? I resign my soul to God and my daughters to my country."

Epitaph: "Here was Buried Thomas Jefferson, Author of the Declaration of Independence, of the Statute of Virginia for Religious Freedom and Father of the University of Virginia." (written by TJ)

JAMES MADISON
Fourth president
1809-17

The Straight Facts

Born: March 16, 1751
Birthplace: Port Conway, Virginia
Ancestry: English
Physical Characteristics: 5'4" tall, blue eyes, blond hair, 100 lbs.
Religion: Episcopalian
Occupation: Lawyer, statesman
Wife: Dorothea "Dolley" Payne Todd Madison (1768-1849)
Date of Marriage: September 15, 1794
Children: None; wife had two sons by previous marriage
College: Princeton University, class of 1771
Military History: None

Political Party: Democrat-Republican
Previous Political Offices: Delegate, Williamsburg Convention (1776); Member, Virginia legislature (1777; 1784-86); Delegate, Virginia state council (1777); Delegate, Continental Congress (1779-83; 1786-88); Member, U.S. House of Representatives (1789-97); Secretary of state (1801-09); (Post presidency) Delegate, Virginia Constitutional Convention (1829)
Vice-President: George Clinton (1739-1812), first term;
   Elbridge Gerry (1744-1814), second term
Died: June 28, 1836, at Montpelier, in Virginia
Burial Place: Montpelier Estate, Montpelier Station, Virginia
Firsts: First president to have been a congressman
   First president to be younger than both his vice-presidents
   First president to have two vice-presidents die while in office
   First president to lead U.S. troops and face enemy fire while in office
Biography in Brief: James Madison was the eldest son of James Madison and Eleanor Rose Conway. Madison was graduated from Princeton, 1771; studied theology, 1772; sat in the Virginia Constitutional Convention, 1776. He was a member of the Continental Congress. He was chief recorder at the Constitutional Convention in 1787, and supported ratification in the *Federalist Papers*, written with Alexander Hamilton and John Jay. He was elected to the House of Representatives in 1789, helped frame the Bill of Rights, and fought the Alien and Sedition Acts. He became Jefferson's secretary of state, 1801.

   Elected president in 1808, Madison was a "strict constructionist," opposed to the free interpretation of the Constitution by the Federalists. He was reelected in 1812 by the votes of the agrarian South and recently admitted western states. Caught between British and French maritime restrictions, the U.S. drifted into war, declared June 18, 1812. The war ended in a stalemate. Madison retired in 1817 to his estate at Montpelier. There he edited his famous papers on the constitutional convention. He became rector of the University of Virginia, 1826.

The More Colorful Facts

Astrological Sign: Pisces
Nicknames: Father of the Constitution, Fugitive President, Jemmy, Little Man in the Palace, Sage of Montpelier, Withered Little Apple John.*
Presidential Notes: The only president to lead troops while in office, he led Barney's Battery, a regiment under the command of Joshua Barney, in the Battle of Bladensburg, nicknamed "the Bladensburg Races," which took place on August 24, 1814. He was trying to defend Washington against the invading British. The troops were retreating as fast as they could towards

*So-called by Washington Irving.

Washington with the British hot on their heels, hence the nickname "race" to see who would reach Washington first.

JM coined the phrase "Mr. President" for what the leader of the country should be called.

JM was the first president to wear long pants; the previous three had worn knickers.

Family Notes: Wife Dolley Madison served as the official White House hostess for 16 years, for her husband and for his immediate predecessor, widower Thomas Jefferson. She also displayed great courage during the invasion of Washington by the British during the War of 1812, refusing to leave until she was sure her husband was safe and until many White House treasures were taken with her. Dolley introduced her distant cousin Angelica Singleton to her future husband, Abraham Van Buren, son of Martin Van Buren.

"Lady Presidentess" was a nickname of Dolley.

Homes: Montpelier, Orange County, Virginia. The architects were William Thornton (who drew the original plans for the U.S. Capitol) and Benjamin Latrobe (who was the architect of the first Hall of Representatives).

Memberships: Agriculture Society of Albermarle County, elected president in 1818.

Last Words: "I always talk better laying down."

"To the grave go sham protectors of 'Free Trade and Sailors' Rights'—and all the people say Amen." This 1814 cartoon by John Wesley Jarvis shows a terrapin, which symbolizes the embargo on trade with Britain, clutching Madison. Madison has managed to sever the terrapin's head, signifying the end of the embargo.

JAMES MONROE

Fifth president

1817-25

The Straight Facts

Born: April 28, 1758
Birthplace: Westmoreland County, Virginia
Ancestry: Scots
Physical Characteristics; 6′ tall, blue-gray eyes, brown hair
Religion: Episcopalian
Occupation: Lawyer, writer
Wife: Elizabeth Kortright Monroe (1768-1830)
Date of Marriage: February 16, 1786
Children: Two daughters, one son
College: College of William and Mary

Military History: Lieutenant colonel, Continental Army

Political Party: Democrat-Republican

Previous Political Offices: Member, Virginia legislature (1780); Member, Virginia House of Delegates (1782); Member, Virginia Continental Congress (1783-86); Member, Virginia assembly (1786; 1810); Member, Virginia state convention (1788); Member, U.S. Senate (1790-94); U.S. minister to France (1794-96; 1803); Governor, state of Virginia (1799-1803; 1811); U.S. minister to Great Britain (1803); Secretary of state (1811-17); Secretary of war (1814-15); Chairman, Virginia Constitutional Convention (1829)

Vice-President: Daniel D. Tompkins (1774-1825)

Died: July 4, 1831, in New York City

Burial Place: Hollywood Cemetery Richmond, Virginia

Firsts: First president to have been a senator
First and only president to serve in two different cabinet posts (secretary of state and war)

Biography in Brief: James Monroe was the son of Spence Monroe and Elizabeth Jones, who were of Scottish and Welsh descent, respectively. He attended the College of William and Mary, fought in the 3rd Virginia Regiment at White Plains, Brandywine, Monmouth, and was wounded at Trenton. He studied law with Thomas Jefferson, 1780, and was a member of the Virginia House of Delegates and of Congress, 1783-86. He opposed ratification of the Constitution because it lacked a bill of rights; was U.S. senator, 1790; minister to France, 1794-96; governor of Virginia, 1799-1802, and 1811. Jefferson sent him to France as minister, 1803. He helped Robert Livingston negotiate the Louisiana Purchase, 1803. He ran against Madison for president in 1808. He was elected to the Virginia Assembly, 1810-11; was secretary of state under Madison, 1811-17.

In 1816 Monroe was elected president; in 1820 reelected with all but one electoral college vote. Monroe's administration became the "Era of

The birthplace of Monroe in Westmoreland County, Virginia.

Good Feeling." He obtained Florida from Spain, settled boundaries with Canada, and eliminated border forts. He supported the antislavery position that led to the Missouri Compromise. His most significant contribution was the "Monroe Doctrine," which became a cornerstone of U.S. foreign policy. Monroe retired to Oak Hill, Virginia. Financial problems forced him to sell his property. He moved to New York City to live with a daughter.

The More Colorful Facts

Astrological Sign: Taurus

Nicknames: James the Lesser, James the Second, Last of the Cocked Hats.

Original Family Name: Munro. The family tree can be traced back to 1520 A.D.

Presidential Notes: The first president to ride a steamship, the S.S. *Savannah*, in May 1829.

JM was the last president to wear knee breeches to his inaugural.

P.K. Moran composed a special march, "March for the Pianoforte," for the inauguration.

William Plumer, a member of the Electoral College from New Hampshire, cast the only dissenting vote against James Monroe. Legend has it that Plumer voted for John Quincy Adams in order to preserve for George Washington the distinction of being the only unanimously elected president of the U.S. The truth is that Plumer disliked both Monroe and his policies.

Family Note: Maria Hester Monroe was the first presidential daughter to be married in the White House. She married a distant cousin, Samuel Lawrence Gouveneur, who proposed to her in the East Room of the White House at the 1819 Christmas Ball. He also served as JM's private secretary.

Homes: Highlands (later called Ashfield, then Ashlawn) near Charlottesville, Virginia, within sight of Thomas Jefferson's Monticello. The house was designed by Thomas Jefferson and constructed under his supervision while JM was serving as the U.S. minister to France. The floor of one patio room is of limestone and shale from pits on JM's land. Imbedded in the flooring are the footprints, tracks, and imprints of the tail and hide of dinosaurs dating from approximately 200 million years ago. JM sold the home in 1826.

Namesakes: Monrovia, the capital of Liberia.

Stamp: James Monroe Issue, a three-cent stamp in honor of the 200th anniversary of JM's birth.

Military Experience: JM served in the 3rd Virginia Regiment during the Revolutionary War. The regiment took part in the battles of White Plains, Brandywine, Monmouth, and Trenton; he was one of the only two Americans wounded in the latter. He was shot in the shoulder and the bullet remained in him for the rest of his life.

Books: *A View of the Conduct of the Executive in the Foreign Affairs of United States*, 1797.

JOHN QUINCY ADAMS

Sixth president

1825-29

The Straight Facts

Born: July 11, 1767
Birthplace: Braintree (Quincy), Massachusetts
Ancestry: English
Physical Characteristics: 5'7" tall, brown eyes, brown hair
Religion: Unitarian
Occupation: Lawyer, statesman

Wife: Louisa Catherine Johnson Adams (1775-1852)
Date of Marriage: July 26, 1797
Children: One daughter, three sons
College: Harvard University, class of 1787
Military History: None
Political Party: Democrat-Republican
Previous Political Offices: U.S. minister to Netherlands (1794); U.S. minister to Portugal (1796); U.S. minister to Prussia (1797); Member, Massachusetts senate (1802); Member, U.S. Senate (1803-08); U.S. minister to Russia (1809-14); U.S. minister to Great Britain (1815-17); Secretary of state (1817-25); (Post presidency) Member, U.S. House of Representatives (1831-48)
Vice-President: John Caldwell Calhoun (1782-1850)
Died: February 23, 1848, in Washington, D.C.
Burial Place: First Unitarian Church Quincy, Massachusetts
Firsts: First president to serve in both the House and Senate
   First and only son of a president to become president
   First and only president elected to the House of Representatives after completing presidency
   First president elected without receiving a majority of the popular vote
   First president married abroad (London, England)
   First president to have a son marry in the White House
Biography in Brief: John Quincy Adams was the son of John and Abigail Adams. His father was the second president. He was educated in Paris, Leyden, and Harvard, graduating in 1787. He served as American minister in various European capitals, and helped draft the War of 1812 peace treaty. He was U.S. senator, 1803-08. President Monroe made him secretary of state, 1817, and he negotiated the cession of the Floridas from Spain, supported exclusion of slavery in the Missouri Compromise, and helped formulate the Monroe Doctrine. In 1824 he was elected president by the House after he failed to win an electoral college majority. His expansion of executive powers was strongly opposed and he was beaten in 1828 by Andrew Jackson. In 1831 he entered Congress and served 17 years with distinction. He opposed slavery, the annexation of Texas, and the Mexican War. He helped establish the Smithsonian Institution. He had a stroke in the House and died in the Speaker's Room, February 23, 1848.

The More Colorful Facts

Astrological Sign: Cancer
Nicknames: The Father of the Smithsonian Institute, John the Second, King John the Second, New England Independent, Old Man Eloquent.
Famous Ancestors: John Alden and Priscilla Mullens Alden (on his maternal side).

Presidential Notes: JQA became the first president to attend a political convention when, in 1808, he turned the Republican caucus meeting into a convention.

The first photo of a president was taken in 1843 of JQA by Albert S. Southworth of the Josiah Dawes Studio in Boston, Massachusetts.

Reporter Anne Royall "stole" JQA's clothes while he was skinny-dipping, to convince him to grant her an interview. It was the first time a president had ever been questioned by a newspaper reporter. Royall is known as the "Mother of Yellow Journalism."

Family Notes: JQA's eldest son, George Washington Adams (1801-29), was born in Berlin, Germany, and named for the first president. He served as a captain in the U.S. Army and as a member of the Massachusetts legislature. He drowned in the Potomac in what historians believe was a suicide.

Second son, John Adams II (1803-34), was the only presidential offspring born on the Fourth of July. He was also the only son of a president to be married in the White House. He wed first cousin Mary Catherine Hellen in a ceremony in the Blue Room.

Homes: For birthplace, see "Homes" in John Adams profile.

Peacefield (now Adams Mansion Historical Site), Quincy, Massachusetts, became JQA's permanent residence from 1801.

Other Positions: Boylston Professor of Rhetoric and Oratory, a title held as a lecturer at Harvard College during 1805.

Coincidences: The sixth president of the U.S., JQA was born in the sixth state to join the union, Massachusetts.

Favorite Game: Billiards

Favorite Book: *The Arabian Nights,* as a child.

Languages Spoken (as a child): Dutch, English, French, German, Greek, Latin, and Russian.

Pseudonyms: Columbus, used in writing articles criticizing the government.

Marcellus, in writing to support neutrality.

Publicola, used in writing letters defending President George Washington's policies.

Publius Valerius, for a series of articles which served to justify his anti-Federalist record in the U.S. Senate

Writings: JQA kept a meticulous diary for 69 years.

"Importance and Necessity of Public Faith in the Well-Being of a Nation," JQA's salutatorian address at Harvard University, 1787.

"Publica," a response to opponent Thomas Paine's "The Rights of Man" because he felt Paine's work was too radical.

Poems of Religion and Society, a 108-page volume of poems published in 1832. JQA was the only president to be a published poet.

"Dermott McMorrogh," a 2,000-line poem about Ireland's conquest by Oliver Cromwell.

Last Words: "This is the last of Earth. I am content."

ANDREW JACKSON

Seventh president

1829-37

The Straight Facts

Born: March 15, 1767
Birthplace: Waxhaw, South Carolina
Ancestry: Scots-Irish
Physical Characteristics: 6'1" tall, blue eyes, brown hair, 140 lbs.
Religion: Presbyterian
Occupation: Soldier
Wife: Rachel Donelson Robards Jackson (1767-1828)

Date of Marriage: January 17, 1794
Children: None
College: None
Military History: General, U.S. Army
Political Party: Democrat
Previous Political Offices: Solicitor, western North Carolina (1788); Delegate, Tennessee state Constitutional Convention (1796); Member, U.S. House of Representatives (1796-97); Member, U.S. Senate (1797-98; 1823-25); Judge, Tennessee Supreme Court (1798-1804); Member, Tennessee state senate (1807); Governor, Florida Territory (1821)
Vice-President: John C. Calhoun (1782-1850), first term;
Martin Van Buren, second term
Died: June 8, 1845, at the Hermitage in Tennessee.
Burial Place: Hermitage Estate, Nashville, Tennessee
Firsts: First president born in a log cabin
First president born west of the Allegheny Mountains
First president born in South Carolina
First president to marry a divorced woman
First president to fight in a duel
First president to be a Democrat
First presidential candidate nominated by a convention
First president to survive an assassination attempt
Biography in Brief: Andrew Jackson was the posthumous son of Andrew Jackson and Elizabeth Hutchinson, who were Irish immigrants. At 13, he joined the militia in the Revolution and was captured.

He read law in Salisbury, North Carolina, moved to Nashville, Tennessee, speculated in land, married, and practiced law. In 1796 he helped draft the constitution of Tennessee and for a year occupied its one seat in Congress. He was in the Senate in 1797, and again in 1823. He defeated the Creek Indians at Horseshoe Bend, Alabama, 1814. With 6,000 backwoods fighters he defeated General Sir Edward Pakenham's 12,000 British troops at the Chalmette, outside New Orleans, January 8, 1815. In 1818 he briefly invaded Spanish Florida to quell Seminoles and outlaws who harassed frontier settlements. In 1824 he ran for president against John Quincy Adams and had the most popular and electoral votes but not a majority; the election was decided by the House, which chose Adams. In 1828 he defeated Adams, carrying the West and South. He was a noisy debater and a duelist and introduced rotation in office called the "spoils sytem." Suspicious of privilege, he ruined the Bank of the United States by depositing federal funds with state banks. Though "Let the people rule" was his slogan, he at times supported strict constructionist policies against the expansionist West. He killed the congressional caucus for nominating presidential candidates and substituted the national convention, 1832. When South Carolina refused to collect imports under his protective tariff he ordered army and naval forces to Charleston. Jackson recognized the Republic of Texas, 1836.

An anti-Jackson cartoon warns voters that if they elect Jackson they will all be hanged because he hanged two Englishmen during the Seminole War.

The More Colorful Facts

Astrological Sign: Pisces
Nicknames: Duel Fighter, Gentleman from Tennessee, Hero of New Orleans, King Andrew the First, L'Enfant Terrible, Mischievous Andy, Napoleon of the Woods, Old Hickory*, Sage of the Hermitage, Tennessee Firecracker.

*Because he was as tough as hickory wood.

Presidential Notes: The only president with both parents born outside of the U.S.; both were born in Ireland. There are some rumors claiming that AJ was born in Ireland, but there appears to be no truth to this story.

AJ was the only president to pay off the national debt.

AJ spent the first night of his presidency at Gadsby's Tavern, nicknamed the "Wigwam," where he had lived before his inauguration. He made a safe getaway from a riotous White House inaugural party by crawling out of a White House window and escaping to Gadsby's.

The first known case of a president being handed a baby to kiss occurred in 1828. AJ declined the invitation, but handed the baby to Secretary of War John Eaton to do it.

The first attempt at bodily harm of a president was made on AJ. On May 6, 1833, AJ sailed on the steamer S.S. *Cygnet* to Fredericksburg, Virginia, to lay the cornerstone on a monument near the grave of Washington's mother, Mary Ball Washington. While on a stopover near Alexandria, Robert B. Randolph, who had been dismissed from the U.S. Navy for embezzlement upon the orders of AJ, struck the president. Before further harm could be done, Randolph fled and was pursued by members of the president's party, including author Washington Irving. AJ did not press charges.

The first president to ride on a railroad train while in office, 1833.

The only president to be born after the death of his father.

The Constitutional Carriage was presented to AJ as a gift from the American people. It was built from the timbers of the famous frigate, the U.S.S. *Constitution.*

Family Notes: AJ was only one of two presidents to adopt a child; he adopted a nephew of his wife and named the child Andrew Jackson, Jr.

AJ met his future wife, Rachel Donelson, at Donelson's Blockhouse where he stayed, as a young prosecutor, during his first visit to Nashville, Tennessee.

Namesakes: Jackson cent, nickname given to a hard times token.

Andrew Jackson Borden, a Fall River, Massachusetts, mortician more famous for being murdered, supposedly by his youngest daughter, Lizzie.

Jackson, Mississippi. This town named itself after AJ on November 28, 1821. It was the first town to name itself after a man who would later become president.

Stamp: Hermitage Issue, a four and one-cent stamp featuring AJ's home, 1959.

Jackson Birthday Issue, a ten-cent stamp in honor of AJ's 200th birthday, March 15, 1967.

Homes: The Hermitage, Hermitage, Tennessee. AJ bought the 425-acre tract in 1804 and built several homes on it. He retired there permanently in 1837 after eight years as president.

Famous Descendants: Actress Jane Darwell (or so she claimed)

Favorite Foods: Blackberry jam

Favorite Christmas Carol: "Shout the Glad Tidings"

Books Read: AJ claimed that *The Vicar of Wakefield,* a novel written by Oliver Goldsmith in 1766, was the only book he ever read.

Early Trade: AJ studied to be a saddler in 1781.

Assassination Attempt: AJ was the victim of the first attempt to assassinate an incumbent president. Richard Lawrence, a house painter, fired two shots at AJ as he left the Capitol rotunda after attending the funeral service for Rep. Warren R. Davis of South Carolina. AJ thought Lawrence was part of a Whig plot to assassinate him. Lawrence was sentenced to St. Elizabeth's Mental Institute for the crime, having been found guilty by reason of insanity. He fancied himself king of England and of the United States; he felt the president was his clerk and had merely taken too much power on himself.

Duels: AJ supposedly fought in 100 duels. His first dueling opponent was Avery Waightstill whom he called out in 1787 for hazing him in court. They met for satisfaction but were persuaded by their seconds to fire the pistols in the air and thus avoid bloodshed.

   AJ killed Charles Dickinson in a duel on May 30, 1806. Dickinson had challenged AJ because of a horse racing wager. Standing 24 feet apart, Dickinson fired first and hit AJ in the chest, grazing his breastbone and breaking two ribs. AJ's .70 caliber ball hit Dickinson in the groin and he died a slow, painful death. Because of the close proximity of the Dickinson bullet to AJ's heart, it was never removed and remained in his body for the rest of his life.

   AJ also dueled with John Sevier, governor of Tennessee from 1796 to 1801 and 1803 to 1809, over a slanderous remark Sevier made about Rachel Jackson. The duel was a draw and neither man was injured.

Songs: "Hunter of Tennessee" was written by Samuel Woodworth to commemorate General AJ's victory in New Orleans over General Pakenham.

Home Remedies: Favorite one was Matchless Senative taken with a glass of wine, because it would calm the mind and keep it "free from perplexing thoughts." AJ also believed it relieved headaches, earaches, and pulmonary symptoms. The medicine could usually be bought from traveling salesmen at a cost of $2.50 per bottle.

Gravestone Inscription: "His faith in the American people never wavered."

MARTIN VAN BUREN

Eighth president

1838-41

The Straight Facts

Born: December 5, 1782
Birthplace: Kinderhook, New York
Ancestry: Dutch

Physical Characteristics: 5'6" tall, blue eyes, reddish hair
Religion: Dutch Reformed
Occupation: Lawyer, statesman
Wife: Hannah Hoes Van Buren (1783-1819)
Date of Marriage: February 21, 1807
Children: Four sons
College: None
Military History: None
Political Party: Democrat
Previous Political Offices: Surrogate, Columbia County, New York (1808); Member, New York senate (1813-20); Attorney general, state of New York (1815-19); Member, U.S. Senate (1821-28); Governor, state of New York (1829); Secretary of state (1829-31); U.S. minister to Great Britain (1831); Vice-president of the United States (1833-37)
Vice-President: Richard Mentor Johnson 1780-1850
Died: July 24, 1862, at Kinderhook, New York
Burial Place: Kinderhook Cemetery, Kinderhook, New York
Firsts: First president born in New York
First president born an American citizen—the first born after the signing of the Declaration of Independence
Biography in Brief: Martin Van Buren was the son of Abraham Van Buren, a Dutch farmer, and Maria Hoes van Alen. He was surrogate of Columbia County, New York state senator and attorney general. He was U.S. senator 1821, reelected 1827, elected governor of New York, 1828. He helped swing eastern support to Andrew Jackson in 1828 and was his secreaty of state 1829-31. In 1832 he was elected vice president. He was a consummate politician, known as "the little magician," and influenced Jackson's policies. In 1836 he defeated William Henry Harrison for president and took office as the panic of 1837 initiated a five-year nationwide depression. He inaugurated the independent treasury system. His refusal to spend land revenues led to his defeat by Harrison in 1840. He lost the Democratic nomination in 1844 to Polk. In 1848 he ran for president on the Free Soil ticket and lost.

The More Colorful Facts

Astrological Sign: Sagittarius
Nicknames: American Talleyrand, Enchanter, Fox of Kinderhook, King Martin the First, Little Magician, Little Wizard, Machiavellian Belshazzar, Martin Van Ruin, Old Kinderhook*, Petticoat Pet, Political Grimalkin, Sweet Sandy Whiskers†, Weazel, Whiskey Van, Wizard of Kinderhook.

---

*Biographer George Berndt claims the expression "O.K." originated from Van Buren backers who referred to him by the initials of this nickname.
†Given to him by New York political "Boss" Thurlow Weed.

Presidential Notes: The first president to grant an exclusive interview to a newsman, James Gordon Bennet, 1839.

   The last sitting vice-president to be elected to the presidency in his own right.

Homes: Kinderhook, New York, his birthplace where he also died. In Dutch Kinderhook means "children's corner."

   Lindenwald, Kinderhook, New York, home purchased in 1839 from William Van Ness. It is said that Washington Irving conceived the idea for his book *The Legend of Sleepy Hollow* while visiting there.

Memberships: Albany Regency, a group of politicans so nicknamed, who ran New York state for 30 years, from 1820 to the mid-1850s. They manipulated patronage, defined party policy, and outmanuevered their foes.

Famous Descendants: Singer Nelson Eddy and actor Glenn Ford.

Hobby: Flying roosters

Coincidences: He was both the eighth president and the eighth vice-president.

Quotes: "As to the presidency, the two happiest days of my life were those of my entrance upon the office and my surrender of it."

In this cartoon, Van Buren thumbs his nose at Andrew Jackson after Van Buren's retirement from the presidency.

WILLIAM HENRY HARRISON

Ninth president
1841

The Straight Facts

Born: February 9, 1773

Birthplace: Charles City County, Virginia

Ancestry: English

Physical Characteristics: 5'8" tall, gray eyes, brown hair

Religion: Episcopalian

Occupation: Soldier

Wife: Anna Tuthill Harrison (1775-1864)

Date of Marriage: November 25, 1795
Children: Four daughters, six sons
College: Hampden-Sydney College
Military History: Major general,
U.S. Army
Political Party: Whig
Previous Political Offices: Secretary,
Northwest Territory (1798-99);
Member, U.S. House of Representa-
tives (1799-1800; 1816-19); Territor-
ial governor, Indiana (1801-13);
Member, Ohio senate (1819-21);
Member, U.S. Senate (1825-28);
U.S. minister to Colombia (1828-29)
Vice-President: John Tyler
Died: April 4, 1841, in the White
House, Washington, D.C.
Burial Place: William Henry
Harrison Memorial State Park, Nortl
Bend, Ohio
Firsts: First Whig president
First president to die in office
First to lie in state in the
White House
First and only president whose
grandson would later be-
come president
Biography in Brief: William Henry
Harrison was the third son of
Benjamin Harrison, a signer of the
Declaration of Independence, and
Elizabeth Bassett. He attended
Hampden-Sydney College. He was
secretary of the Northwest Territory
1798; its delegate in Congress, 1799
first governor of Indiana Territory,
1800; and superintendent of Indian
affairs. With 900 men he routed
Tecumseh's Indians at Tippecanoe,
November 7, 1811. A major general,

IN MEMORY
OF

PRESIDENT

WM. H. HARRISON,

WHO DEPARTED
THIS LIFE,
APRIL 4, 1841,
AGED 68,

Deeply lamented
by 16 Millions of
people.

Harrison was the first president to die in
office. Many wore black arm bands or
special ribbons like the one shown above.

he defeated British and Indians at Battle of the Thames, October 5, 1813.
He served in Congress, 1816-19; Senate, 1825-28. In 1840, when 68, he was
elected president with a "log cabin and hard cider" slogan. He caught pneumonia during the inauguration and died April 4, 1841, 35 days later.

The More Colorful Facts

Astrological Sign: Aquarius

Nicknames: Cincinnatus of the West, Farmer President, Father of the West, Granny Harrison, General Mum*, Hero of Tippecanoe, Log Cabin President, Old Buckeye, Our Hero Farmer, Old Tip, Old Tippecanoe, Tippecanoe, Washington of the West.

Original Family Name: Harryson. It can be traced back to 1632.

Ancestors: Colonel John Harrison, an ancestor of both William Henry and Benjamin Harrison, was one of the judges who tried and condemned Charles I of England. Harrison, himself, was later hanged for his part in the deed.

Presidential Notes: WHH was the only president to study medicine; he studied at Hampden-Sydney College, which he left before graduation. He studied under Dr. Benjamin Rush, a signer of the Declaration of Independence and treasurer of the U.S. Mint. In 1791, Harrison's father, Benjamin, and his close friend George Washington decided young William should drop medicine and pursue a career in the army instead.

When president-elect WHH boarded the steamer S.S. *Ben Franklin* on January 26, 1841, in Cincinnati, Ohio, to sail to Washington, D.C., for his inauguration, his family didn't realize that it would the last time they would see him alive.

Family Notes: Anna Tuthill Symmes was the only First Lady to never live in the offical residence of the president. She had not yet left her North Bend, Ohio, home when her husband died after only 31 days in office. She is not the only First Lady not to reside in the White House. The White House was not inhabitable until the later part of John Adams' term. Martha Washington did reside in the official residence, which was in Philadelphia. WHH had 48 grandchildren, the most of any president. One of them, Benjamin, became the 23rd President.

He had 106 great-grandchildren, also the most of any president.

Campaign Notes: The slogan "Keep the ball rolling" comes from a large paper ball that served as the Whig campaign banner for the 1840 presidential campaign. It was "rolled" from Kentucky to Baltimore where the Whig nominating convention was held and nominated WHH and John Tyler.

Theme of 1840 campaign between WHH and incumbent Martin Van Buren was "Log Cabin and Hard Cider Democracy."

Another Whig Theme or slogan in 1840, "Tippecanoe and Tyler, Too," was coined by Cleveland, Ohio, lawyer James A. Briggs. It was also the name of the campaign theme song with lyrics by Alexander C. Ross of Zanesville, Ohio, and music to the tune of "Little Pig's Tail."

Campaign songs included: "Harrison's Song" a Whig song written in

*So-called because during the 1840 presidential campaign he wouldn't speak out on major issues.

1840 by Thomas Powers; "Log Cabin Quick Step," another 1840 Whig campaign theme song, written in 1836 by Henry Schmidt; and "Ye Jolly Young Lads of Ohio."

Homes: Grouseland, original name of the Vincennes, Indiana, home of military governor WHH and family. It is located at 3 West Scott Street. The name was recently reinstated. It was nicknamed "White House of the West."

Namesakes: Jack Dempsey, the heavyweight boxing champion from 1919 to 1926, whose real name was William Harrison Dempsey.

Harrison's Walk, a path on the grounds of Rutherford B. Hayes' home, Spiegel Grove, named for the trail General WHH cut across the land during the War of 1812. The trail is in the southwest corner of the estate and is marked with a large boulder.

Descendants: Robert Harrison (1885-1953), the Hollywood actor and director who was a descendent of WHH, Benjamin Harrison, and Jefferson Davis.

Pets: His Whiskers, a goat.

Books: *Discourses on the Aborigines of the Valley of Ohio*, the only book written by WHH was published in 1830.

Curse: Tecumseh, the Shawnee Indian chief who led his tribe against the American forces at the Battle of the Thames on October 5, 1813, was killed in the battle, supposedly by Colonel Richard Mentor Johnson, later vice-president under Martin Van Buren. (This proved to be just a rumor started by Johnson to glorify his part in the battle.) Tecumseh's brother, the Prophet, avenged his death by placing a curse on the leader of the troops, General William Henry Harrison. (See The Presidential Curse, p. 233)

JOHN TYLER
Tenth president
1841-45

The Straight Facts

Born: March 29, 1790
Birthplace: Charles City County, Virginia
Ancestry: English
Physical Characteristics: 6' tall, blue eyes, light brown hair
Religion: Episcopalian

Occupation: Lawyer
Wife: Letitia Christian Tyler 1790-1842; Julia Gardiner Tyler 1820-89
Date of Marriage: March 29, 1813; June 26, 1844
Children: Seven daughters, eight sons
College: College of William and Mary, class of 1807
Military History: Captain, Virginia Militia
Political Party: Whig
Previous Political Offices: Member, Virginia house (1811-16; 1823-25; 1839); Member, Virginia council of state (1816); Member, U.S. House of Representatives (1817-21); Governor, state of Virginia (1825-27); Member, U.S. Senate (1827-36); President pro tempore, U.S. Senate (1835-36); Member, Virginia Constitutional Convention (1829-30); Vice-president of the United States (1841); (Post presidency) Delegate, Confederate Provisional Congress (1861)
Vice-President: None
Died: January 18, 1862, in Richmond, Virginia
Burial Place: Hollywood Cemetery, Richmond, Virginia
Firsts: First vice president to succeed to presidency on death of predecessor
First president to face impeachment hearings
First president to have wife die while in office
First president to marry while in office
First president to marry on his birthday (first wife)
First president to have no vice-president during his entire term
First and only to serve as president pro tempore of the Senate
Biography in Brief: John Tyler was the son of John Tyler and Mary Armistead. His father was governor of Virginia, 1808-11. Tyler was graduated from William and Mary, 1807. In 1840 he was elected vice-president and, on Harrison's death, succeeded him. He favored preemption, allowing settlers to get government land; he rejected a national bank bill and thus alienated most Whig supporters; he refused to honor the spoils system. He signed the resolution annexing Texas, March 1, 1845. He accepted renomination, 1844, but withdrew before election. In 1861, he chaired an unsuccessful Washington conference called to avert civil war. After its failure he supported secession, sat in the provisional Confederate Congress, became a member of the Confederate House, but died in Richmond before it met.

The More Colorful Facts

Astrological Sign: Aries
Nicknames: Honest John, Young Tippecanoe.
Presidential Notes: Vice-president JT took the oath of office as president of the United States after the death of William Henry Harrison at the Indian Queen Hotel, in Washington, D.C. The oath was administered by Chief Justice William Cranch on April 6, 1841. At the time, Tyler, 51, was the youn-

First Lady Julia Gardiner
Tyler was nicknamed "Rose
of Long Island."

gest president ever to serve. He was sworn in 53 hours after Harrison's death, the longest amount of time the United States, since its inception, has gone without a president.

Legend has it that Vice-president JT was playing marbles with his sons when State Department courier Fletcher Webster arrived to inform him of the death of President Harrison. There appears to be no truth to this story. Tyler claimed that he was in the parlor of his Virginia home and answered the door himself upon Webster's knock.

The words of "Hail to the Chief," the official song of the president, were adapted by First Lady Julia Tyler for her husband. The words are by Sir Walter Scott from "The Lady of the Lake," Canto II, and the music is by James Sanderson from *The Knight of Snowdon*, a musical of Sir Henry Rowland Bishop.

Family Notes: How JT and Julia Gardiner met (the official version): when the Peacemaker, a cannon on the U.S.S. *Princeton* misfired, JT was below deck and not injured in the blast that killed 12 people, including two cabinet ministers and Mr. David Gardiner. Mr. Gardiner's daughter, Julia, was on board and fainted into the arms of the president when she learned of her father's death. Unofficially, the couple had already met and were secretly dating. They later married.

Tyler and Julia Gardiner were married in a secret ceremony on June 29, 1844, at the Church of Ascension on Fifth Avenue in New York City. On their wedding day, they sailed on a cruise on *The Essex,* a New York City harbor pleasure boat. They spent their honeymoon in the Hartwell Hotel in Philadelphia, occupying the apartments normally occupied by Daniel Webster.

"Rose of Long Island" was a nickname for First Lady Julia Tyler.

"Fairy Girl was JT's nickname for Julia Tyler.

JT had fifteen children, eight by his first wife and seven by his second; the last, Pearl Tyler, was born on June 20, 1860, when he was 70.

Letitia Tyler, a granddaughter, was the first girl born in the White House.

Homes: Gloucester Place, the Charles City County, Virginia, estate Tyler purchased for his first wife, Letitia, in 1829.

Sherwood Forest, an estate in Charles City County, Virginia, purchased in 1842. Originally called Creek Plantation, JT claimed he renamed it because he felt he was a political outlaw.

Horse: The General was his favorite horse. The mount is buried on the grounds of the Sherwood Forest estate in Virginia. The grave is marked by an inscription by JT which reads "Here lies the body of my good horse 'The General.' For twenty years he bore me around the circuit of my practice and in all that time he never made a blunder. Would that his master could say the same."

Last words: "I am going, perhaps it is for the best."

JAMES KNOX POLK
Eleventh president
1845-49

The Straight Facts

Born: November 2, 1795
Birthplace: Mecklenburg, North Carolina
Ancestry: Scots-Irish
Physical Characteristics: 5'8" tall, gray eyes, white hair
Religion: Presbyterian
Occupation: Lawyer
Wife: Sarah Childress Polk (1803-91)
Date of Marriage: November 1, 1824
Children: None
College: University of North Carolina, class of 1818
Military History: None
Political Party: Democrat

Previous Political Offices: Chief Clerk, Tennessee senate (1821-23); Member, Tennessee house (1823-25); Member, U.S. House of Representatives (1825-39); Speaker of the U.S. House (1835-39); Governor, state of Tennessee (1839-41)

Vice-President: George Mifflin Dallas (1792-1864)

Died: June 15, 1849, in Nashville, Tennessee

Burial Place: State Capitol grounds, Nashville, Tennessee

Firsts: First president born in North Carolina
First and only president to serve as Speaker of the House of Representatives
First dark horse candidate for president
First president to be survived by his mother
First president to voluntarily retire after one term

Biography in Brief: James Knox Polk was the son of Samuel Polk, farmer and surveyor of Scotch-Irish descent, and Jane Knox. He served as a member of the Tennessee state legislature, 1823-25. He served in Congress 1825-39 and as speaker 1835-39. He was governor of Tennessee 1839-41, but was defeated 1841 and 1843. In 1844, when both Henry Clay and Martin Van Buren announced opposition to annexing Texas, the Democrats made Polk the first

An 1845 engraving shows Polk on his way to the White House.

dark horse nominee because he demanded control of all Oregon and annexation of Texas. Polk reestablished the independent treasury system originated by Van Buren. His expansionist policy was opposed by Clay, Daniel Webster, and John C. Calhoun; he sent troops under Zachary Taylor to the Mexican border and, when Mexicans attacked, declared war existed. The Mexican War ended with the annexation of California and much of the Southwest as part of America's "manifest destiny." He compromised on the Oregon boundary ("54-40 or fight!") by accepting the 49th parallel and giving Vancouver to the British.

The More Colorful Facts

Astrological Sign: Scorpio

Nicknames: First Dark Horse, Handy Jim of Tennessee, Polk the Mendacious, Punctilious James, Napoleon of the Stump.

Mr. Polk's War was a nickname given to Mexican-American War of 1846.

Original Family Name: Pollock, or Pollok, and can be traced back to 1593.

Campaign Notes: "All of Oregon," "Fifty-four-forty or fight," and "New Yankee Doodle" were themes of JKP's 1844 presidential campaign. "Who is James K. Polk?" was the Whig campaign slogan that backfired when Henry Clay lost to Polk.

Homes: 318 West Seventh Street, Columbia, Tennessee, was JKP's own home where he resided from 1825 on.

Polk Place, in Nashville, Tennessee, was originally named Grundy Place, but changed when Polk bought it from his mentor, Congressman Felix Grundy. JKP retired to and died in this home. It was demolished in 1901.

Health: At age 16, he had gallstones removed without anesthesia, by frontier surgeon, Dr. Ephraim McDowell.

Last Words: "I love you Sarah, for all eternity, I love you." Polk lived only 103 days after leaving office.

ZACHARY TAYLOR

Twelfth president

1849-50

The Straight Facts

Born: November 24, 1784
Birthplace: Orange County, Virginia
Ancestry: English
Physical Characteristics: 5'8" tall, gray eyes, black hair, 170 lbs.

Religion: Episcopalian
Occupation: Soldier
Wife: Margaret Mackall Smith Taylor (1788-1852)
Date of Marriage: June 21, 1810
Children: Four daughters, two sons
College: None
Military History: General, U.S. Army
Political Party: Whig
Previous Political Offices: None
Vice-President: Millard Fillmore
Died: July 9, 1850, in Washington, D.C.
Burial Place: Springfield Cemetery, Louisville, Kentucky
Firsts: First president to have held no previous political office
First president elected from a state west of the Mississippi River—
Louisiana
First president to never have voted in any election, including his own
Biography In Brief: Zachary Taylor, who served only 16 months, was the son of Richard Taylor, later collector of the port of Louisville, Kentucky, and Sarah Strother. Taylor was commissioned first lieutenant, 1808; he fought in the War of 1812; the Black Hawk War, 1832; and the second Seminole War, 1837. He was called "Old Rough and Ready." He settled on a plantation near Baton Rouge, Louisiana. In 1845 Polk sent him with an army to the Rio Grande. When the Mexicans attacked him, Polk declared war. Taylor was successful at Palo Alto and Roseca de la Palma, 1846; he occupied Monterrey. Polk made him major general but sent many of his troops to Gen. Winfield Scott. Outnumbered 4-1, he defeated Santa Anna at Buena Vista, 1847. A national hero, he received the Whig nomination in 1848, and was elected president. He resumed the spoils system and, though once a slaveholder, worked to have California admitted as a free state. He died in office.

The More Colorful Facts

Astrological Sign: Sagittarius
Nicknames: Hero of Buena Vista, Old Buena Vista, Old Fuss and Feathers, Old Rough and Ready, Old Zach.
Presidential Notes: ZT died in office, but had no formal state burial; five days after his death, he was quietly interred in the family crypt.
Campaign Notes: "Old Zach's Quick Step" was a Whig campaign song written by Edward White.
Namesakes: Fort Zachary Taylor, the Key West, Florida, military base constructed in 1845. It was a key part of the U.S. coastal defense system and has recently been designated a National Monument.
Homes: Cypress Grove, Jefferson County, Mississippi, an estate he purchased in 1841 for $95,000, including 81 slaves.

"Questioning a candidate." A political cartoon from the 1848 presidential campaign comments on Taylor's reluctance to speak out on issues.

Military Career: On October 31, 1812, ZT was promoted to the rank of brevet major, the first brevet promotion in U.S. Army history.

He established Fort Seldon, a military camp located in the Louisiana Territory in 1821.

He established Fort Snelling, a military camp in the Northwest Territory (now Minnesota) in 1828.

In 1829, ZT was assigned to Fort Crawford, a military camp at Prairie du Chien in the Michigan Territory (now Wisconsin). One of his aides was a recent West Point graduate, future son-in-law and future Confederate president, Jefferson Davis.

Favorite Christmas Carol: "It Came Upon a Midnight Clear"

Coincidences: There are 13 letters in his name; upon ZT's death Millard Fillmore became the 13th president.

Last words: "I am about to die, I expect the summons soon. I have endeavored to discharge all my official duties faithfully. I regret nothing, but am sorry that I am about to leave my friends."

Cause of Death: The suspected cause of his death was gastroenteritis. On July 4, 1850, while attending the ceremony laying the cornerstone of the Washington Monument, ZT consumed large quantities of iced milk, cold cherries, and pickled cucumbers; he was dead five days later. Other medical experts have argued that he died of typhus or cholera.

MILLARD FILLMORE
Thirteenth president
1850-53

The Straight Facts

Born: January 7, 1800
Birthplace: Cayuga County, New York
Ancestry: English
Physical Characteristics: 5'9" tall, blue eyes, graying hair
Religion: Unitarian
Occupation: Lawyer

Wife: (1) Abigail Powers Fillmore (1798-1853); (2) Caroline Carmichael Mc-
intosh Fillmore (1813-81)
Date of Marriage: (1) February 16, 1826; (2) February 10, 1858
Children: (1) One daughter, one son; (2) none
College: None
Military History: Home Guard, New York state militia
Political Party: Whig
Previous Political Offices: Member, New York state assembly (1828-31);
Member, U.S. House of Representatives (1833-35; 1837-43); Controller,
state of New York (1848-49); Vice-president of the United States (1849-50)
Vice-President: None
Died: March 8, 1874, in Buffalo, New York
Burial Place: Forest Lawn Cemetery, Buffalo, New York
Firsts: First president to have a stepmother
First president to have been an indentured servant
Biography in Brief: Millard Fillmore was the son of Nathaniel Fillmore and
Phoebe Millard. He taught school and studied law; was admitted to the bar,
1823. He was a member of the state assembly, 1829-32; in Congress, 1833-
35 and again 1837-43. He opposed the entrance of Texas as a slave territory
and voted for a protective tariff. In 1844 he was defeated for governor of
New York. In 1848 he was elected vice-president and succeeded as president July 10, 1850, after Taylor's death. Fillmore favored the Compromise
of 1850 and signed the Fugitive Slave Law. His policies pleased neither ex-
pansionists nor slave-holders and he was not renominated in 1852. In 1856 he
was nominated by the American (Know Nothing) party and accepted by the
Whigs, but was defeated by James Buchanan.

The More Colorful Facts

Astrological Sign: Capricorn
Nicknames: American Louis Philippe, Last of the Whigs, Woolcarder
President.
Original Family Name: Phillmore. Ancestors can be traced back to ca.1700
A.D.
Presidential Notes: First Lady Abigail Fillmore began the first White House
library, donating many of the family books to start the collection. She also
had the first bathtub installed in the White House, in 1852.
Campaign Notes: "Know Nothing Party" was the nickname of the American
Party, which chose MF and Andrew Jackson Donelson, nephew of Andrew
Jackson, as their standard bearers in 1852. The Know-Nothings were origi-
nally a secret organization that got its nickname because members would
deny knowing anything about party matters.
Homes: 24 Shearer Avenue, East Aurora, New York. The home MF built after
he finished law school in 1826 and where he lived with his wife until 1830.

52 Niagara Street, Buffalo, New York. MF's retirement home.

Other positions: Formed a law partnership, Hall and Fillmore, in 1830 with Nathan K. Hall. The partnership later became one of western New York's most prestigious firms.

Elected president of the Buffalo Historical Society in 1862.

Elected president of the Buffalo General Hospital in 1870, and served for four years.

Elected as the first president of the Buffalo Club, a New York society, in 1886.

Favorite color: Fuchsia

Pen name: Juridicious, used in writing his views of the relevance of religious testing of witnesses in legal cases.

Honors Refused: In 1846, MF, who had no classical education, refused an honorary doctorate of civil law from Oxford University, claiming that he wouldn't accept a degree he couldn't read.

Last Words: "The nourishment is palatable."

"The Right Man for the Right Place." Here, as an elder statesman, Fillmore is depicted as a peacemaker, between Republican John C. Fremont (left) and Democrat James Buchanan (right) in the 1865 presidential campaign.

FRANKLIN PIERCE

Fourteenth president

1853-57

The Straight Facts

Born: November 23, 1804
Birthplace: Hillsboro, New Hampshire
Ancestry: English

Physical Characteristics: 5'10" tall, dark gray eyes, black hair
Religion: Episcopalian
Occupation: Lawyer, politician
Wife: Jane Means Appleton (1806-63)
Date of Marriage: November 10, 1834
Children: Three sons
College: Bowdoin College, class of 1824
Military History: Brigadier general, U.S. Army
Political Party: Democrat
Previous Political Offices: Member, New Hampshire house of representatives (1829-33); Speaker of the house (1832); Member, U.S. House of Representatives (1833-37); Member, U.S. Senate (1837-42); President, New Hampshire fifth state Constitutional Convention (1850)
Vice-President: William Rufus DeVane King (1786-1853)
Died: October 8, 1869, in Concord, New Hampshire
Burial Place: Old North Cemetery Concord, New Hampshire
Firsts: First president born in New Hampshire
   First president who affirmed oath
   First president whose vice-president never served, as he died before assuming any responsibilities
   First and only president to retain his original cabinet during his four year term
Biography in Brief: Franklin Pierce was the son of Benjamin Pierce, veteran of the Revolution and governor of New Hampshire, 1827, and Anna Kendrick. He was graduated from Bowdoin, 1824. A lawyer, he served in the state leg-

From the 1852 presidential campaign, a Whig cartoon shows Gen. Winfield Scott pulling the presidential chair out from under Pierce. Pierce, however, won the election.

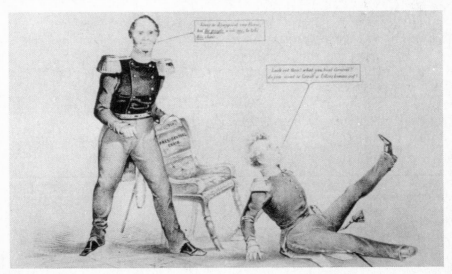

islature 1829-33; in Congress, supporting Andrew Jackson, 1833-37; as U.S. senator, 1837-42. He enlisted in the Mexican War, became brigadier general under Gen. Winfield Scott. In 1852 Pierce was nominated on the 49th ballot over Lewis Cass, Stephen A. Douglas, and James Buchanan, and defeated General Scott, a Whig. Though against slavery, Pierce was influenced by proslavery Southerners. He ignored the Ostend Manifesto that the U.S. either buy or take Cuba. He approved the Kansas-Nebraska Act, leaving slavery to popular vote ("squatter sovereignty"), 1854. He signed a reciprocity treaty with Canada and approved the Gadsden Purchase from Mexico, 1853. Denied renomination by the Democrats, he spent most of his remaining years in Concord, New Hampshire.

The More Colorful Facts

Astrological Sign: Sagittarius

Nicknames: The Dictator*, Handsome Frank, Purse, Young Hickory of the Granite Hills.

Presidential Notes: Central heating was installed for the first time in the White House in 1853, during the Pierce administration. FP was the first to deliver his inaugural as an oration, not a speech. After his vice-president, William Rufus King, died in office, FP served the rest of his term without a vice-president.

Family Notes: First Lady Jane Appleton Pierce wore only black after the death of her third son. Franklin, Jr. died after only three days of life; Frank Robert died of typhus at age 4; and Benjamin was killed in a train crash in January 1853 while the family was on the way to Washington for his father's inauguration as 14th president of the United States.

FP always insisted that grace be said before every meal.

Campaign Notes: FP was nominated as a dark horse candidate by the Democrats on the 49th ballot. "Our Country Right or Wrong," and "We Polked You in '44, We shall Pierce you in '52" were themes of the 1852 Democratic campaign.

Homes: Homestead, Hillsboro, New Hampshire, FP's boyhood home.

Spigel Grove, Concord, New Hampshire, 1857-69.

Other Positions: When elected to the state legislature of New Hampshire, 1828, FP was selected as chair of the Committee of Education because he was college educated.

In 1844, he established a law firm, Pierce and Minot, in Concord, New Hampshire with Josiah Minot.

Education: FP was graduated from Bowdoin College in 1824, third in his class, with a Bachelor of Arts degree. Pierce's future father-in-law, Jessee Apple-

*Given to him by his political enemies in his home state of New Hampshire.

ton, was president of the College at the time he attended. Among his classmates were Henry Wadsworth Longfellow and Nathaniel Hawthorne.

His senior year Latin dissertation was entitled "De Triumphis Romanorum."

He received an honorary LL.D. from Dartmouth College in 1850.

Memberships: Aztec Club, a society of Mexican War veterans.

Literary Note: Against his publisher's wishes, Nathaniel Hawthorne dedicated his book, *Our Old Home* (1863), to his good friend and former classmate Franklin Pierce.

Cause of Death: Stomach inflation.

JAMES BUCHANAN

Fifteenth president

1857-61

The Straight Facts

Born: April 23, 1791
Birthplace: Cove Gap, Pennsylvania
Ancestry: Scots-Irish
Physical Characteristics: 6' tall
Religion: Presbyterian
Occupation: Lawyer, statesman
Wife: None
Children: None
College: Dickinson College, class of 1809
Military History: Infantryman, U.S. Army
Political Party: Democrat
Previous Political Offices: Member, Pennsylvania house of representatives (1814-15); Member, U.S. House of Representatives (1821-31); U.S. minister to Russia (1832-33); Member, U.S. Senate (1834-45); Secretary of state (1845-49); U.S. minister to Great Britain (1853)
Vice-President: John Cabel Breckinridge (1821-75)
Died: June 1, 1868, at Wheatland in Pennsylvania
Burial Place: Woodward Hill Cemetery, Lancaster, Pennsylvania
Firsts: First president born in Pennsylvania
First president to be a bachelor when elected
First and only president to never marry
Biography in Brief James Buchanan was the son of James Buchanan, a merchant born in Ireland, and Elizabeth Speer. He was graduated from Dickinson, 1809; was a volunteer in the War of 1812; member, Pennsylvania legislature, 1814-16; Congress, 1821-31; Jackson's minister to Russia, 1831-33; U.S. senator 1834-45. As Polk's secretary of state, 1845-49, he ended the Oregon dispute with Britain, supported the Mexican War, and annexation of Texas. As minister to Britain, 1853, he signed the Ostend Manifesto. Nominated by Democrats, he was elected, 1856, over John C. Fremont (Republican) and Millard Fillmore (American Know Nothing and Whig tickets). On slavery he favored popular sovereignty and choice by state constitutions; he accepted the proslavery Dred Scott decision as binding. He denied the right of states to secede. A strict constructionist, he desired to keep peace and found no authority for using force. He died at Wheatland, near Lancaster, Pennsylvania.

The More Colorful Facts

Astrological Sign: Taurus
Nicknames: Bachelor President, Do Nothing President, Old Buck, Old Fogey, Old Fossil, Old Obliquity, Old Public Functionary, Ten-cent Jimmy*.

*Also a nickname given to politicians who advocated low tariffs, low wages, and a wage of 10 cents a day.

"A Serviceable Garment, or Reverie of a Bachelor." Louis Maurer, in an 1856 cartoon, shows Buchanan contemplating the Cuba patch in his coat. He had pressed unsuccessfully for the purchase of Cuba.

Presidential Notes: During JB's administration, Albert Edward, later Edward VII of England, was the first member of the immediate royal family to visit the U.S. He visited the country in 1860 and stayed at the White House as a guest of JB. The prince was given Buchanan's bedroom and the president slept on a couch in a hallway.

Harriet Lane (1830-1906), Buchanan's niece, served as his official White House hostess. The song "Listen for the Mocking Bird" was written in her honor in 1855 by Septimus Winner. In 1857, a Coast Guard cutter was commissioned and named in her honor. According to Coast Guard records, this cutter fired the first shot at sea during the Civil War. In 1982, another cutter was commissioned in her honor, with the wife of Transportation Secretary Drew Lewis doing the honors.

The first president to send and receive a transatlantic telegram: on August 16, 1858, he exchanged greetings with Queen Victoria of Britain.

Campaign Notes: "Buck and Breck" was poster slogan for the 1855 Democratic candidates, JB and John Breckenridge, his vice-presidential running mate.

Namesakes: James "Diamond Jim" Buchanan Brady, New York financier and gourmet, who was born in the year JB became president.

Homes: Wheatland, 1120 Marietta Avenue, Lancaster, Pennsylvania, purchased at a cost of $6,750 in 1848.

Love Life: Anne Caroline Coleman, his financee, died of an overdose of laudanum in December 1819 after a lovers' quarrel. It was fashionable for ladies to take laudanum to sleep in those days. No one is certain if Anne deliberately tried to kill herself or if she was so distraught that she took a little extra to help her sleep. Buchanan vowed to never marry after her death.

Education: JB was graduated from Dickinson College in Carlisle, Pennsylvania on September 7, 1809. At one point, he was expelled from Dickinson for wild behavior and bad conduct. He pleaded for another chance and three years later graduated with honors.

Other Positions: Prizefighter

Favorite color: Maroon

Quotes: "Crown of Thorns"—on the burdens of the presidency.

"If you are as happy in entering the White House as I feel on returning to Wheatland, you are a happy man indeed!"—to Abraham Lincoln on March 4, 1861.

Songs: "Buchanan's Union Grand March," written by Nathan Richardson in honor of JB's inauguration.

Books: *Mr. Buchanan's Administration of The Eve of the Rebellion,* published in 1866 by Appleton Publishers of New York City, was the only book written by JB.

ABRAHAM LINCOLN
Sixteenth president
1861-65

The Straight Facts

Born: February 12, 1809
Birthplace: Hogdenville, in Hardin County (today, Larue), Kentucky
Ancestry: English
Physical Characteristics: 6'4" tall, gray eyes, black hair, 180 lbs.
Religion: No particular denomination
Occupation: Lawyer
Wife: Mary Ann Todd Lincoln (1818-82)
Date of Marriage: November 4, 1842
Children: Four sons
College: None
Military History: Captain, U.S. Army Volunteers
Political Party: Whig; Republican
Previous Political Offices: Postmaster, New Salem, Illinois (1833); Member, General Assembly of Illinois (1835-36); Member, U.S. House of Representatives (1847-49)
Vice-President: Hannibal Hamlin (1809-91), first term; Andrew Johnson (1808-75), second term
Died: April 15, 1865, in Washington, D.C.
Burial Place: Oak Ridge Cemetery, Springfield, Illinois
Firsts: First president to be assassinated
First president born in Kentucky
First president born in a state not of the original 13
First and only president granted a patent
First president to have a beard;
First Republican president
Biography in Brief: Abraham Lincoln was born in a log cabin on Sinking Spring Farm. He was the son of Thomas Lincoln, a carpenter, and Nancy Hanks.
 The Lincolns moved to Spencer County, near Gentryville, when Abe was seven. In 1830 the family moved to Macon County, Illinois. Lincoln lost election to the General Assembly of Illinois, 1832, but later won four times, beginning in 1834. He enlisted in the militia for the Black Hawk War, 1832. In New Salem he ran a store, surveyed land, and was postmaster.
 In 1837 Lincoln was admitted to the bar and became partner in a Springfield, Illinois, law office. He was elected to Congress, 1847-49. He opposed the Mexican War. He supported Zachary Taylor in 1848. He opposed

the Kansas-Nebraska Act and extension of slavery in 1854. He failed in his bid for the Senate in 1855. He supported John C. Fremont in 1856.

In 1858 Lincoln had Republican support in the Illinois legislature for appointment to the Senate, but was defeated by Stephen A. Douglas, Democrat, who had sponsored the Kansas-Nebraska Act.

Lincoln was nominated for president by the Republican party on an antislavery platform in 1860. When he won the election, South Carolina seceded from the Union December 20, 1860, followed in 1861 by ten southern states.

The Civil War erupted when Fort Sumter was attacked April 12, 1861. On September 22, 1862, five days after the battle of Antietam, he announced that slaves in territory then in rebellion would be free January 1, 1863, date of the Emancipation Proclamation. His speeches, including his Gettysburg and Inaugural addresses, are remembered for their eloquence.

Lincoln was reelected, 1864, over Gen. George B. McClellan, Democrat. Gen. Robert E. Lee surrendered April 9, 1865. On April 14, Lincoln was shot by actor John Wilkes Booth in Ford's Theatre, Washington. He died the next day.

The More Colorful Facts

Astrological Sign: Aquarius

Nicknames: Abolitionist Emperor*, Ancient, Gorilla, Great (or Grand) Wrestler, Great Emancipator, Honest Abe, Illinois Beast, Long Abe, Massa Linkum, Ourang-Outang at the White House*, Rail Splitter, The Right Man in the Right Place, Sectional President, Tyrant, Uncle Abe.

Presidential Notes: The first president to be photographed at his inauguration (his second). In the photo, Lincoln conspirators John Wilkes Booth, John Surratt, and George Atzerdot can all be seen in close proximity to AL.

The Bixby Letter, one of condolence written to Mrs. Lydia Bixby of Boston whom he thought had lost five sons in the Civil War, was one of AL's most famous pieces of correspondence. Lincoln had been misinformed about their fates, but the letter still shows his great humanity.

The original manuscript for AL's Emancipation Proclamation, signed January 1, 1863, was destroyed in the Chicago Fire of 1871.

The $10 demand note, issued July 17, 1861, was the first U.S. paper currency to feature a living president.

Family Notes: AL's wife, Mary Ann Todd Lincoln, was a southern belle; four of her brothers and four brothers-in-law fought on the side of the Confederacy during the Civil War. This caused many rumors to the effect that she was a southern spy. AL was so distressed upon hearing these rumors that he testified at a senate hearing denouncing them.

The inscription on wife Mary's wedding band read: "A.L. to Mary Nov. 4, 1842. 'Love is Eternal'"

AL called Mary "Molly" while he was courting her, and "Mother" affectionately after they were married.

Mary preferred to be called "Madame President."

Son Robert Todd Lincoln (1842-1926) was the only one to live to manhood. He served as secretary of war for Presidents James Garfield and Chester Arthur. He was the only man to be in the vicinity of and attend the funerals of the first three assassinated presidents. After the death of Pres. William McKinley, he vowed never to appear in public again with an incumbent American president.

William Wallace Lincoln (1850-62) was the son who died in the White House on February 20. AL had all the government departments closed. It was the only time the U.S. government has ceased operating in honor of the death of a presidential child.

AL's youngest son Thomas (1853-71) was nicknamed "Tad" because his father thought he looked like a tadpole due to the fact that his head appeared to be too large for his body. The White House staff called him "Little Tyrant" because he was spoiled and always wanted to have his own way. Tad

---

*So-called by the Confederate press

was given his own Union lieutenant colonel's uniform and he would march White House guards and staff around for hours.

Campaign Notes: "Don't Swap Horses" was the 1864 Republican presidential campaign theme. (However, AL did, in swapping Andrew Johnson for Vice-president Hannibal Hamlin.)

Namesakes: Lincoln Memorial, Washington, D.C. The cornerstone was laid on February 12, 1915, and the memorial was dedicated on May 30, 1922. Robert Todd Lincoln attend the dedication. The architect was Henry Bacon, and the 19-foot-high figure of AL in the memorial was sculpted by Daniel Chester French.

Lincoln Logs, a children's building toy invented by John Lloyd Wright, the son of famed architect Frank Lloyd Wright, were named after the logs used to reproduce AL's birthplace. Alfred W. Dennett had actually built a replica of the cabin transplanting it to the Pan-American Exposition in Buffalo, New York, in 1901.

Lincoln Rocker, a highback upholstered rocking chair with open arms that was popular in the mid-1800s, and the type of chair AL was sitting in when he was shot. This chair is now on display at the Henry Ford Museum in Dearborn, Michigan.

Lincoln Penny, a copper cent first circulated in 1909, was the first to bear the portrait of a president. It was designed by Victor David Brenner and based on a photo taken of AL by Mathew Brady. The reverse side was changed in 1959 from the original sheaves of wheat to the Lincoln Memorial.

Mister Lincoln Rose, a dark crimson rose that is a cross between a Chrysler Imperial and a Charles Mallerin.

Homes: 526 South Seventh Street, Springfield, Illinois. This was the only home AL ever owned. Purchased in 1844, the price was $1,500 ($300 for the land and $1,200 for the house), which represented an entire year's salary.

Other Positions: Saloon owner. In 1833, AL took out a saloon license for the store he owned in Springfield, Illinois, with William Franklin Berry. The store folded two years later due to Berry's death and left AL $1,000 in debt; it took him 15 years to pay off the debt.

Steamboat pilot. On the *Talisman,* on the Mississippi River, 1832.

Law partner. First in Stuart & Lincoln, in Springfield, Illinois, in 1837. John Stuart was a cousin of wife Mary. Second, with William Henry Herndon, from 1844 to 1861. Herndon was also a Lincoln biographer, considered by many to be the best.

Pets: Bob, a grey and white Maltese. A pet of the young AL, it was so named because when a kitten a spark from a coal fireplace burned one inch of tail off, giving him a bobtail.

Jack, the family pet turkey of the Lincoln sons, which received a reprieve from AL and was spared from being the main course for Thanksgiving dinner.

Jib, a pet mongrel, which liked to sit on Lincoln's lap and eat morsels from the table.

Early Love Life: Ann Rutledge, his first fiance, died of malarial fever with AL at her bedside. They first met when he boarded at her parents' tavern in 1833. She was reportedly the love of his life, although Mary Lincoln claimed the story of their romance was made up.

After the death of Ann Rutledge, AL proposed to Mary Owen. She refused him because she said he was, among other things, deficient in the little things which make up the chain of a woman's happiness. She later married farmer Jesse Vineyard.

Health: For most of his adult life, AL suffered from bunions.

AL had smallpox while in office. One story claimed that he had contracted the disease when a female Confederate spy, dressed in widow's weeds and seeking a favor, kissed the president.

Some claim AL suffered from Marfan's disease, a nervous disorder hereditary in the Lincoln family. The disease is a genetic condition that causes elongation of the skeletal system, uncoordinated and cold limbs, heart failure, and visual problems.

Boot Size: 12B

Hat Size: 7½

Favorite Poem: "Immortality, or Oh, Why Should the Spirit of Mortal Man be Proud," by William Knox.

A *Vanity Fair* cartoon shows Lincoln doing the Highland fling while waiting for a train to Washington.

Favorite Ballad: "Twenty Years Ago," a melancholy tale of a man revisitng the haunts of his youth and the graveyard where his friends are buried.

Favorite Christmas Carol: "We Three Kings"

Favorite Food: Fricasseed chicken

Coincidences: AL's grandfather, Abraham Lincoln (1744-85), was also married to a woman named Mary (Shepley), had a son named Thomas, and was shot and murdered (by Indians).

AL kept an envelope entitled "Assassinations" in his desk in which he used to save all the threatening letters he received, and he often reread them. At one point, it is said to have contained over 80 letters.

Edwin Thomas Booth, the famous nineteenth century American actor and brother of Lincoln's assassin John Wilkes Booth, saved the life of Robert Todd Lincoln. Early in the Civil War, young Lincoln was waiting to board a train at Jersey City, New Jersey, when, pressed by the crowds, he slipped between the platform and a moving car. Booth hauled him back to safety.

Just hours before he was shot, AL said to his bodyguard Col. William Crooks, "I believe there are men who want to take my life. And I have no doubt they will do it."

Defeats: Before being elected to the presidency, AL suffered eleven major defeats in his life.

1831	Failed in business
1832	Defeated in a bid for the Illinois legislature
1833	Death of Ann Rutledge
1834	Second failure in business
1836	Suffered a nervous breakdown
1838	Defeated in bid for speaker of the Illinois house
1840	Defeated in bid for being a Whig elector
1848	Defeated in bid for the U.S. House of Representatives
1855	Defeated in a bid for U.S. Senate
1856	Defeated in a bid for the Republican vice-presidential nomination
1858	Again defeated in a bid for the U.S. Senate

Duels: James Shields, an Illinois state auditor, challenged AL to a duel in 1842 over a slanderous newspaper article. Shields believed Lincoln wrote the anonymous piece sent to *The Sangamo Journal* by "Aunt Becca," but many claim that it was actually written by Mary Todd Lincoln and her friend Julia Jayne and that AL was defending her honor. Historians now believe that all three had a part in the writing of the article. Shields was a suitor of Mary Todd and there is a discrepancy as to who actually dumped whom. As the challengee, AL had the choice of weapons and chose the longsword. Shields took one look at the six-foot-plus AL swinging a sword with his long arms and called off the duel after the seconds worked out a compromise.

Inventions: AL received U.S. patent 6469 for a complicated device that lifted ships over dangerous shoals with buoyant air chambers.

Honorary citizenship: San Marino bestowed such on AL and he was also depicted on one of their postage stamps.

Assassination Attempt: In the so-called Baltimore plot, secessionist sympathizers planned to assassinate president-elect AL as he passed through Baltimore in 1861 on the way to his inauguration. The eight men involved drew lots to see who would get the red marker and either shoot or stab Lincoln. The winner was to keep it a secret and not tell anyone until the appointed time. Unknown to the other plotters, organizer Sipriano Fernandino actually placed three red markers in the hat so if one would back out, there were always two others who could possibly strike. Government operative Harry Davies, who infiltrated the gang (and drew a white marker) reported the plot to Allan Pinkerton who was able to sneak AL through the town in the middle of the night.

Assassination: AL was shot by John Wilkes Booth with a .44 caliber derringer at Ford's Theater in Washington, D.C., on April 14, 1865. The president was at the theater for Laura Keene's last performance in *Our American Cousin.* AL died the next day.

In all, ten people were implicated in the plot first to kidnap and, then, because the war had ended, murder AL and key members of his cabinet. The average age of the ten conspirators was 28.3 years.

Name	Role	Fate
Samuel Arnold	Conspirator	Life; paroled 1869
George Atzerodt	Kill VP Johnson	Hanged July 7, 1865
John Wilkes Booth	Kill Lincoln	Shot April 26, 1865
David Herold	Aid escape	Hanged July 7, 1865
Dr. Samuel Mudd	Conspirator	Life; paroled 1869
Michael O'Laughlin	Kill U.S. Grant	Life; died in prison
Lewis Paine (Powell)	Kill W. H. Seward	Hanged July 7, 1865
Edward Spangler	Douse theater lights	Life; paroled 1869
John Surratt	Conspirator	Tried 1867; hung jury
Mary Surratt	Conspirator	Hanged July 7, 1865

Last Words: "They won't think anything of it," spoken in response to wife Mary's question as to whether he thought the audience would mind if they held hands.

ANDREW JOHNSON
Seventeenth president
1865-69

The Straight Facts

Born: December 29, 1808
Birthplace: Raleigh, North Carolina
Ancestry: English
Physical Characteristics: 5'10" tall, blue eyes, brown hair, 168 lbs.
Religion: No specific denomination
Occupation: Tailor, politician
Wife: Eliza McCardle Johnson (1810-76)
Date of Marriage: May 5, 1827
Children: Two daughters, three sons
College: None
Military History: Brigadier General, Tennessee Volunteers
Political Party: Democrat (elected vice-president on National Union Ticket)
Previous Political Offices: Alderman, Greeneville, Tennessee (1828-29); Mayor, Greeneville, Tennessee (1830-33); Member, Tennessee legislature

(1835-40); Member, Tennessee senate (1841-43); Member, U.S. House of Representatives (1843-53); Governor, state of Tennessee (1853-57); Member, U.S. Senate (1857-62); Vice-president of the United States (1865); (Post presidency) Member, U.S. Senate (1875)

Vice-President: None
Died: July 31, 1875, in Tennessee
Burial Place: Andrew Johnson National Cemetery, Greeneville, Tennessee
Firsts: First president to be impeached
First mayor elected president
First and only president elected to the Senate after completing term of office

Biography in Brief: Andrew Johnson was the son of Jacob Johnson, porter at an inn and a church sexton, and Mary McDonough. He was apprenticed to a tailor but ran away and eventually settled in Greeneville, Tennessee. He became an alderman, 1828; mayor, 1830; state representative and senator, 1835-43; member of Congress, 1843-53; governor of Tennessee, 1853-57; U.S. senator, 1857-62. He supported John C. Breckinridge against Abraham Lincoln in 1860. He had held slaves, but opposed secession and tried to prevent his home state, Tennessee, from seceding. In March 1862, Lincoln appointed him military governor of occupied Tennessee. In 1864 he was nominated for vice-president with Lincoln on the National Union ticket to win Democratic support. He succeeded Lincoln as president April 15, 1865. In a controversy with Congress over the president's power over the South, he proclaimed, May 26, 1865, an amnesty to all Confederates except certain leaders if they would ratify the 13th Amendment abolishing slavery. States doing so added antiNegro provisions that enraged Congress, which restored military control over the South. When Johnson removed Edwin M. Stanton, secretary of war, without notifying the Senate, thus repudiating the Tenure of Office Act, the House impeached him for this and other reasons. He was tried by the Senate, and acquitted by only one vote, May 26, 1868. He returned to the Senate in 1875.

The More Colorful Facts

Astrological Sign: Capricorn
Nicknames: Andy the Sot, Constitution Defender, Daddy of the Baby, Demagogue*, Great Commoner, Grim Presence†, King Andy, Last Jacksonian, Man Without a Party, Old Andy, Plebian Andy, Sir Veto, Tennessee Tailor.

Andyjohnsonianisms: Nickname given to radical and novel proposals of Andrew Johnson as a Tennessee state senator.

*So-called as vice-president by Mary Todd Lincoln.
†Called by the White House staff.

Presidential Notes: Queen Emma, Queen of the Sandwich Islands (Hawaii), on August 14, 1866, paid the first visit by a queen to an American president.

Family Notes: Wed at age 18 years, 115 days, AJ married at the youngest age of all presidents. He married Eliza McCardle, 16 years and 213 days, on May 17, 1827.

Education: None; he was the only unschooled man to become president.

Early Profession: AJ was a tailor. James J. Selby, a tailor in Raleigh, North Carolina, offered a $10 reward for the return of his runaway apprentice, Andrew Johnson. He had been apprenticed in 1822. He had run to Carthage, fifty miles southwest of Raleigh, and opened his own shop. The reward was advertised in the Raleigh *Gazette*.

Political Education: AJ considered *American Speaker*, a collection of famous speeches, given to him by a friend, a Raleigh, North Carolina, school master, to be his political textbook.

Resignations: AJ resigned from several positions, including Tennessee state solicitor (1830), U.S. attorney (1831), U.S. congressman (1837), U.S. senator (1838), and justice of the Tennessee Supreme Court (1839).

Assassination Escape: Vice-president AJ lived in Suite 68 at Kirkwood, a Washington, D.C., hotel, located at 12th Street and Pennsylvania Avenue. It was here he was informed by his friend Leonard Farwell of the shooting of President Abraham Lincoln. Johnson had a cold on the night of the shooting and did not accompany Farwell to Ford's Theatre as he had planned. Chief Justice Salmon P. Chase administered the oath of office to Johnson in his suite on April 15, 1865. Lincoln conspirator George Atzerodt, who was assigned to kill Johnson was also living at the Kirkwood, in Room 136, which was immediately above Johnson's suite. Atzerodt was to have knocked on the door of Johnson's room at precisely 10:15 P.M. to shoot the vice-president, but had a change of heart and did not go through with the plan.

Quotes: "She kept the nest that hatched the egg"—about Mary Surratt.

Song: "President Johnson's Grand March and Quick Step" written by E. Mack in 1865.

Burial Request: His remains were put to rest with a copy of the Constitution as a pillow and the American flag as a blanket.

ULYSSES SIMPSON GRANT

Eighteenth president

1869-77

The Straight Facts

Born: April 27, 1822
Birthplace: Point Pleasant, Ohio
Ancestry: Scots-Irish
Physical Characteristics: 5′8½″ tall, blue eyes, sandy brown hair

Religion: Methodist
Occupation: Soldier
Wife: Julia Boggs Dent Grant (1826-1902)
Date of Marriage: August 22, 1848
Children: One daughter, three sons
College: United States Military Academy (West Point), class of 1843
Military History: General of the Army
Political Party: Republican
Previous Political Offices: Secretary of war (1867-1868)
Vice-President: Schuyler Colfax (1823-85), first term; Henry Wilson (1812-75), second term
Died: July 23, 1885, at Mt. McGregor, New York
Burial Place: Grant National Memorial, New York City, New York
Firsts: First president born in Ohio
First president to change his name (from Hiram Ulysses)
First president to have both parents alive when taking oath of office
First president to have a female run against him for president
Biography in Brief: Ulysses S. Grant was the son of Jesse Root Grant, a tanner, and Hannah Simpson. The year after his birth the family moved to George-town, Ohio. He was graduated from West Point in 1843; served under Gen-erals Zachary Taylor and Winfield Scott in the Mexican War; resigned, 1854; worked in St. Louis until 1860; then went to Galena, Illinois. With the start of the Civil War, he was named colonel of the 21st Illinois Volunteers, 1861, then brigadier general; took Forts Henry and Donelson; fought at Shi-loh; took Vicksburg. After Grant's victory at Chattanooga, Pres. Abraham Lincoln placed him in command of the Union Armies. He accepted Confed-erate Gen. Robert E. Lee's surrender at Appomattox, April 1865. Pres. An-drew Johnson appointed Grant secretary of war when he suspended Edwin M. Stanton, but Grant was not confirmed. He was nominated for president by the Republicans in 1868 and elected over Horatio Seymour, Democrat. The 15th Amendment, amnesty bill, and civil service reform were events of his administration. The liberal Republicans and Democrats opposed him with Horace Greeley, 1872, but he was reelected. An attempt by the Stal-warts (Old Guard) to nominate him in 1880 failed. In 1884 the collapse of Grant & War, investment house, left him penniless. He wrote his personal memoirs while ill with cancer and completed them four days before his death. The book realized over $450,000.

The More Colorful Facts

Astrological Sign: Taurus
Nicknames: American Sphinx, Bulldog, Butcher Grant*, Country Sam, The

*Mary Todd Lincoln was especially fond of this one.

An 1872 Republican campaign poster emphasizes the humble background of Grant and his vice-presidential running mate Henry Wilson.

Fighting Tanner, Great Hammerer, Great Peacemaker, H.U.G.†, Hero of Appomattox, Hero of Heroes, Little Beauty‡, Man Who Won the War, Unconditional Surrender, Union Safeguard, United States Grant, United We Stand Grant.

Real Name: His given name was Hiram Ulysses Grant. He dropped it for two reasons. First, the appointment to West Point read Ulysses Simpson (mother's maiden name) Grant due to a clerical error. Thomas Lyon Hamer (1800-46), the Ohio congressman (1833-39) who arranged the appointment to West Point could not remember the boy's correct name; he knew one of his names was Ulysses and that his mother's maiden name was Simpson and that was how the appointment came in. Second, USG did not like his initials with the given name (H.U.G.).

Presidential Notes: The temperature at USG's second inaugural was -4° F, the second coldest in Washington history.

†Hated this childhood nickname which stood for his real name, Hiram Ulysses Grant. He went unnamed for the first six weeks of his life until his mother decided on the name Hiram.
‡So-called by the officers of his regiment, because of his rosy complexion and soft, melodious voice.

USG was driving his racing horse, Julia, when arrested for speeding on M Street between 11th and 12th in Washington, D.C. The police officer, William West, did not recognize the president. USG paid the $20 fine, which he forfeited when he failed to appear for the trial and sent in a commendation for West.

King David Kalakaua, king of the Sandwich Islands (now Hawaii), was the first ruling monarch to be entertained in the White House, in 1874.

Family Notes: As a lieutenant, Grant wooed and wed Miss Julia Dent at White Haven, her family home near St. Louis. They were married on August 22, 1848.

First Lady Julia Dent Grant was cross-eyed. When it was suggested to Grant that she have an operation to correct the condition, he replied that he liked her that way.

Daughter Ellen Wrenshall (Nellie) Grant was married in the White House East Room on May 21, 1874, to Algernon Charles Frederick Sartoris, an Englishman. Poet Walt Whitman wrote "A Kiss for the Bride" for the occasion. Sartoris turned out to be an alcoholic and the two separated in 1889.

Campaign Notes: "A Smokin His Cigar," (1868) and "Grant at the Head of the Nation" (1868), written by W.G. Fiske, "Grant at the Head of the Nation" (1868), also by Fiske, and "Ulysses Is His Name" (1868) by Dexter Smith were campaign songs.

Namesakes: Ulysses S. Grant "Lil" Stoner (1899-1966), the major league baseball pitcher for Detroit, Pittsburgh, and Philadelphia. He threw the pitch that Babe Ruth hit in what is baseball's longest home run.

Homes: Hardscrabble, the crude log cabin Ulysses S. Grant built for his new wife Julia on a 60-acre tract of land about 12 miles from St. Louis presented to them as a wedding gift by her father. The Grants lived there from 1855 to 1858. The cabin still exists, now on the grounds of the Anheuser Busch estate in St. Louis, Missouri.

511 Bouthillier Street, Galena, Ohio, home purchased and given to the Grants by the citizens of Galena.

Early Professions: USG was taught the tanning trade by his father, Jesse, who, in turn, had been taught the trade by Owen Brown, the father of abolitionist John Brown.

Military Rank: USG was the first to hold the rank of lieutenant general, created by Congress in 1864.

Favorite Breakfast: Cucumbers soaked in vinegar.

Preferred Brand of Whiskey: Old Crow

Favorite Snack: Fried apples

Favorite Book: *Ivanhoe*, written by Sir Walter Scott in 1820.

Horses: His chestnut sorrel mount, York, set West Point's high jump over record in 1843, a record that held for 24 years. The height is questionnable, some claim it to be better than six feet.

Cincinnatus, a favorite horse, was used as a model for an equestrian statue standing in front of the U.S. Capitol.

Books: *Personal Memoirs,* his autobiography, was written to pay his debts.

Last words: "Water"

Burial: USG is buried in Grant's Tomb. Buried with him in the structure (technically they are not buried in the ground) is his wife. A public subscription drive was held to build the memorial on New York City's Riverside Drive. The architect was John H. Duncan. The tomb was dedicated in 1897 by President William McKinley.

The inscription on the tomb is "Let Us Have Peace."

RUTHERFORD BIRCHARD HAYES

Nineteenth president

1877-81

The Straight Facts

Born: October 4, 1822
Birthplace: Delaware, Ohio
Ancestry: Scottish
Physical Characteristics: 5'8" tall, blue eyes, reddish-brown hair, 170 lbs.
Religion: Methodist
Occupation: Lawyer
Wife: Lucy Ware Webb Hayes (1831-89)
Date of Marriage: December 30, 1852
Children: One daughter, seven sons
College: Kenyon College, class of 1842
Military History: Major general, Ohio Volunteer Army
Political Party: Republican

Previous Political Offices: Solicitor, city of Cincinnati, Ohio (1857-59); U.S. House of Representatives (1865-67); Governor, state of Ohio (1868-72; 1876-77)

Vice-President: William Almon Wheeler (1819-1887)

Died: January 17, 1893, at Fremont, Ohio

Burial Place: Rutherford B. Hayes State Park, Fremont, Ohio

Firsts: First president to visit the West Coast while in office

First president to use the telephone while in office

First president to celebrate his golden wedding anniversary while in office

Biography in Brief: Rutherford B. Hayes was the posthumous son of Rutherford Hayes, a farmer, and Sophia Birchard. He was raised by his uncle Sardis Birchard. He was graduated from Kenyon College, 1842, and Harvard Law School, 1845. He practiced law in Lower Sandusky, Ohio, now Fremont; was city solicitor of Cincinnati, 1858-61. In the Civil War, he was major of the 23d Ohio Volunteers, was wounded several times, and rose to the rank of brevet major general, 1864. He served in Congress 1864-67, supporting Reconstruction and Pres. Andrew Johnson's impeachment. He was elected governor of Ohio, 1867 and 1869; beaten in the race for Congress, 1872; reelected governor, 1875. In 1876 he was nominated for president and believed he had lost the election to Samuel J. Tilden, Democrat. But a few Southern states submitted two different sets of electoral votes and the result was in dispute. An electoral commission of eight Republicans and seven Democrats appointed by Congress awarded all disputed votes to Hayes, al-

In the late 1900s it was common for advertisers to use pictures of presidents to promote their products; here Hayes and his wife extol the virtues of an iron.

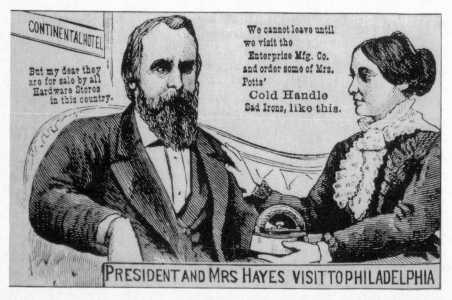

lowing him to become president by one electoral vote. Hayes, keeping a promise to southerners, withdrew troops from areas still occupied in the South, ending the era of Reconstruction. He proceeded to reform the civil service, alienating political spoilsmen. He advocated repeal of the Tenure of Office Act. He supported sound money and specie payments.

The More Colorful Facts

Astrological Sign: Libra

Nicknames: Dark Horse President, Fraud President, Granny Hayes, Great Unknown, Hero of '77, His Fradulency, Old Eight to Seven*, President De Facto, Rud, Rutherfraud, Rutherford The Rover†.

Presidential Notes: First Lady Lucy Hayes started the traditional White House Easter Egg Roll. Previously, the event had been held on the Capitol Lawn, but Congress claimed it wrecked the grass.

RBH was the first president to cross the continent while in office.

Family Notes: "Lemonade Lucy" was the nickname of RBH's wife, Lucy, who did not serve any distilled spirits in the White House, would not allow smoking, dancing, or card playing. She was also the first wife of a president to attend college, Wesleyan Female College, now called Ohio Wesleyan. She delivered a commencement address entitled "The Influence of Christianity on National Prosperity" for her June 1850 graduation. RBH served as a trustee of this school from 1884 until his death in 1893.

Campaign Notes: "Hayes and Wheeler Grand March Waltz," "Hayes the True and Wheeler Too," written by "R.E.Publican," "Hurrah for Hayes and Honest Ways," and "Roll Along, Shout The Campaign Battle Song," were songs from the 1876 presidential campaign.

Namesakes: Presidente Hayes, an eastern department (state) of the central South American country of Paraguay.

Home: Spiegel Grove, 1337 Hayes Avenue, Fremont, Ohio. He inherited the estate from his uncle Sardis Birchard in 1874.

Education: As valedictorian at Kenyon College, RBH gave the address "College Life." Awarded an honorary LL.D. from Kenyon in 1868, and another from Johns Hopkins in 1881.

Other Positions: Began a law partnership, Buckland and Hayes, in Sandusky, Ohio, with Ralph Buckland on April 1, 1846. It lasted three years.

On December 26, 1853, he formed a law partnership with Richard M. Corwine and William X. Rogers: Corwine, Hayes, and Rogers. Rogers later became his private secretary.

Favorite Sport: Croquet

Slogan: "He serves his party best who serves his country best."

---

*Referring to his narrow victory over Samuel J. Tilden.
†So-called by the Chicago *Tribune* because he traveled so much, his longest trip was 71 days.

Clubs: Historical and Philosophical Society of Ohio, in Cincinnati.
Literary Club of Cincinnati
Philomathesian Society, at Kenyon College
Military Order of the Loyal Legion of the United States; he briefly served as national commander.
Trusteeships: Mt. Union College
Ohio State University (1887-93)
Western Reserve University (1881-93)
Songs: "Hayes Grand Triumphal March," written in 1877 by F.W. Belwick
Horse: Whitey; Gen. RBH's war horse was buried on the grounds of his estate, Spiegel Grove, marked with a slab which reads "Old Whitey A Hero of Nineteen Battles 1861-1865."
Last words: "I know that I'm going where Lucy is."

JAMES ABRAM GARFIELD

Twentieth president

1881

The Straight Facts

Born: November 19, 1831
Birthplace: Orange, Ohio
Ancestry: English
Physical Characteristics: 6' tall, blue eyes, reddish-brown hair, 210 lbs.
Religion: Disciples of Christ
Occupation: Teacher, minister
Wife: Lucretia Randolph Garfield (1832-1918)

Date of Marriage: November 11, 1858
Children: Two daughters, five sons
College: Williams College, class of 1856
Military History: Major general, U.S. Army
Political Party: Republican
Previous Political Offices: Member, Ohio senate (1859); Member, U.S. House of Representatives (1863-80); Member, U.S. electoral commission (1877); Member, U.S. Senate (1881)
Vice-President: Chester Alan Arthur
Died: September 19, 1881, at Elberon, New Jersey
Burial Place: Lakeview Cemetery, Cleveland, Ohio
Firsts: First left-handed president
First president to have been a minister
First president to have campaigned for national office in more than one language
Biography in Brief: James A. Garfield was the son of Abram Garfield and Eliza Ballou. His father died in 1833. He worked as a canal bargeman, farmer, and carpenter; attended Western Reserve Eclectic, later Hiram College, and was graduated from Williams in 1856. He taught at Hiram, and later became principal. He was in the Ohio senate in 1859. Antislavery and antisecession, he volunteered for the war, became colonel of the 42nd Ohio Infantry and brigadier in 1862. He fought at Shiloh, was chief of staff for Gen. William S. Rosecrans and was made major general for gallantry at Chickamauga. He entered Congress as a radical Republican in 1863; supported specie payment as against paper money (greenbacks). On the electoral commission in 1877 he voted for Republican Rutherford B. Hayes against Democrat Samuel J. Tilden on strict party lines. He was senator-elect in 1880 when he became the Republican nominee for president. He was chosen as a compromise over General Grant, James G. Blaine, and John Sherman. This alienated the Grant following but Garfield was elected. On July 2, 1881, Garfield was shot by a mentally disturbed office-seeker, Charles J. Guiteau, while entering a railroad station in Washington, D.C.

The More Colorful Facts

Astrological Sign: Scorpio
Nicknames: Boatman Jim, Canal Boy*, Last of the Log Cabin Presidents, Plow Boy of Ohio, Praying Colonel, Preacher President†, Scholar President, Teacher President.

*He once worked on the Erie Canal. On the flatboat *Evening Star,* captained by his cousin Amos Letcher, leading the horses on one side, Garfield claimed he got dunked 14 times before he got the horses to cooperate.

†He was pastor of the Franklin Circle Disciples of Christ in Ohio City, Ohio. The sect was known as the Campbellites.

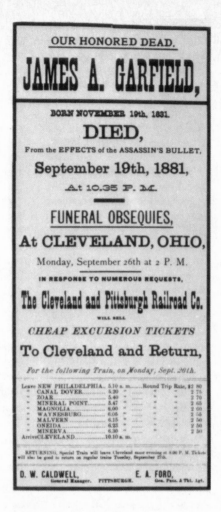

OUR HONORED DEAD.

JAMES A. GARFIELD,

BORN NOVEMBER 19th, 1831.

DIED,

From the EFFECTS of the ASSASSIN'S BULLET,

September 19th, 1881,

At 10.35 P. M.

FUNERAL OBSEQUIES,

At CLEVELAND, OHIO,

Monday, September 26th at 2 P. M.

IN RESPONSE TO NUMEROUS REQUESTS,

The Cleveland and Pittsburgh Railroad Co.

WILL SELL

CHEAP EXCURSION TICKETS

To Cleveland and Return,

For the following Train, on Monday, Sept. 26th.

Leave NEW PHILADELPHIA	5.10 a. m.	Round Trip Rate,	$2 80
" CANAL DOVER	5.20 "	" "	2 75
" ZOAR	5.40 "	" "	2 70
" MINERAL POINT	5.47 "	" "	2 65
" MAGNOLIA	6.00 "	" "	2 60
" WAYNESBURG	6.05 "	" "	2 55
" MALVERN	6.15 "	" "	2 50
" ONEIDA	6.23 "	" "	2 50
" MINERVA	6.30 "	" "	2 50
Arrive CLEVELAND	10.10 a. m.		

RETURNING, Special Train will leave Cleveland same evening at 8.00 P. M. Tickets will also be good to return on regular trains Tuesday, September 27th.

D. W. CALDWELL, General Manager. PITTSBURGH.   **E. A. FORD,** Gen. Pass. & Tkt. Agt.

Ancestors: Henry I of France (ca.1005-60). Garfield was 28th in line of descent.

Rhys ap Tewdwr (?-1093), King of Deheubarth.

Presidential Notes: JAG's mother, Eliza(beth) Ballou Garfield (1801-88) was the first presidential mother to witness her son's inauguration.

Family Trivia: JAG called his wife Lucretia "Crete."

Garfield met his future wife, Lucretia Randolph, at Geauga Seminary which was located at Chester and E. 100 Street in Cleveland. They first attended in March of 1848.

"Trot" was the nickname of Garfield's eldest daughter, Eliza Arbella, who died of diphtheria at 4 years, 5 months.

Campaign Notes: "His name is General G.," written by Knapp and Wilson, was a song in the 1880 presidential campaign.

Homes: Lawnfield, 8095 Mentor Avenue, Mentor, Ohio. He purchased the

160-acre rundown "Dickey place" in October 1876. It remained in use by the family until 1936 when it became the property of the Western Reserve Historical Society.

Other Positions: At age 23, JAG taught at Western Reserve Eclectic Institute, the original name of Hiram College. He later served as its president.

Physical Traits: Ambidextrous; JAG could write efficiently with either hand.

Hobbies: Juggling Indian clubs to build his muscles.

Songs: "Garfield Funeral March" was written for JAG by Fred W. Klein in 1881.

"Ho, Reapers of Life's Harvest," a favorite hymn, was played often at his funeral.

Favorite Operetta: *H.M.S. Pinafore*

Clubs: Philologians, literary society at Williams College, which he joined. Williams College. He was nicknamed "Poet" and elected president in his senior year.

He was elected editor of *The Quarterly*, the literary magazine, in 1855. Also at Williams, he became associated with the Theological Society in 1854.

Assassination: JAG was shot by Charles A. Guiteau at 9:20 A.M. EST, at the Baltimore & Ohio railway station in Washington, D.C.

Dr. D.W. Bliss was the chief attending physician of the mortally wounded president. Mrs. Dr. Susan Edson was the chief nurse. Dr. Edson, a homeopathic practitioner, was the family physician of the Garfields. She was nicknamed by the Garfield children as "Dr. Edson, full of med'cine."

Guiteau used a British Bulldog, a five barrel, .44 caliber pistol, to shoot JAG. He claimed he selected it because it would look good in a museum someday. "My God, what is this?" was JAG's reaction to being shot. Garfield lived for 80 days after he was shot.

Guiteau was led to the gallows on June 30, 1882 at 12:40 P.M. before a crowd of over 250, some of whom paid as much as $300 to watch.

Last Words: "The People . . . trust," in Elberon, New Jersey, where he had been moved because the doctors felt the sea air might do him some good.

CHESTER ALAN ARTHUR

Twenty-first president

1881-85

The Straight Facts

Born: October 5, 1830
Birthplace: Fairfield, Vermont
Ancestry: Scots-Irish
Physical Characteristics: 6′2″ tall, black eyes, brown hair
Religion: Episcopalian
Occupation: Lawyer
Wife: Ellen Lewis Herndon Arthur (1837-80)
Date of Marriage: October 25, 1859
Children: One daughter, two sons

In a *Puck* cartoon, Arthur is shown weathering the many serious schisms in the Republican Party.

College: Union College, class of 1848
Military History: Brigadier general, U.S. Army
Political Party: Republican
Previous Political Offices: Collector, Port of New York (1871-78); Vice-president of the United States (1881)
Vice-President: None
Died: November 18, 1886
Burial Place: Rural Cemetery, Albany, New York
Firsts: First president born in Vermont
First president to have his citizenship questioned (many believe he was born in Canada)
First president to take the oath of office at his own home
Biography in Brief: Chester A. Arthur was the son of the Reverand William Arthur, from County Antrim, Ireland, and Malvina Stone. He was graduated from Union College, 1848; taught school at Pownall, Vermont; studied law in New York. In 1853, in a fugitive slave case he argued that slaves transported through New York State were thereby freed. He was made collector

of the Port of New York, 1871. Pres. Rutherford B. Hayes, reforming the civil service, forced Arthur to resign, 1879. This made the New York machine stalwarts enemies of Hayes. Arthur and the stalwarts tried to nominate Ulysses S. Grant for a third term in 1880. When Garfield was nominated, Arthur received second place in the interests of harmony. When Garfield died, Arthur became president. He supported civil service reform and the tariff of 1883. He was defeated for renomination by James G. Blaine.

The More Colorful Facts

Astrological Sign: Libra

Nicknames: America's First Gentleman, Arthur the Gentleman, Chet, Dude President, Elegant Arthur, First Gentleman of the Land, Friend of the Stalwarts, Gentleman Boss, Gentleman President, Prince Arthur.

Ancestry: Genealogists suggest the family is descended from the MacArthurs, Clan Campbell of Scotland, whose ancestors can be traced back to the fifteenth century.

Birthplace Controversy: Some historians believe his actual birthplace was Canada. In 1882, A. P. Hinman claimed in a published book that during the period CAA's minister father preached on both sides of the Vermont-Canada border, a son was born in Canada during 1828 and another in America in 1830. It was well known that CAA, due to vanity, changed the date of his birth. Hinman speculated that he had actually been born in Canada and took his stillborn brother's birthdate enable him to become president. No evidence can be found to prove or disprove the story.

Presidential Notes: CAA was the first president to smoke cigarettes.

Adelina Patti, the operatic soprano, was the first person to appear, at CAA's specific request, in a presidential command performance at the White House.

Daughter Ellen "Nellie" hosted the first White House Christmas Party for needy children in 1883.

CAA netted $8000 in selling 26 wagonloads of old White House furniture, some priceless. Former president Rutherford B. Hayes bought two wagonloads and the furniture now is in place at his Spiegel Grove home in Fremont, Ohio.

Home: 123 Lexington Avenue, New York, New York, a two-story brownstone where he took the oath of office.

Namesakes: Blues singer Howlin', Wolf, whose real name was Chester Arthur Burnett.

Other Positions: Teacher, at District School 14 at Schaghticoke, New York, at a salary of $15 per month. He had previously taught summer school in this town.

Favorite Meal: Mutton chops

Favorite Poet: Robert Burns—he was fond of quoting passages from his work.

Favorite Song: "Robin Adair"

Civil War Rank: Quartermaster general

Clubs: Century Club, an exclusive New York social club (a main criterion for membership at the time was that the man be distinguished in intellectual and social life). Other members at the time included actor Edwin Booth and financier J. Pierpont Morgan.

Personal Accomplishments: CAA was the first person to walk across the Brooklyn Bridge when it was officially opened to the public on May 24, 1883.

Cause of Death: Bright's disease, a kidney disease. He knew he was terminally ill while he was still in office, but decided to keep it a secret and not worry the nation as his predecessor, James Garfield, had just been lost to an assassin's bullet.

(STEPHEN) GROVER CLEVELAND

Twenty-second and Twenty-fourth president

1885-89; 1893-97

The Straight Facts

Born: March 18, 1837
Birthplace: Caldwell, New Jersey
Ancestry: English-Irish
Physical Characteristics: 5'11" tall, blue eyes, brown hair
Religion: Presbyterian
Occupation: Lawyer, politician
Wife: Frances Folsom Cleveland (1864-1947)
Date of Marriage: June 2, 1886
Children: Three daughters, two sons
College: None
Military History: None
Political Party: Democrat

Previous Political Offices: Ward supervisor, Buffalo, New York (1862); Asst. district attorney, Erie County, New York (1863-65); Sheriff, Erie County, New York (1871-73); Mayor, Buffalo, New York (1882); Governor, state of New York (1883-85)

Vice-President: Thomas Andrews Hendricks (1819-85), first term; Adlai Ewing Stevenson (1835-1914), second term

Died: June 24, 1908, at Princeton, New Jersey

Burial Place: Princeton, Cemetery, Princeton, New Jersey

Firsts: First president elected to two nonconsecutive terms
First and only president married in the White House
First president to have a child born in the White House
First president born in New Jersey
First Democratic president after the Civil War

Biography in Brief: *(According to a ruling of the State Department, Grover Cleveland is both the 22d and the 24th president, because his two terms were not consecutive. By individuals, he is only the 22d.)*

Grover Cleveland was the son of Richard Falley Cleveland, a Presbyterian minister, and Anne Neal. He was named Stephen Grover, but dropped the Stephen. He clerked in Clinton and Buffalo; was admitted to the bar in Buffalo, 1859; became assistant district attorney, 1863; sheriff,

In a *Puck* cartoon after the 1884 election, Cleveland braves dangerous waters, threatened by spoilsmen on one side and, as the nation's most eligible bachelor, by wedding bells on the other.

1871; mayor, 1881; governor of New York, 1882. He was an independent, honest administrator who hated corruption. He was nominated for president over Tammany Hall opposition, 1884, and defeated Republican James G. Blaine. He enlarged the civil service, vetoed many pension raids on the Treasury. In 1888 he was defeated by Benjamin Harrison, although his popular vote was larger. Reelected over Harrison in 1892, he faced a money crisis brought about by lowering of the gold reserve, circulation of paper, and exorbitant silver purchases under the Sherman Act; obtained a repeal of the latter and a reduced tariff. A severe depression and labor troubles racked his administration but he refused to interfere in business matters and rejected Jacob Coxey's demand for unemployment relief. He broke the Pullman strike, 1894. In 1896, the Democrats repudiated his administration and chose silverite William Jennings Bryan as their candidate.

The More Colorful Facts

Astrological Sign: Pisces

Nicknames: Beast of Buffalo*, Draft Dodger†, Dumb Prophet, Grover the Good, Hangman of Buffalo‡, His Complacency, His Obstinancy, Perpetual Candidate, Pretender, Reform Governor, Sage of Princeton, Stubborn Old Grover, Stuffed Prophet.

First Name: Stephen, after his father's friend, the Reverand Stephen Grover, who had been pastor of the Presbyterian Church in Caldwell, New Jersey.

Presidential Notes: Cleveland exercised 413 vetoes during his first term of office, and a two-term total of 584 vetoes, second only to Franklin D. Roosevelt.

Esther Cleveland, Cleveland's second daughter, born on September 9, 1893, was the only child of a U.S. president born in the White House.

Cleveland married Frances Folsom (1864-1947), daughter of Grover Cleveland's law partner, in the White House Blue Room, the only White House wedding of a president. She had become his ward fifteen years earlier after her father's death. At age 21, she became the youngest First Lady ever; the groom was 49 years of age. Thirty-one guests were invited to the ceremony. The bride came down the front staircase with a 12-foot train. In 1913, five years after Cleveland's death, she married Thomas J. Preston, Jr., a professor at Princeton University. Cleveland did not use the word "obey,"

---

*Given by his political enemies while mayor of Buffalo, New York.

†So-called by political opponents because he paid a Polish immigrant, George Benninski, $150 to substitute for him in the Civil War. Even though he was one of the first drafted under the Conscription Act of March 3, 1863, GC needn't have done this. As assistant district attorney for Erie County, New York, he could have had a convict serve in his place for free. Benninski served briefly with the 76th New York but injured his back. He later became a hospital orderly and never served as a combatant in battle.

‡As sheriff of Buffalo, New York, GC officiated at the public execution of two men. On September 6, 1872, Patrick Morissey was hung for stabbing his mother. On February 14, Jack Gaffney met his death for killing a man during a card game.

promising only to love, honor, comfort, and keep her. John Philip Sousa, director of the Marine Corps Band, played at wedding.

GC set sail in July 1893 on board the *Oneida,* a private yacht of Commodore Elias C. Benedict, for what his wife and public thought was a fishing vacation. In actuality, GC was secretly operated on for a malignant growth in his mouth. So secret was the operation that no one outside of the immediate party knew anything about it until 1917 when one of the attending physicians let it slip out.

Family Notes: It is believed that the Baby Ruth candy bar was named after GC's eldest daughter, although some candy officials claim otherwise. During GC's first term, Ruth would often play on the front lawn of the White House, but this was soon stopped after too many people picked her up and passed her around. From then on, she only played out of sight of tourists, causing newspaper columnists to comment that she must be deformed because no one saw her anymore. Ruth died in 1904 at the age of 13 years, a victim of cerebral palsy.

Campaign Notes: The 1884 presidential campaign was nicknamed "The Great National Fishing Match" because both GC and Republican candidate, James G. Blaine, were avid fisherman.

Democratic campaign songs included "Cleveland's Grand March" (1884) by J.J. Freeman, "Cleveland's March and Victory" (1884) by George Schleifforth, and "Blaine, Blaine. James G. Blaine, Continental Liar from the State of Maine." The latter aimed ridicule at Blaine's questionnable business practices and honesty.

"Rum, Romanism and Rebellion": The Reverend Samuel D. Burchard, a supporter of James G. Blaine, claimed a vote for GC was a vote for this, thereby attempting to link the Democrats with whiskey, the Catholic church, and the southern cause during the Civil War.

Homes: Westland, 15 Hodge Street, Princeton, New Jersey. He lived here between terms and in his later years. It was named for Princeton University Professor Andrew F. West.

Other Positions: Assistant teacher at the New York Institution for the Blind, 1853.

Law clerk at Rogers, Bowen, and Rogers (Millard Fillmore was a former member of the firm).

Law partner in Vanderpool and Cleveland, 1863-66.

Law partner in Bass, Cleveland and Bissell, Buffalo, New York,

Law partner in Lanning, Cleveland, and Folsom, Buffalo, New York.

Mistress: On July 2, 1884, the headline story of *The Buffalo Telegraph* revealed the details of Mrs. Maria Halpin and her affair with presidential candidate Grover Cleveland and the subsequent birth of her illegitimate child. Oscar Folsom Cleveland, supposedly the illegitimate son of Maria Halpin and GC, was born on September 14, 1874. The boy was named after his godfather and GC's law partner, Oscar Folsom (father of Frances). Cleveland never admitted paternity but did support the child and later arranged for his adoption when Halpin became a hopeless alcoholic.

Favorite Food: Corned beef and cabbage

Favorite Shotgun: GC called his favorite hunting shotgun "Death and Destruction."

Drinking Spots: The Boas, a Buffalo, New York, saloon located in the White Building.

The Shades; at Main and Swan in Buffalo, New York.

Memberships: Association of Life Insurance (served as president in 1907) City Club of Buffalo. Cleveland was a founding member in 1877 and a member of the original board of directors.

Books: *American Shorthand Handbook 1855-1861,* written with his uncle Lewis Allen.

Influence of Sea Power Upon History 1660-1783, published in 1890.

Principles and Purposes of Our Form of Government, 1892.

Presidential Problems, 1904.

Fishing and Good Shooting Sketches, 1906, published by Outing Publishers of New York City.

Good Citizenship, 1908, published by H. Altemus Company of Philadelphia, Pennsylvania.

Magazine Articles: GC wrote a total of 18 stories for the *Saturday Evening Post,* including "Some Fishing Pretenses and Affectations," the September 24, 1904, cover story.

Last words: "I have tried so hard to do so right."

BENJAMIN HARRISON
Twenty-third president
1889-93

The Straight Facts

Born: August 20, 1833
Birthplace: North Bend, Ohio
Ancestry: English
Physical Characteristics: 5'6" tall, blue eyes, light brown hair
Religion: Presbyterian
Occupation: Lawyer
Wife: (1) Caroline Scott Harrison (1832-92); (2) Mary Lord Dimmick Harrison (1832-1892)
Date of Marriage: (1) October 20, 1853; (2) April 6, 1896

Children: (1) One daughter, one son; (2) one daughter
College: Miami University, class of 1852
Military History: Brigadier general, U.S. Army
Political Party: Republican
Previous Political Offices: Reporter of Decisions, Indiana Supreme Court (1864-68); Member, Mississippi River Commission (1879); Member, U.S. Senate (1881-87)
Vice-President: Levi Parsons Morton, (1824-1920)
Died: March 13, 1901, in Indianapolis, Indiana
Burial Place: Crown Hill Cemetery, Indianapolis, Indiana
Firsts: First grandson of a president (William Henry Harrison) to serve as president
First president to have a child born after leaving the White House
Biography in Brief: Benjamin Harrison's great-grandfather, Benjamin Harrison, was a signer of the Declaration of Independence; his grandfather, William Henry Harrison, was the ninth president; his father, John Scott Harrison, was a member of Congress. His mother was Elizabeth Ramsey Irwin. He attended school on his father's farm; was graduated from Miami University at Oxford, Ohio, 1852; admitted to the bar, 1853, and practiced in Indianapolis. In the Civil War, he rose to the rank of brevet brigadier general, fought at Kennesaw Mountain, Peachtree Creek, Nashville, and in the Atlanta campaign. He failed to be elected governor of Indiana, 1876, but became senator, 1881. In 1888 he defeated Grover Cleveland for president despite having fewer popular votes. He expanded the pension list, signed the McKinley high tariff bill and the Sherman Silver Purchase Act. During his administration, six states were admitted to the union. He was defeated for re-election, 1892. He represented Venezuela in a boundary arbitration with Great Britain in Paris, 1899.

The More Colorful Facts

Astrological Sign: Leo
Nicknames: Chinese Harrison, Grandfather's Hat, His Hirsute Highness, Kid Gloves Harrison, Little Ben*, Minority President, Son of His Grandfather, White House Iceberg.
Presidential Notes: Edison Electric Company installed the first electricity in the White House during 1891. After receiving an electrical shock, the Harrisons refused to touch the switches and often would go to bed with the lights on.

Six states were admitted to the union during his presidency, the most of any administration since the time of George Washington (South Dakota, North Dakota, Montana, Washington, Idaho, and Wyoming).

*So-called by his civil war regiment, the 70th Indiana Volunteers.

In an 1892 cartoon, Harrison is shown as too small for "His Grandfather's Hat," one of his nicknames.

Family Notes: BH's grandson Benjamin Harrison McKee, nicknamed "Baby McKee," was his constant companion.

Elizabeth Harrison, born February 21, 1897 to BH and his second wife, was younger than four of his grandchildren by his first wife: Marthene (1888), William Henry (1896), Benjamin (1887), and Mary (1888).

Campaign Notes: 1888 Republican presidential campaign songs included "Grandfather's Hat Fits Ben," "Harrison's Victory" written by Clifford Hale, and "His Grandfather's Hat," written by Henry Clay Work.

Homes: 1230 North Delaware Street, Indianapolis, Indiana, built in 1874.

Namesakes: Benjamin Harrison Memorial Drawbridge, over the James River in Virginia, is one of the largest vertical lift bridges in North America, 363 feet at its longest span.

Other positions: Law partner, Harrison and Wallace, 1855-61. Partner William Wallace was the brother of General Lew Wallace, the author of *Ben Hur* and son of David Wallace, governor of Indiana from 1837-40.

Law partner, Harrison and Fishback, 1861-70.

Law partner, Harrison, Hines, and Miller, formed in April 1874

Memberships: Union Literary Society, a debating society at Miami University.

Fraternity: While a student at Miami University BH helped found the Phi Delta Theta fraternity. He was the thirteenth charter member.

Books: *This Country of Ours,* written in 1897, published by Scribner's in New York City and first serialized by *Ladies Home Journal.*

Magazine articles: Harrison wrote several on federal government for the *Ladies Home Journal.*

WILLIAM McKINLEY
Twenty-fifth president
1897-1901

The Straight Facts

Born: January 29, 1843
Birthplace: Niles, Ohio
Ancestry: Scots-Irish
Physical Characteristics: 5'7" tall, blue-gray eyes, about 200 lb.
Religion: Methodist
Occupation: Lawyer
Wife: Ida Saxton McKinley (1847-1907)
Date of Marriage: January 25, 1871
Children: Two daughters

College: Allegheny College
Military History: Brevet major, U.S. Army
Political Party: Republican
Previous Political Offices: Prosecuting attorney, Stark County, Ohio (1869-71); member, U.S. House of Representatives (1877-83, 1885-91); Governor, state of Ohio (1892-96)
Vice-President: Garret Augustus Hobart (1844-99), first term; Theodore Roosevelt, second term
Died: September 14, 1901, in Buffalo, New York
Burial Place: Westlawn Cemetery, Canton, Ohio
Firsts: First president to campaign by telephone
Biography in Brief: William McKinley was the son of William McKinley, an ironmaker, and Nancy Campbell Allison. McKinley attended school in Poland, Ohio, and at Allegheny College, Meadville, Pennsylvania, and enlisted for the Civil War at 18 in the 23rd Ohio. He studied law in the Albany, New York, law school; opened an office in Canton, Ohio, in 1867; and campaigned for Ulysses S. Grant and Rutherford B. Hayes. He served in the House of Representatives, 1877-83, 1885-91, and led the fight for passage of the McKinley Tariff, 1890. Defeated for reelection on the issue in 1890, he was governor of Ohio, 1892-96. He had support for president in the convention that nominated Benjamin Harrison in 1892. In 1896 he was elected president on a protective tariff, sound money (gold standard) platform over William Jennings Bryan, Democratic proponent of free silver. McKinley was reluctant to intervene in Cuba but the loss of the battleship *Maine* at Havana crystallized opinion. He demanded Spain's withdrawal from Cuba; Spain made some concessions but Congress announced a state of war as of April 21. He was reelected in the 1900 campaign, defeating Bryan's anti-imperialist arguments with the promise of a "full dinner pail." McKinley was respected for his conciliatory nature, but conservative on business issues. On September 6, 1901, while welcoming citizens at the Pan-American Exposition, Buffalo, New York, he was shot by Leon C. Czolgosz, an anarchist.

The More Colorful Facts

Astrological sign: Aquarius
Nicknames: Idol of Ohio, Napoleon of Protection, Prosperity's Advance Agent, Stockingfoot Orator, Wobbly Willie, Young Napoleon*.
Presidential Notes: "Full Dinner Pail" was the theme of WMcK's presidency, referring to the Republican advocacy of full employment.

First Lady Ida McKinley banned yellow in the White House because she didn't like it. When the forsythia bloomed, she ordered all the flowers pulled.

*So-called by the newspapers when he was a congressman.

A political cartoon shows McKinley's frustration with Congress' tortoise-like progression in dealing with his programs.

Ida McKinley suffered from petit mal, a form of epilepsy. WMcK broke White House tradition by having her sit at his right at dinner parties and not at on the other end of the table, so he could watch over her. If she appeared to be exhibiting signs of a seizure, he would gently place a napkin over her face until the symptoms subsided and then continue on as if nothing had happened.

Family Notes: His future wife, Ida Saxton, was working at the First National Bank of Canton, where she met WMcK. She was the first president's wife to be employed in a profession other than teaching.

"My Precious" was Ida's favorite endearment for her husband.

The William McKinleys lived in the Neil Hotel in Columbus, Ohio, while he was governor of the state. Every morning upon entering the Capitol Building, he would lift his hat in a smiling farewell greeting. Every day at 3 P.M. regardless of his official duties, WMcK would go to a statehouse window and wave his handkerchief at his invalid wife, Ida, who would be sitting on the front porch of the Neil Hotel, awaiting his wave.

Campaign Notes: "Front Porch Campaign" was the nickname given to McKinley's 1896 presidential campaign against William Jennings Bryan because McKinley stayed at his home on North Market Street in Canton, Ohio, and gave rehearsed speeches as he refused to leave his wife for tours of the country.

"Sound Money" and "The Advance Agent of Prosperity" were Republican campaign themes in 1896.

"McKinley drinks soda water, Bryan drinks rum; McKinley is a gentleman, Bryan is a bum" was an uncomplimentary Republican campaign slogan in 1900 campaign. In truth, the Democratic candidate, William Jennings Bryan, was a teetotaler.

Home: North Market Avenue and Eighth Street, Canton, Ohio. This is the home from which WMcK campaigned in 1896.

Namesakes: Mt. McKinley, the highest point in the United States, is located in Alaska and stands 20,320 feet above sea level in Denali National Park.

William McKinley Memorial Library, 40 Main Street, Niles, Ohio.

Indian Name: Big White Feather, given by Indian tribesmen at the 1901 Pan Am Exposition.

Famous Descendants: Martha Scott, the Hollywood actress, whose mother was a second cousin of McKinley.

Military Career: During the Civil War, Sgt. WMcK was given a battlefield commission to lieutenant because of his ability to obtain needed food and supplies. The colonel who promoted him was Rutherford B. Hayes.

Favorite Card Game: Cribbage

Favorite Plays: *The Cricket on the Hearth* and *Rip Van Winkle*, especially when the lead was played by Joseph Jefferson, a noted comedian of the day, who played the role off and on for over 40 years.

Favorite Cigar: Garcias; he reportedly smoked 20 a day.

Favorite Poems: "Recompense," by Myron Herrick; "Song of the Mystic by Abraham Ryan.

Favorite Hymn: "Lead, Kindly Light"

Hallmark: Usually wore a red carnation in his lapel for good luck. It is the state of flower of Ohio, his home state.

Fraternity: Sigma Alpha Epsilon at Allegheny College

Memberships: Knights of Pythias, a Canton, Ohio society McKinley joined in 1869.

Books: *The Tariffs in the Days of Henry Clay and Since*, written in 1896 by presidential candidate WMcK. It was published by the Henry Clay Publishing Company.

Assassination: WMcK was assassinated by Leon F. Czolgosz at 4:07 P.M. on September 6, 1901. McKinley lived for 8 days after being shot. Czolgosz was found guilty after only two days in the trial that lasted 8 hours and 26 minutes. He was electrocuted at Auburn state prison on October 29, 1901, 54 days after shooting the president and 45 days after his death.

McKinley lived, died, and lay in state at Milburn House, 1168 Delaware Avenue, in Buffalo, during his ill-fated trip to the 1901 Pan Am Exposition.

Assassin Czolgosz lived at the Raines Law Hotel, 1078 Broadway, atop John Nowak's Saloon in Buffalo, New York. He rented the room on August 31 as John Doe, paying the bill of $2 a week in advance.

Last words: Moments before he died, WMcK was whispering the words of "Nearer, My God to Thee."

THEODORE ROOSEVELT
Twenty-sixth president
1901-09

The Straight Facts

Born: October 27, 1858
Birthplace: New York, New York
Ancestry: Dutch
Physical Characteristics: 5'8" tall, blues eyes, brown hair, 200 lb.
Religion: Dutch Reformed
Occupation: Rancher, statesman
Wife: (1) Alice Hathaway Lee Roosevelt (1861-84); (2) Edith Kermit Carow Roosevelt (1861-1948)
Date of Marriage: (1) October 27, 1880; (2) December 2, 1886
Children: (1) One daughter; (2) one daughter, four sons
College: Harvard University, class of 1880
Military History: Colonel, U.S Army
Political Party: Republican
Previous Political Offices: Member, New York state assembly (1882-84); Member, U.S. Civil Service commission (1889-95); Police commissioner, New York City (1895-97); Asst. secretary of the Navy (1897-98); Governor, state of New York (1899-1901); Vice-president of the United States (1901)
Vice-President: None, first term; Charles Warren Fairbanks (1852-1918), second term
Died: January 6, 1919, at Oyster Bay, New York
Burial Place: Young's Memorial Cemetery, Oyster Bay, New York
Firsts: First president to win the Nobel Peace Prize
First president to visit a foreign country while in office
First former president to survive an assassination attempt
Biography in Brief: Theodore Roosevelt was the son of Theodore Roosevelt, a glass importer, and Martha Bulloch. He was a fifth cousin of Franklin D. Roosevelt, and an uncle of Eleanor Roosevelt. Roosevelt was graduated from Harvard, 1880; attended Columbia Law School briefly; sat in the New York state assembly, 1882-84; ranched in North Dakota, 1884-86; failed election as mayor of New York City 1886; member of U.S. Civil Service Commission, 1889; president, New York Police Board, 1895, supporting the merit system; assistant secretary of the Navy under McKinley, 1897-98. In the war with Spain, he organized the 1st U.S. Volunteer Cavalry (Rough Riders) as lieutenant colonel; led the charge up Kettle Hill at San Juan. Elected New York governor, 1898-1900, he fought the spoils system and achieved taxation of corporation franchises. Nominated for vice president, 1900, he

became the nation's youngest president when McKinley died. As president he fought corruption of politics by big business; dissolved Northern Securities Co. and others for violating antitrust laws; intervened in coal strike on behalf of the public, 1902; obtained Elkins Law forbidding rebates to favored corporations, 1903; Hepburn Law regulating railroad rates, 1906; Pure Food and Drugs Act, 1906, Reclamation Act, and employers' liability laws. He organized conservation; mediated the peace between Japan and Russia, 1905; won the Nobel Peace Prize. By recognizing the new Republic of Panama he made Panama Canal possible. He was reelected in 1904.

In 1908 he obtained the nomination of William H. Taft, who was elected. Feeling that Taft had abandoned his policies, Roosevelt unsuccessfully sought the nomination in 1912. He bolted the party and ran on the Progressive "Bull Moose" ticket against Taft and Woodrow Wilson, splitting the Republicans and insuring Wilson's election. He was shot during the campaign but recovered. In 1916 he supported Charles E. Hughes, Republican. A strong friend of Britain, he fought American isolation in World War I.

The More Colorful Facts

Astrological Sign: Scorpio

Nicknames: Bull in a China Shop*, Driving Force, Dynamo of Power, First Modern President, Four Eyes, Great White Chief, Haroun-al-Roosevelt, Hero of San Juan Hill, Man on Horseback, Meddler, Old Lion, Teddy the Meddler, Teddy, Telescope Teddy, Terrible Teddy, Trust Buster, Typical American.

Presidential Notes: John R. Hazel, federal district court judge of New York, administered the oath of office to Vice-president Theodore Roosevelt upon the death of President William McKinley. The ceremony took place in the parlor of the Ansley Wilcox home on September 14, 1901. Reportedly, the new president took the oath with his left hand on a Bible and his right in a rigid military salute.

The members of the press formed the Ananias Club in 1906. Membership was restricted to those who had been called a liar by TR. Among the first members were E. H. Harrison, Judge Alton Brooks, and Senator Benjamin Tilman. Ananias was a biblical character who was put to death for lying.

TR is the only president not to use the word "I" in his inaugural address.

TR was the first White House jogger. He ran daily around the Washington Monument.

"Tennis Cabinet" was the nickname given to TR's cabinet.

On New Year's Day 1907, TR shook hands at the White House with a record 8,513 people.

Booker T. Washington, the educator who founded Tuskegee Institute in 1881, was the first black to be invited to dinner at the White House. TR shocked quite a few people by having him to dinner on October 16, 1901.

TR was shaved by the White House barber everyday at 12:40 P.M

Theodore Roosevelt was the first president to ride in a submerged submarine when he sailed on the U.S.S. *Plunger* during training exercises on August 25, 1905. He remained submerged for about one hour.

The "Square Deal" was the program initiated in 1903, designed not to play favorites and to assure that every citizen should have a square deal.

"Big Stick Diplomacy" was another theme of TR's presidency.

TR called the White House the "Bully Pulpit."

TR was the first president to ride in a horseless carriage, a Columbia Electric Victoria. Accompanied by Colonel Jacob Lyman-Green, he drove through the streets of Hartford, Connecticut, on August 22, 1902, in a parade. Twenty-two horsedrawn carriages followed the purple-lined car driven by the president.

The first time a president flew was on October 11, 1910, at the Aero Club Meet, in St. Louis. The four-minute flight at St. Louis's Aviation Field

---

*Given to TR as assistant secretary of the Navy by Secretary of the Navy John Long.

was in a type B pusher plane built by the Wright Brothers in 1910 and reached an average altitude of 50 feet.

Alice Lee Roosevelt, TR's daughter, married Nicholas Longworth, U.S. Representative from Ohio, in the White House on February 17, 1906, with the Right Reverend Henry Yates Satterlee, Episcopal Bishop of Washington, officiating. Longworth would later serve as Speaker of the House from 1925-31.

When TR went on the *U.S.S. Louisiana* to inspect the Panama Canal, it was the first time a president left the United States while in office.

TR was the only president to see action in the Spanish-American War.

John L. Sullivan, the last of the bare-knuckle heavy-weight boxing champions, gave up drinking on the very day that TR took the oath of office as president of the United States, because he was a hero of the hard-drinking Sullivan.

Family Notes: TR's mother and his first wife, Alice Lee, both died on January 14, 1914; his mother of typhoid, and his wife of Bright's disease three days after giving birth to daughter Alice.

The "White House Gang" was the nickname given to his children.

His best man at his second wedding to Edith Kermit Carow was Cecil Spring-Rice, later British Ambassador to the United States then Secretary at the British Legation. The wedding took place at St. George's Church in Hanover Square, London, England on December 2, 1886; the maid of honor was Emily Carow. He was affectionately known as "Springy" to the Roosevelt children.

Daughter Alice inspired the song "Alice Blue Gown."

Campaign Notes: "Roosevelt the Peace Victor" was a campaign song written for TR in 1904 by Irving J. Morgan.

"Same Old Flag and Victory—Stand Pat" and "Peacemaker" were slogans used in 1904 campaign. TR's theme song was "Hot Time in The Old Town".

In the 1912 presidential campaign, TR was the standard bearer for the Bull Moose Party, also known as the Progressive Party.

Home: Sagamore Hills, Oyster Bay, Long Island. TR's permanent home, it was named for the Indian chieftain Sagamore Mohannis. The home was built in 1884 at a cost of $16,975 and designed by Lamb & Rich of 486 Broadway, New York, New York, with help from TR. The original name of the house was supposed to be Leeholm, after first wife Alice Lee.

Namesakes: Theodore Roosevelt National Park, located on 70,416 acres near Medora, North Dakota.

U.S.S. *Theodore Roosevelt,* 30-ton nuclear-powered aircraft carrier.

Theodore Roosevelt Island, originally called Analostan Island, a small 88-acre island located in the Potomac River near the nation's capital in Washington, D.C., that was purchased in 1932 for $364,000 by the Theodore Roosevelt Association. It was donated to the Federal government by the Association and renamed Theodore Roosevelt Island. Analostan was the original Indian name but it has also been called My Lord's Island (1632), Barbadoes (1681), and Masons Island (1717).

Roosevelt elk, the largest of the American elk, now restricted to the Olympic peninsula of Washington State. Named after TR by naturalist C. Hart Merriam, it is officially called *cervus Roosevelti*.

Roosevelt Trout, a fish of North America, similar to the golden trout but considered a different species.

The Teddy Bear, cuddly child's toy bear, created by Morris Michton in 1902. The original is now on display in the Smithsonian Institution.

Rio Roosevelt (or Rio Tedoro). Originally called the River of Doubt, it is the 900-mile river TR went to Brazil to explore after losing the election of 1912 to Woodrow Wilson.

Stamp: Sagamore Hill issue, a three-cent stamp featuring TR's Oyster Bay home, September 14, 1953.

Famous Quotes: "A fifth wheel to a coach"—on the vice presidency.

College Days: TR edited the *Advocate,* the Harvard newspaper.

TR belonged to the Dicky social club.

Military Career: The Rough Riders, the U.S. Army Volunteer Regiment of the First Cavalry led by Colonel TR up Kettle (not San Juan as is popularly believed) Hill, were a collection of college athletes, polo players, cowboys, and Harvard friends of Roosevelt. Included in their ranks were Harvard quarterback Dudley Dean; the world's greatest polo player, Joe Sampson Stevens; U.S. Tennis champ Bob Wrenn, the ex-captain of Columbia's rowing team, Hamilton Fish; and Theodore Westwood Miller, brother-in-law of

"Why Not?" A 1909 NEA Service cartoon that originally appeared in the *Cincinnati Times-Star*, the newspaper owned by Charles P. Taft, the brother of the incoming president.

Thomas Edison (the latter two were killed in action); as well as Col. Webb Cook Hayes I, son of former President Rutherford B. Hayes.

Rain-in-the Face was the name of the horse TR rode up Kettle Hill.

Family Pets: Algonquin, Icelandic calico pony (Kermit and Quentin once sneaked the pony up the White House elevator into the sickroom of brother Archie who had the measles).

Allen, terrier of Kermit Roosevelt

Bill, horned toad

Black Jack, dog

Bob Evans, guinea pig

Dewey, Sr. and Dewey, Jr., guinea pigs

Eli Yale, blue Brazilian macaw

Emily Spinach, Alice's garter snake

Father Grady, guinea pig

Fidelity, Ethel's pony

Gem, Edith Roosevelt's dog

Jessie, Scottish terrier

Jonathan Edward, bear (later became the property of the Washington Zoo).

Josiah, badger

Manchu, Alice's spaniel

Peter, bull terrier who distinguished himself by biting through the trousers of French Ambassador Jusseraud.

Peter, dog

Sailor Boy, Chesapeake Bay retriever. He liked to go boating with the Roosevelt children and if they forgot him, he would simply swim out to the boat.

Scamp, terrier

Skip, a mongrel

Slippers, cat with six toes on one paw.

Susan, a large male dog (no one knows why the he was called a she)

Tom Quartz, Kermit's cat

Personal Data: TR was blinded in the left eye during a 1904 boxing match with a White House military aide. He kept the fact secret for the rest of his life.

Favorite Book: *Wind in The Willows,* by Kenneth Graham

Advertising: TR is credited with giving Maxwell House coffee its slogan. After drinking a cup at the Hermitage, Andrew Jackson's home, Roosevelt is supposed to have said, "Delicious, this coffee is good to the last drop!" The blend was concocted by Joel Cheek in 1880 and served at the Maxwell House Hotel in Nashville, Tennessee, hence giving the brew its name.

Books: *Naval War of 1812,* 1886
Wilderness Hunter, 1893
History of New York City, 1890
Historic Towns, 1890

Essays on Practical Politics, 1892

The Deer Family, a scholarly book published while in office

Life of Gouverneur Morris, 1887

Ranch Life and Hunting Trail, 1888

Summer Birds of the Adirondacks in Franklin County, New York, 1878 (published by Henry Minot).

The Winning of the West, 2 volumes published in 1889, a third in 1894. Considered his greatest book.

African Game Trails, written to defray costs of his 1909 African Safari. Also appeared in *Scribner's* Magazine.

Other Writing: "About Man-eating Lions", cover story of November 1913 issue of *Boy's Life.*

Assassination Attempt: The site was the Gilpatrick Hotel, in Milwaukee, Wisconsin. TR was attending a small dinner in his honor at the inn before delivering a speech at the Milwaukee Auditorium. Upon exiting, he was shot in the chest by John Nepomuk Schrank, but delivered the speech anyway. Afterward, TR was rushed to the Johnston Emergency Room where it was discovered that the bullet had nicked his glasses case, slowing the impact of the bullet. It was the first assassination attempt against a former president.

TR had written the speech he was to deliver that day by hand on single pieces of paper in large letters with wide spaces for easier reading. The speech was folded in half in his left breast pocket as Schrank's bullet struck Roosevelt. The 100-page thickness slowed the bullet, which missed Roosevelt's right lung by one-half inch, cracking and lodging against a rib.

Last Words: "Please put out the light."

WILLIAM HOWARD TAFT
Twenty-seventh president
1909-13

The Straight Facts

Born: September 15, 1857
Birthplace: Cincinnati, Ohio
Ancestry: English
Physical Characteristics: 6'2" tall, blue eyes, chestnut hair
Religion: Unitarian
Occupation: Lawyer
Wife: Helen Herron Taft (1861-1943)
Date of Marriage: June 19, 1886
Children: One daughter, two sons
College: Yale University, class of 1878

A 1905 cartoon depicts the breadth of Taft's experience, as well as of his girth.

Military History: None
Political Party: Republican
Previous Political Offices: Asst. prosecuting attorney, Cincinnati, Ohio (1881-82); Asst. city solicitor, Cincinnati, Ohio (1887); Judge, Superior Court of Cincinnati, Ohio (1887-90); U.S. solicitor general (1890-92); Judge, U.S. federal circuit court (1892-1900); President, Philippines Commission (1900-01); Governor general, Philippine Islands (1901); Secretary of war (1904-08); Provisional governor of Cuba (1907); (Post presidency) Chief justice, United States Supreme Court (1921-30)
Vice-President: James Schoolcraft Sherman (1855-1912)
Died: March 8, 1930, at Washington, D.C.
Burial Place: Arlington National Cemetery, Arlington, Virginia

Firsts: First president of the 48 states

First president to serve in the Supreme Court

First president buried in Arlington National Cemetery

Biography in Brief: William Howard Taft was the son of Alphonso Taft and Louisa Maria Torrey. His father was secretary of war and attorney general in Grant's cabinet and minister to Austria and Russia under Arthur. Taft was graduated from Yale, 1878; Cincinnati Law School, 1880; was assistant prosecuting attorney, 1881-83; assistant county solicitor, 1885; judge, superior court, 1887; U.S. solicitor-general, 1890; federal circuit judge, 1892. In 1900 he became head of the U.S. Philippines Commission and was first civil governor of the Philippines, 1901-04; secretary of war, 1904; provisional governor of Cuba, 1906. He was groomed for president by Roosevelt and elected over William Jennings Bryan, 1908. His administration dissolved Standard Oil and tobacco trusts; instituted the Department of Labor; drafted direct election of senators and income tax amendments. His tariff and conservation policies angered progressives; though renominated he was opposed by Roosevelt; the result was Democrat Woodrow Wilson's election. Taft, with some reservations, supported the League of Nations. He was professor of constitutional law at Yale, 1913-21; chief justice of the U.S. Supreme Court, 1921-30; illness forced him to resign.

The More Colorful Facts

Astrological Sign: Virgo

Nicknames: Big Bill, Peaceful Bill, Smiling Bill, William The Improbable.

Original Family Name: Taffe. Ancestors can be traced back to 1678 A.D.

Presidential Notes: First Lady Helen Taft had 3,500 imported Yoshino variety (single white flower) cherry trees planted along the banks of Potomac in 1912, a gift from the wife of the Japanese Prime Minister. Only 25 percent of the original plantings are alive today, as the first were killed by disease within a few years.

Archie Butt, private secretary and aide to WHT, was lost in the *Titanic* disaster. WHT had a memorial fountain built in his memory on the south lawn of the White House.

"Dollar Diplomacy" was a theme of the WHT presidency.

Malacanan Palace was a nickname for the White House during WHT's term.

WHT's pet Holstein cow, Pauline Wayne, used to graze on the White House lawn. The White House staff often called her Mooly-Wooly.

A special bathtub capable of holding four regular-sized men was installed in the White House for WHT's use in 1909; he weighed 350 pounds.

Family Notes: WHT's half brother, Charles Taft, was at one time co-owner of the Philadelphia Phillies baseball team.

Violets were a trademark of First Lady Helen Taft.

Homes: 2038 Auburn Avenue, Cincinnati, Ohio, WHT's birthplace.

Campaign Notes: The 1908 campaign songs included "Get in Line for Big Bill Taft," written by Frederick W. Mills and D.M. Kinnon; "Get on the Raft with Taft;" and "Possum—The Latest Craze."

Other Positions: Law reporter, *Cincinnati Times*, 1886-1887.

Memberships: American Bar Association, elected president in 1913.

Famous Quotes: "Loneliest Place in the World"—on the presidency

Sports: An avid golfer, WHT, in 1909, bet $1,000 that he could beat 100 on the course at the Myopia Golf Club, in Boston, Massachusetts, considered to be one of the most difficult at the turn of the century. He shot a 98.

Dramatic Achievements: Starred in *Scrap of Paper*, a play presented in his mother's drawing room in 1880. His future wife, Helen Herron, also starred. Other performances of the Cincinnati amateur group were *She Stoops To Conquer* and *Sleeping Beauty*.

Books: *Four Aspects of Civic Duty*, 1906

Ethics in Service, 1915

Recollections of Full Years, 1914, autobiography of Helen Taft, his wife.

(THOMAS) WOODROW WILSON

Twenty-eighth president

1913-21

The Straight Facts

Born: December 28, 1856
Birthplace: Staunton, Virginia
Ancestry: Scots-Irish
Physical Characteristics: 5'11" tall, blue-gray eyes, brown hair
Religion: Presbyterian
Occupation: Teacher

Wife: (1) Ellen Louise Axson Wilson (1860-1914); (2) Edith Bolling Galt Wilson (1872-1961)

Date of Marriage: (1) June 24, 1886; (2) December 18, 1915

Children: Three daughters

College: Princeton University, class of 1879

Military History: None

Political Party: Democrat

Previous Political Offices: Governor, state of New Jersey (1911-13)

Vice-President: Thomas R. Marshall (1854-1925)

Died: February 3, 1924, in Washington, D.C.

Burial Place: National Cathedral, Washington, D.C.

Firsts: First president to earn a Ph.D.

First president to have been a president of a major university

First president to hold open press conferences

First president to cross the Atlantic while in office

First president to have two daughters marry in the White House

Biography in Brief: Woodrow Wilson was the son of a Presbyterian minister, the Reverand Joseph Ruggles Wilson, and Janet (Jessie) Woodrow. He attended Davidson College, 1873-74; was graduated from Princeton, A.B., 1879; A.M., 1882; read law at the University of Virginia, 1881; practiced law, Atlanta, 1882-83; Ph.D., Johns Hopkins, 1886. He taught at Bryn Mawr, 1885-88; at Wesleyan, 1888-90; was professor of jurisprudence and political economy at Princeton, 1890-1910; president of Princeton, 1902-1910; governor of New Jersey, 1911-13. In 1912 he was nominated for president with the aid of William Jennings Bryan, who sought to block James "Champ" Clark and Tammany Hall. Wilson won the election because the Republican vote for William H. Taft was split by the Progressives under Roosevelt.

Wilson protected American interests in revolutionary Mexico and fought for American rights on the high seas. His sharp warnings to Germany led to the resignation of his secretary of state, Bryan, a pacifist. In 1916 he was reelected by a slim margin. Wilson's attempts to mediate in the war failed.

Wilson proposed peace January 8, 1918, on the basis of his "Fourteen Points," a state paper with worldwide influence. His doctrine of self-determination continues to play a major role in territorial disputes.

Wilson went to Paris to help negotiate the peace treaty, the crux of which he considered the League of Nations. The Senate demanded reservations that would not make the U.S. subordinate to the votes of other nations in case of war. Wilson refused to consider any reservations and toured the country to get support. He suffered a stroke, October 1919. An invalid for months, he clung to his executive powers while his wife and doctor sought to shield him from affairs which would tire him.

He was awarded the 1919 Nobel Peace Prize, but the treaty embodying the League of Nations was rejected by the Senate in 1920.

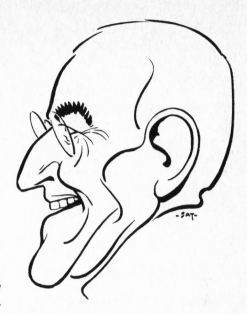

A 1919 caricature of Wilson by
Satterfield (NEA Service).

The More Colorful Facts

Astrological Sign: Capricorn

Nicknames: Coiner of Weasel Words, Phrasemaker, Professor, Schoolmaster in Politics, Tiger*.

Presidential Notes: The first president to appoint a woman, Anne(tte) Abbott Adams, to a subcabinet post, as assistant attorney general in 1920.

WW popularized the slogan "America First."

First president to show a motion picture in The White House. It was *Birth of a Nation*, shown on February 15, 1915.

"Duumvirate" was the nickname given to WW and his friend and aide, Colonel Edwin House during World War I. The word dates to Roman times where two officers were united in administering one public office. House was such a confidant of WW that the Europeans thought of them as one.

WW is the only president buried in Washington, D.C., at the National Cathedral.

Family Notes: Then a widower, WW married Edith Bolling Galt on December 18, 1915. She is often called the First Woman President because when a disabling stroke felled WW during his second term many believed she made all the decisions.

It was Admiral Cary Travers Grayson, WW's personal physician, who introduced him to the widow Edith Galt in 1915.

After his first night with his new wife Edith, WW supposedly broke out

*Given to him by his cousin Helen Bones because he was "caged in The White House."

and sang "Oh What a Beautiful Doll" to the White House staff. The song was composed in 1911 by A. Seymour Brown (words) and Nat D. Ayer (music).

Edith Wilson claimed to be a ninth generation descendant of Pocahantas and John Rolfe.

"Presidentress" was a nickname given to Edith Wilson.

Edith Wilson attended the inauguration of John F. Kennedy in 1961. It was her last public appearance before her death later that year.

Jessie Woodrow Wilson, another daughter of WW, married Francis Sayre (1885-1973) in the White House on November 25, 1913. Their son, Francis Jr., became Dean of the Washington National Cathedral.

Eleanor Randolph Wilson, WW's daughter married William Gibbs McAdoo in a ceremony at the White House on May 7, 1914. They were divorced in 1934.

Campaign Notes: 1912 Campaign songs included "Be Good to California, Mr. Wilson (California was Good to You)" by Andrew Sterling and Keoser, and "Wilson, That's All" by Ballard MacDonald and George Walter Brown. Another song, "We Take Our Hats Off to You, Mr. Wilson" was a definite reference to opponent Theordore Roosevelt's declaration that his "hat was in the ring."

The 1912 political platform was "New Freedom" and dealt with reform of the federal government.

Campaign themes from the 1916 reelection campaign included "Wilson and Peace with Honor, or Hughes with Roosevelt and War," "He Kept Us Out of War" and "He Proved the Pen Mightier Than the Sword."

Namesakes: American folk singer Woodie Guthrie, whose real name was Woodrow Wilson Guthrie.

Homes: 24 North Coalter Street, Staunton, Virginia, Wilson's birthplace. It was built in 1846 as the home of the Presbyterian minister. The Wilsons were the second family to live there as their father, Rev. Joseph Ruggles Wilson, served the local area. WW was actually born at "12¾ o'clock in the morning" on December 29, 1856 but his father recorded it as December 28th. The home was restored in 1979 and is now a National Historic Landmark.

2340 S Street N.W., the Washington, D.C., home ex-President Woodrow Wilson purchased for his wife Edith on their fifth wedding anniversary. He followed Scottish custom by presenting her with a key to the front door and a piece of sod from the garden. Mrs. Wilson would live there for the rest of her life. When she died at age 90 on December 28, 1961, it was the 105th anniversary of Woodrow's birth.

Adolescent Aspirations: At age 16, WW hung a picture of William Gladstone over his bed. He told his father: "This Gladstone is the greatest statesman who ever lived. I intend to be a great statesman too."

College Years: In his junior year at Princeton, WW served as manager and writer for the *Princetonian.*

WW held the position of speaker of the Whig Society while at Princeton and belonged to the Witherspoon Gang dormitory club; joined the Alligator Eating Club, a private society.

At Davidson, Wilson belonged to the Eumenean Club, a debating society.

His doctoral thesis for his Ph.D. from Johns Hopkins University was entitled "Congressional Government, A Study in American Politics."

Other Positions: Law partner, Renick and Wilson, Atlanta, Georgia, 1882.

Professor and football coach, Wesleyan University, Middletown, Connecticut, 1889.

Professor, Bryn Mawr college. WW was the first department head for history and political economy, 1885-88.

President, Princeton University, 1902-10.

Pets: Old Ike, a tobacco-chewing ram that grazed on the White House lawn. Mrs. Wilson kept 20 sheep grazing on the White House lawn. She once donated over 90 pounds of their wool to the Red Cross.

First Book Ever Read: *Weem's Life of Washington*

Favorite Foods: Chicken salad for lunch.

Grapefruit juice and raw eggs for breakfast.

Favorite Mystery Writer: J.S. Fletcher

Favorite Comic Strip: Krazy Kat

Favorite Actress: Katherine MacDonald

Books: *An Old Master,* 1893

Congressional Government and the State, 1885

Constitutional Government in the United States, 1911

Division and Reunion, 1893

George Washington, 1896

History of The American People, 5 volumes, 1902

International Ideals, 1919

Mere Literature, 1896

On Being Human, 1916

The State, 1889

Explusion: As president of Princeton, he expelled would-be playwright Eugene O'Neill for throwing a bottle of beer through his office window.

Famous Quotes: "Great Melting Pot." These words were first used by WW in a speech delivered on October 16, 1916 at the Cincinnati Music Hall.

"There is very little to be said about the vice-presidency . . . . His importance consists in the fact that he may cease to be vice-president," 1885.

Last words: 'Edith, I'm a broken machine, but I'm ready."

WARREN GAMALIEL HARDING

Twenty-ninth president

1921-23

The Straight Facts

Born: November 2, 1865
Birthplace: Corsica, Ohio
Ancestry: English, Dutch
Physical Characteristics: 6' tall, gray eyes, white hair
Religion: Baptist
Occupation: Newspaper editor
Wife: Florence Kling De Wolfe Harding (1860-1924)
Date of Marriage: July 8, 1891
Children: None, wife had son by previous marriage
College: Ohio Central College
Military History: None
Political Party: Republican

Previous Political Offices: City auditor, Marion, Ohio (1895); Member, Ohio Senate (1899-1903); Lieutenant governor, state of Ohio (1904-05); Member, U.S. Senate (1915-21)

Vice-President: Calvin Coolidge

Died: August 2, 1923, in San Francisco, California

Burial Place: Marion Cemetery, Marion, Ohio

Firsts: First president survived by his father
First president whose father was a physician
First president to ride to his inaugural in an auto
First president whose election returns were broadcast over radio
First president to visit Alaska
First president to visit Canada

Biography in Brief: Warren Gamaliel Harding was the son of Dr. George Tyron Harding, a physician, and Phoebe Elizabeth Dickerson. He attended Ohio Central College. He was state senator, 1899-1903; lieutenant governor, 1904-05; defeated for governor, 1910; chosen U.S. senator, 1915. He supported William H. Taft, opposed federal control of food and fuel; voted for antistrike legislation, woman's suffrage, and the Volstead prohibition enforcement act over President Woodrow Wilson's veto; and opposed the League of Nations. In 1920 he was nominated for president and defeated James M. Cox in the election. The Republicans capitalized on war weariness and fear that Wilson's League of Nations would curtail U.S. sovereignty. Harding stressed a return to "normalcy;" worked for tariff revision and repeal of excess profits law and high income taxes. Two Harding appointees, Albert B. Fall (interior) and Harry Daugherty (attorney general), became involved in the Teapot Dome scandal that embittered Harding's last days. He called the International Conference on Limitation of Armaments, 1921-22. Returning from a trip to Alaska he became ill and died in San Francisco.

The More Colorful Facts

Astrological Sign: Scorpio

Nicknames: Babbit in the White House, Great Handshaker, Standard Oil Senator, Wobbly Warren.

Presidential Notes: The Gayety Burlesque in Washington, D.C., built a special viewing box for WGH so he could watch the show and not be seen by other patrons.

"Poker Cabinet" was the nickname given to WGH's cigar-smoking, poker-playing, hard-drinking political advisors.

WGH insisted that boxes of toothpicks be placed in easily accessible, strategic places in the White House.

WGH made the first presidential speech by air over WEAR (today WFBR). The occasion was the dedication of the Francis Scott Key Memorial in Baltimore on June 14, 1922.

His inaugural address, which lasted 37 minutes, was the first to be amplified so all those on the Capitol grounds could hear it.

Family Notes: WGH called his wife Florence "Duchess." Her friends called her "Flossie."

"The End of a Perfect Day," composed in 1901 by Carrie Jacobs Bond, was Mrs. Harding's favorite song. The Marine Band would always include this song in their repertoire as a tribute to her.

Campaign Notes and Songs: "Back to Normalcy," "Americanism," and "Normalcy for the Nation" were themes of the 1920 presidential campaign.

"Harding, You're The Man For Us," composed by Al Jolson, and "Loyal American," written by F. Chantereau, were campaign songs.

Homes: 380 Mount Vernon Avenue, Marion, Ohio, now site of the Harding Museum. Warren and Florence Harding were married at the foot of the staircase in the house built in 1891 shortly before their wedding. Senator WGH rarely left the front porch during his campaign for the presidency and after being elected, the porch had to be rebuilt from overuse by crowds of supporters and pressmen.

Other Positions: Printer's apprentice at the *Caldonia Argus*, Marion, Ohio, at the age of ten.

Reporter, Marion *Democratic Mirror,* 1884. He was paid one dollar a week for his efforts. He was fired by editor Colonel James Vaughan in 1885 for spending too much time at the local Republican headquarters; Vaughan was a Democrat.

Editor, Marion *Star.* WGH bought the newspaper for $300 in 1884 with his friends from the Marion People's Band (which he founded and in which he played cornet), Jack Warwick, and Johnnie Sickle. WGH became the sole owner when he won Warwick's share in a poker game and Sickle sold

"If the Dream Comes True." A 1921 cartoon by Dorman H. Smith (NEA Service).

out. He served as its editor for over 35 years. WGH sold the paper in 1922 for $480,000.

Pets: Bob, Mrs. Harding's canary. When she left the White House, she gave Bob to Maggie Rogers of *Backstairs at the White House* fame.

Laddie Boy, pet airedale of Warren Harding, real name Caswell Laddie Boy. Laddie Boy once presided at his own White House birthday party, hosting other neighborhood dogs. The cake was made of layers of dog biscuits topped with icing. There is a bronze statue of him in the Smithsonian Institute by Bashka Paeff.

Mistress: Nan Britton was the mistress of WGH who supposedly bore his illegitimate daughter. The child, Elizabeth Ann Christian Britton (Christian was the name Britton would use when registering at hotels; George Christian was Harding's personal secretary), was born in 1919. WGH suggested to Britton that she take Doctor Humphrey's Number 11 Tablets to induce an abortion in February 1919 after he learned she was pregnant. She refused and the child was born on October 22. Supposedly, WGH never saw her. After WGH's death, Britton asked for a part of his estate for the girl's support but was denied. She later wrote a book called *The President's Daughter* on their affair. Britton disappeared in 1933 and was not heard from again. Elizabeth Ann, now Mrs. Henry Blaesig, was adopted in 1921 by Britton's sister and, as of 1980, was a housewife living in southern California.

Carrie Phillips was another mistress of WGH. Their 15-year affair was only discovered in 1960 when his love letters to her were found. Republican party bosses had paid her off to keep quiet during WGH's presidential campaign and term.

Memberships: National Horseshoe Pitching Association, as a senator elected honorary president, 1917.

Favorite Foods: Knockwurst and sauerkraut

Favorite Song: "La Paloma"

Favorite Hymn: "My Redeemer Liveth;" it was played at each stop of the funeral train carrying his body back to Marion, Ohio, for burial.

Hobbies: Favorite was "bloviating," his name for shooting the breeze.

Poker was another. His poker playing buddies, including Harry Daugherty, John R. McClean, and Jesse Smith, were nicknamed the Ohio Gang.

Golf, and betting on golf. Six Dollars Nassau was WGH's favorite golf bet, at Chevy Chase Golf Club. He would bet $6 out, $6 in, and $6 across. WGH usually shot in the 90's.

Musical Achievements: WGH played the althorn in the Ohio Central College band; he also played the B flat cornet.

WGH played B flat cornet in and helped found the Caledonia Aeolian Band. Reportedly, barring the bass drum, no other band member made as much noise as WGH.

WGH played trombone for the Silver Cornet Band

Quotes: Harding coined the phrase "Our Founding Fathers" for the American Revolutionary leaders.

Coined "Normalcy."

Coincidences: Dr. Charles Sawyer (1860-1924), friend and personal physician of WGH, died of mysterious ailments one year after WGH. As with the case of WGH, the only person with him at the time of death was Mrs. Harding.

Two was a number that kept reoccuring during WGH's life. He was born on November 2, (1865); accepted the nomination for president on July 22 (1920); was elected president November 2, (1920); his supposed illegitimate child was born on October 2 (1919); and he died on August 2 (1923).

Scandals: Teapot Dome, a Navy oil reserve in Wyoming, was the subject of a scandal during WGH's administration. Secretary of the Interior Albert Fall accepted a bribe for $300,000 in cash and bonds and a $100,000 loan for leasing the reserves to private interests. It is believed WGH knew nothing of this.

(JOHN) CALVIN COOLIDGE
Thirtieth president

1923-29

The Straight Facts

Born: July 4, 1872
Birthplace: Plymouth, Vermont
Ancestry: English
Physical Chracteristics: 5'9", blue eyes, sandy-red hair
Religion: Congregationalist
Occupation: Lawyer
Wife: Grace Anna Goodhue Coolidge (1879-1957)
Date of Marriage: October 4, 1905
Children: Two sons

College: Amherst College, class of 1895
Military History: None
Political Party: Republican
Previous Political Offices: City councilman, Northampton, Massachusetts (1899); City solicitor, Northampton, Massachusetts (1900-01); Clerk of courts, Hampshire County (1903-04); Member, Massachusetts house of representatives (1907-08); Mayor, Northampton, Massachusetts (1910-11); Member, Massachusetts senate (1912-15); President, Massachusetts senate (1914-15); Lieutenant governor, state of Massachusetts (1916-18); Governor, state of Massachusetts (1919-20); Vice-president of the United States (1921-23)
Vice-President: None, first term; Charles Gates Dawes (1865-1951), second term
Died: November 5, 1933, in Northampton, Massaschusetts
Burial Place: Notch Cemetery, Plymouth Notch, Vermont
Firsts: First president to be sworn in by his father
First president to be sworn in by a former president
First president born on the Fourth of July
Biography in Brief: Calvin Coolidge was the son of John Calvin Coolidge, a storekeeper, and Victoria Josephine Moor, and was named John Calvin Coolidge. Coolidge was graduated from Amherst in 1895. He entered Republican state politics and served as mayor of Northampton, Massachusetts, state senator, lieutenant governor, and, in 1919, governor. In September 1919, Coolidge attained national prominence by calling out the state guard in the Boston police strike. He declared: "There is no right to strike against the public safety by anybody, anywhere, anytime." This brought his name before the Republican convention of 1920, where he was nominated for vice-president. He succeeded to the presidency on Harding's death. He opposed the League of Nations; approved the World Court; vetoed the soldiers' bonus bill, which was passed over his veto. In 1924 he was elected by a huge majority. He reduced the national debt by $2 billion in three years. He twice vetoed the McNary-Haugen farm bill, which would have provided relief to financially hard-pressed farmers. With Republicans eager to renominate him he announced, August 2, 1927: "I do not choose to run for president in 1928."

The More Colorful Facts

Astrological Sign: Cancer
Nicknames: Cautious Cal, Last of the Yankees, Mr. Status Quo, Puritan President, Puritan in Babylon, Red, Silent Cal*, Little Fellow†.

*Actually a misnomer as he enjoyed talking to others.
†So-called by the White House staff behind his back.

AS SEEN BY THE CARTOONIST OF THE DAILY BLAT (REP.) AND BY THE CARTOONIST OF THE EVENING PUFF (DEM.)

Political cartoonist Dorman H. Smith shows how political leaning may affect the caricaturist's art when the victim is Coolidge (NEA Service).

Original Family names: Cooledge. The family can be traced back to the late 1500s.

Presidential Notes: CC's father, Colonel John C. Coolidge (1845-1926), the justice of the peace of Plymouth Notch, Vermont, administered the oath of office to his son upon Harding's death.

CC officially designated Christmas Eve as a holiday in 1928.

The first coin to carry a portrait of a living president was the 1926 Sesquicentennial half-dollar featuring CC and George Washington on one side and the original Liberty Bell on the reverse. The net coinage was 141,120 and they were struck at the Philadelphia Mint.

Term in office was called "Era of Wonderful Nonsense."

CC was the first president to broadcast a speech from the White House by radio. On February 22, 1924, he delivered an address commemorating George Washington's birthday.

White House staff nicknamed Mrs. Coolidge "Sunshine."

Campaign Notes: "Keep Cool and Keep Coolidge" was a theme of 1924 presidential campaign (also a song from "Gentlemen Prefer Blondes").

The first talking pictures of presidential candidates were taken on August 11, 1924 by Theodore Case and Lee A.E. LaForest of Republican candidate CC on the White House lawn and Progressive Candidate Robert LaFollette on the steps of the Capitol.

Namesakes: Coolidge Dam, a high, multiple concrete irrigation dam that generates electric power and supplies water for the San Carlos irrigation project in Florence-Casa Grande Villa, Arizona. Built in 1928 at a cost of $5.5 million.

First Annual President Calvin Coolidge Week: A resolution passed by the Democratically-controlled House declared the week of August 1 to August 7, 1983, in tribute to the late Republican president.

Homes: 21 Massasoit Street, Northampton, Massachusetts. The Coolidges first rented the home in 1906 for $28 a month. They resided there until they went to Washington in 1919.

Beeches, Northampton, Massachusetts, where CC fled after the presidency to be less visible.

Other positions: Vice-president, Northampton Savings Bank, elected in 1898.

Pets: Many dogs (several collies and chows), cats, canaries, a donkey named Ebeneezer, and Enoch, a white goose given to the Coolidges by actress Marie Dressler, who was starring in the Broadway play, *The White Goose.*

Famous Descendants: Television wit Orson Bean, whose real name is Dallas Frederick Burrows, is a third cousin.

College Years: CC was elected Grove Orator at Amherst for the Spring 1895 commencement. His task was to amuse classmates and alumni at Class Day exercises.

CC joined the Phi Gamma Delta fraternity at Amherst in December of 1894. He had previously been rejected by four other fraternities. He remained interested in "Fiji" affairs for the rest of his life.

"Principles Fought for in the American Revolution" was the topic of an essay CC wrote as a senior at Amherst. He won the silver medal awarded by the Sons of the American Revolution. As regional winner he was automatically entered in the national competition. CC won that award also. The prize was a gold medal worth $100. In typical fashion, he never told his family of the award.

Favorite Cigar: Fonesca Corona Fines deLuxe. CC paid $21 per hundred; he kept these for himself and would give others three-cent stogies.

Favorite Actor: Will Rogers

Preferences: He liked to have his head rubbed with petroleum jelly while eating breakfast in bed.

Preferred Speed Limit: CC had his chauffeur adhere to 16 miles per hour.

Sleep: CC reportedly slept 11 hours a day.

Shoe Size: 7½

Memberships: American Antiquarian Society. CC became president of this society in April 1930, serving until his death in 1933.

Honorary member of the Sioux Indian tribe from 1927. His Indian name was Chief Leading Eagle

Northampton Literary Club, an exclusive men's club in Northampton, Massachusetts. CC claimed membership was mostly comprised of those who could regularly afford to smoke expensive cigars.

Sports: Riding his electric horse. In 1927, CC had one installed in his bedroom at the White House, and rode it almost every day.

Books: *Have Faith in Massachusetts,* 1919

Famous Quotes: "I do not choose to run for president in 1928." This was written in a note personally handed to members of the press corps by CC on August 3, 1927, with no additional comment. Many politicos had expected him to run again in 1928 and were surprised by the announcement. Years later it would be revealed that CC had suffered a heart attack a few months earlier and his doctors did not believe he was up to the strain of another term.

Last words: "Good Morning, Robert."

HERBERT CLARK HOOVER

Thirty-first president

1929-33

The Straight Facts

Born: August 10, 1874
Birthplace: West Branch, Iowa
Ancestry: Swiss-German
Physical Characteristics: 5'11", hazel eyes, brown hair
Religion: Society of Friends (Quaker)
Occupation: Engineer
Wife: Lou Henry Hoover (1875-1944)
Date of Marriage: February 10, 1899
Children: Two sons
College: Stanford University, class of 1895
Military History: None
Political Party: Republican
Previous Political Offices: Chairman, American Relief Commission (1914-

15); Chairman, Commission for the Relief of Belgium (1915-18); Chairman, Supreme Economic Council (1919); Chairman, European Relief Council (1920); U.S. Food Administrator (1917-19); Secretary of commerce (1921-28)

Vice-President: Charles Curtis (1860-1936)
Died: October 20, 1964, in New York, New York
Burial Place: Herbert Hoover National Historic Site, West Branch, Iowa
Firsts: First president born in Iowa
  First president born west of the Mississippi River
  First president to visit China
  First president to serve in the cabinet in a position other than war or state
Biography in Brief: Herbert C. Hoover was the son of Jesse Clark Hoover, a blacksmith, and Hulda Randall Minthorn. Hoover grew up in Indian Territory (now Oklahoma) and Oregon; won his A.B. in engineering at Stanford, 1891. He worked briefly with the U.S. geological survey and western mines; then was a mining engineer in Australia, Asia, Europe, Africa, and the U.S. While chief engineer of the imperial mines in China, he directed food relief for victims of the Boxer Rebellion, 1900. He directed American Relief Committee, London, 1914-15; was U.S. Commissioner for Relief in Belgium 1915-19; U.S. Food Administrator, 1917-19; American Relief Administrator, 1918-23, feeding children in defeated nations; Russian Relief, 1918-1923. He was secretary of commerce, 1921-28. He was elected president over Alfred E. Smith, 1928. In 1929 the stock market crashed and the economy collapsed. During the depression, Hoover opposed federal aid to the unemployed. He was defeated in the 1932 election by Franklin D. Roosevelt. Pres. Harry S. Truman made him co-ordinator of European Food Program, 1947, and chairman of the Commission for Reorganization of the Executive Branch, 1947-49. He founded the Hoover Institution on War, Revolution, and Peace at Stanford University.

The More Colorful Facts

Astrological Sign: Leo
Nicknames: Hail Columbia*, Chief, Friend of Helpless Children, Grand Old Man, Hermit Author of Palo Alto, Hardest Working President†, Knight of The Lean Garbage Can, Man of Great Heart, Quaker Engineer, Weary Titan, World Humanitarian.
Original Family Name: Huber. Ancestors can be traced back to around 1700.
Presidential Notes: "Medicine Ball Cabinet" was the nickname given to his political advisors.

*So-called by Australian miners.
†So-called by the White House staff.

First president to receive an absolute monarch, Prajadhipok, King of Siam, at the White House, on April 29, 1931.

HCH officially approved the "Star Spangled Banner" as the national anthem.

HCH held 89 honorary degrees, the most awarded to any president.

Mrs. Hoover always left a $1,000 bill laying on top of her dresser. The White House staff was always puzzled and thought she just might be testing them.

Campaign Notes: "A Chicken in Every Pot" was a 1928 Republican campaign slogan. It was attributed to HCH, but in reality was said by his Democractic opponent, Al Smith, in a 1928 Boston speech.

"Hoover is the Man," written by B.J. McPhee, was a 1928 Republican campaign song.

Homes: Encina Hall, Room 38, Stanford University. Tradition has it that he was the first person to sleep under its roof.

Rapidan (later Camp Hoover), presidential retreat in the Blue Ridge Mountains. HCH donated the tract to Shenandoah National Park in 1933 to be used as a retreat for future presidents, but it never served as such.

"San Juan Hill," 623 Mirada Avenue, Palo Alto, California. After his wife's death, HCH gave the house to Stanford University to use as its President's House.

Namesakes: Hoover Dam, located near Las Vegas, Nevada, on the Colorado River, is one of the largest in the United States. It impounds the waters of Lake Mead and is 726 feet at its maximum height. The dam was completed in 1936 but not named for HCH until 1947.

"Memories," a 1929 NEA
Service cartoon alludes to
Hoover's war-relief work.

Hoovera, plant discovered in 1920.

Hooveria, an asteroid discovered by Austrian astronomer Professor Johann Palisan of the University of Vienna, in March 1920. Professor Palisan named his discovery after HCH, who at the time was helping world relief efforts after the first World War. He is the first president to have an asteroid named for him.

Hooverville, nickname given to a collection of ramshackle dwellings erected on a dump or urban wasteland and occupied by disposed, unemployed persons during the Great Depression, named after HCH.

Hooverize, a popular verb in the late 1920's synonomous with saving food.

Pets: Various dogs, including Tut, a German shepherd. No staff member was allowed to pet the dog because it would never come when HCH called it.

Other positions: Gold mine operator in Australia, 1897-98.

Founder, Chinese Engineering & Mining Company, 1900. The Hoover family was caught in China in the midst of the 1900 Boxer Rebellion.

Engineer with the British firm Bewick, Moreing, and Company, 1897-1908.

Memberships: Barbs, short for Barbarians, society which HCH joined at Stanford. The membership was made up of poor students who were not considered "worthy enough" to belong to fraternities or sororities. HCH served as treasurer of the Barbs in 1894.

Angler's club, a Florida social club Hoover joined to enjoy bonefishing.

Favorite Sport: Bonefishing

Quotes: "Depression"—Hoover was the first to use this economic term.

Books: *America's First Crusade,* 1943

American Individualism, 1922

An American Epic, 3 volumes, 1959-61

Fishing For Fun and To Wash Your Soul, 1963

Principles of Mining, 1908. Until it went out of print in 1967, it was a classic textbook for engineering students.

Problems of Lasting Peace, 1942

FRANKLIN DELANO ROOSEVELT

Thirty-second president

1933-45

The Straight Facts

Born: January 30, 1882
Birthplace: Hyde Park, New York
Ancestry: Dutch
Physical Characteristics: 6'1", blue eyes, dark hair

Religion: Episcopalian
Occupation: Lawyer
Wife: Anna Eleanor Roosevelt (1884-1962)
Date of Marriage: March 17, 1904
Children: One daughter, five sons
College: Harvard University, class of 1903
Military History: None
Political Party: Democrat
Previous Political Offices: Member, New York senate (1911-13); Asst. secretary of the navy (1913-20); Governor, state of New York (1929-33)
Vice-President: John Nance Garner (1868-1967), first and second term; Henry Agard Wallace (1888-1965), third term; Harry S. Truman, fourth term.
Died: April 12, 1945, at Warm Springs, Georgia
Burial Place: Roosevelt family estate, Hyde Park, New York
Firsts: First president elected to four terms
First president whose mother was eligible to vote for him
First presidential candidate to appear at a nominating convention
First president to appear on television
First president-elect to survive an assassination attempt
Biography in Brief: Franklin D. Roosevelt was born the son of James Roosevelt and Sara Delano. He was graduated from Harvard, 1904; attended Columbia Law School; was admitted to the bar. He went to the New York senate, 1910 and 1913. In 1913 Pres. Woodrow Wilson made him assistant secretary of the navy.

Roosevelt ran for vice-president, 1920, with James Cox and was defeated. From 1920 to 1928 he was a New York lawyer and vice president of Fidelity & Deposit Company.

Roosevelt was elected governor of New York, 1928 and 1930. In 1932, he was nominated by the Democrats for the presidency. The depression and the promise to repeal prohibition insured his election. He asked for emergency powers, proclaimed the New Deal, and put into effect a vast number of administrative changes. Foremost was the use of public funds for relief and public works, resulting in deficit financing. He greatly expanded the controls of the central government over business, and by an excess profits tax and progressive income taxes produced a redistribution of earnings on an unprecedented scale. The Wagner Act gave labor many advantages in organizing and collective bargaining.

When the Supreme Court nullified some New Deal laws, Roosevelt sought power to "pack" the court with additional justices, but Congress refused to give him that authority. He was openly hostile to fascist governments before World War II and launched a lend-lease program on behalf of the Allies. He wrote the principles of fair dealing into the Atlantic Charter, August 14, 1941 (with Winston Churchill), and urged the Four Freedoms (freedom of speech, of worship, from want, from fear) January 6, 1941.

When Japan attacked Pearl Harbor, December 7, 1941, the U.S. entered the war. He conferred with allied heads of state at Casablanca, January 1943; Quebec, August 1943; Teheran, November to December 1943; Cairo, December 1943; Yalta, February 1945.

The More Colorful Facts

Astrological Sign: Aquarius

Nicknames: Alphabet King, Boss, Champion of the Four Freedoms, Crisis President, Dr. Jekyll of Hyde Park, Eleanor's Husband, Fireside Chatterer, Franklin the First, Great Humanitarian, Houdini in The White House, Hudson Valley Aristocrat, Mob's Friend, New Deal President, Sphinx, Squire of Dutchess County, Supreme Court Packer, That Man in The White House, That Red in The White House.

Presidential Notes: FDR was the last president inaugurated on March 4 (1933) and the first inaugurated on January 20 (1937).

Political enemies nicknamed FDR's social programs "alphabet soup."

FDR's political advisors, which included Judge Sam Rosenbaum, Bernard Baruch, and Herbert Lehman, were nicknamed the "Brain Trust."

FDR was the first U.S. president to speak in a foreign country and broadcast back to the U.S., in Cartagena, Colombia.

FDR banned the Chicago *Daily Tribune* from The White House during his entire presidency because he didn't like the paper's editorial policies.

FDR turned on the lights with a special switch at the White House for the first night game ever played in the major baseball leagues on May 24, 1935. The Reds beat the Philadelphia Phillies 4-1 with the Phils' Lou Chiozza as the game's first batter. The game was played at Crosby Field in Cincinnati, Ohio.

"Dixie Clipper" was the nickname of the first presidential aircraft. Rented by the Secret Service, the plane flew FDR to Casablanca to meet with British prime minister Winston Churchill.

FDR was the first president to broadcast a radio speech to the people of France in their native language, on November 2, 1942.

As president-elect, FDR picked Miss Louise Hachmeister as chief White House operator because she was good at detecting important voices. She was nicknamed "Hacky" by the White House staff.

Eleanor Roosevelt cooked hot dogs for the King and Queen of England during their stay at the White House. Eleanor was a self-admitted terrible cook, claiming to know how to cook only hot dogs and scrambled eggs.

FDR was the first president to visit Hawaii while in office. He traveled on the U.S.S. *Houston* and landed at Hilo on July 25, 1934.

Louis McHenry Howe (1871-1936), friend, confidant, and political advisor to Franklin D. Roosevelt, was a permanent guest in the FDR White House. His favorite breakfast was codfish cakes with catsup and tabasco, cornmeal pone with no shortening. The staff was aghast because whenever he called, FDR came running.

The first Fireside Chat was broadcast on March 12, 1933, from the White House Diplomatic Reception Room.

FDR appointed the first woman ambassador to a foreign country, Ruth Bryan Owens, who served in Denmark. She was the daughter of William Jennings Bryan.

FDR had a passion for peanuts; he had the White House staff place out bowls for him to munch.

FDR named the first woman to a cabinet post, Frances Perkins, who served as secretary of labor from 1933 to 1945. The two met in 1911 while FDR was a member of the New York assembly and Perkins was a representative of the National Consumers League.

FDR had "Stolen from the White House" imprinted on White House matchbooks.

Family Notes: FDR's pet nickname for Eleanor was "Babs."

FDR and Eleanor called their children "chicks."

First Lady Eleanor Roosevelt hosted the "The Eleanor Roosevelt Program," a WNBC radio weekly program, heard Monday through Friday at 12:30 P.M. and first broadcast in 1933. The orchestra leader for the 15-minute show was Leo Reisman and the vocalist was Lee Riley. She has been the only First Lady to host a radio series.

Faye Emerson, a Hollywood actress, became FDR's daughter-in-law when she married his son Elliott on December 3, 1944. Elliott took Faye Emerson for his third wife on a platform in the Grand Canyon. The two were divorced in 1949. "At Home with Faye and Elliott" was the radio series that featured husband and wife. The program first was broadcast in 1946.

Eleanor was nicknamed "First Lady of the World".

"His" and "Hers" were the nicknames of the two pistols FDR and Eleanor kept under their pillows at night.

In January 1936, Eleanor began writing, "My Day," a syndicated newspaper column.

Campaign Notes: The "New Deal" was a general theme of the FDR presidency, but especially of the 1932 presidential campaign.

"Happy Days Are Here Again" was the theme song of that campaign. Words by Jack Yellen and music by Milton Ager, the song was from the movie *Chasing Rainbows.* Other songs from that campaign included "The Road is Open Again" by Irving Kabel and Sammy Fain, and "Roosevelt, Garner, and Me," written by Al Lewis and Al Sherman.

"Sunflowers Die in November" was a Democratic slogan used in the 1936 campaign to refer to Republican candidate Alf Landon's symbol, the flower of his home state of Kansas.

In the 1940 campaign opponent Wendell Willkie used the slogan "Roosevelt for Ex-President."

In the 1944 campaign the Democratic theme song was "Let's Re-Re-

In 1944, Dorman H. Smith comments on Roosevelt's decision to run for a fourth term. (NEA Service).

Re-Elect Roosevelt," and Republicans campaigned with "Had Enough?"

Homes: Springwood, Hyde Park, New York, birthplace, home, also burial place (in the Rose Garden).

Campobello, vacation home in New Brunswick, Canada, on the Bay of Fundy.

Namesakes: Roosevelt dime, designed by John Sinnock. Under FDR's neck are the small initials JS, which stand for Sinnock. The Roosevelt dime was first issued in 1946, the year after FDR's death.

Stamp: Roosevelt Birthday Issue, a six-cent stamp in honor of FDR's 84th birthday, January 29, 1966.

Monuments: A statue of FDR stands in Grosvenor Square in London, England.

Pets: Fala, a Scotty, originally named Big Boy became rather famous during his master's term in office, as he was FDR's constant companion. Fala's full name was Murray of Fala Hill. The press corps called Fala the "Informer," because they knew that wherever Fala was, FDR wasn't far away.

Blaze, Elliott's pet mastiff that mauled Fala. After the incident, Blaze had to be put to sleep.

Cricky, Eleanor's Scotty, banned to Hyde Park from the White House for biting columnist Bess Furman on the lip.

Major, the German shepherd FDR acquired after his beloved Scotty, Fala, died. Major bit Senator Hattie Caraway (the first woman ever elected in her own right to the U.S. Senate), British Prime Minister Ramsay Mac-Donald, and Canadian Prime Minister Mackenzie King.

Military Career: In 1898, FDR and a Groton classmate ran away from school to join the Army to fight in the war against Spain. They escaped by hiding in a pie wagon. During the two-day trip to the recruiting station, both complained of fever and parched throats. It turned out both had the measles, and that ended FDR's military career.

Mistress: Lucy Mercer was first employed as Eleanor's social secretary in 1913. Eleanor was willing to give Franklin a divorce in 1919 so he could marry Lucy but two things prevented that: Lucy was a Catholic and would not marry a divorced man; and Sara Delano Roosevelt threatened to cut off her son without a cent if the divorce went through. Lucy left him and later married Wintie Rutherford. They later resumed their relationship, and she was with FDR at Warm Springs, Georgia, when he died.

Health: FDR was struck by poliomyelitis on August 21, 1921. He learned to walk with leg braces and a cane.

Memberships: Eagle Engine Company of Hyde Park, volunteer fire department young FDR joined in 1907, following in the footsteps of his father and grandfather before him.

Rescue Hook and Ladder Company of Dutchess County, volunteer fire department FDR joined in 1907.

Chevy Chase Golf Club, joined in 1913 while serving as assistant secretary of the navy.

Cuff Links Club, made up of friends of FDR who helped him in the unsuccessful vice presidential run in 1920. He presented them all with gold cuff links; thereafter they met each year on his birthday.

Dutchess Golf and Country Club. On December 15, 1923, FDR resigned his membership. In his letter to the board of this New York club FDR explained that "he was recovering from polio and still using crutches to get around and that he believed it would be at least a year or two before he got around to playing golf again."

Philanthropies: FDR founded the March of Dimes for the benefit of the National Foundation for Infantile Paralysis. It was comedian Eddie Cantor, on January 3, 1938, who coined the campaign name "March of Dimes." Red Skelton served as the master of ceremonies for the first fund raising program.

Allied Code Names (WWII): Rover (for Eleanor because she traveled so much); Cargo (for FDR)

Favorite Dessert: Apple pie and fruitcake

Favorite Vermouth: Argentine Vermouth was the only brand FDR enjoyed in his martinis.

Favorite Foods: Frog legs, pig knuckles, scrambled eggs (each Sunday Eleanor would prepare them in a chafing dish for the whole family).

Brand of Cigarettes: Camels

Favorite Christmas Carol: "Art Thou Weary, Art Thou Laden?"

Favorite Card Game: Solitaire

Favorite Mystery Writer: Dorothy L. Sayers (particularly her Lord Peter Wimsey novels.)

Boats: *Amberjack II,* a 45-foot sailboat

   Half-Moon, a 40-foot yacht FDR had as a teenager; first launched in July 1891.

   Larooco, the houseboat FDR used for his winter cruise in 1924. The name was short for Lawrence and Roosevelt Company, as he purchased it with Boston banker John S. Lawrence.

   New Moon, 21-foot knockabout FDR had as a sixteen-year-old.

Awards: Punctuality prize, at Groton

Assassination Attempt: Bay Front Park in Miami, Florida, located on 40 acres on Biscayne Bay, was the site of the only assassination attempt on the life of a president-elect. On February 15, 1933, Guiseppe Zangara aimed for FDR, who was riding in a limousine with Miami mayor R.B. Gauthier and George T. Hussey, chair of the reception committee. Zangara fatally shot Mayor Anton Cermak of Chicago. Also wounded were Russell Caldwell of Coconut Grove, Florida (head wound), Miss Margaret Kruis of Newark, New Jersey (head wound), Mrs. Joseph H. Gill of Miami (the wife of the president of Florida Power and Light Company, shot in abdomen) and vacationing New York police detective William J. Sinnot (head wound).

Last words: "I have a terrific headache."

HARRY S. TRUMAN
Thirty-third president
1945-53

The Straight Facts

Born: May 8, 1884
Birthplace: Lamar, Missouri
Ancestry: English, Scots-Irish
Physical Characteristics: 5'10", blue eyes, brown hair
Religion: Baptist
Occupation: Haberdasher, politician
Wife: Elizabeth "Bess" Virginia Wallace Truman (1885-1982)
Date of Marriage: June 28, 1919
Children: One daughter
College: None
Military History: Major, U.S. Army
Political Party: Democrat
Previous Political Offices: Judge of the Jackson County court, Missouri (1922-24); Presiding judge, Jackson County, Missouri (1926-34); Member,

U.S. Senate (1935-1945); Vice-president of the United States (1945)

Vice-President: None, first term; Alben William Barkley (1877-56), second term

Died: December 26, 1972, in Kansas City, Missouri

Burial Place: Truman Memorial Library and Museum, Independence, Missouri

Firsts: First president born in Missouri

First president to televise a speech from the White House

First former president to address Congress

Biography in Brief: Harry S. Truman was the son of John Anderson Truman and Martha Ellen Young. A family disagreement on whether his middle name was Shippe or Solomon, after the names of two grandfathers, resulted in his using only the middle initial S. He attended public schools in Independence, Missouri, worked for the *Kansas City Star,* 1901; as railroad time-keeper; and as a helper in Kansas City banks up to 1905. He ran his family's farm, 1906-17. He was commissioned a first lieutenant and took part in the Vosges, Meuse-Argonne, and St. Mihiel actions in World War I. After the war he ran a haberdashery; became judge of Jackson County court, 1922-24; attended Kansas City School of Law, 1923-25.

Truman was elected U.S. senator in 1934; reelected 1940. In 1944 with Roosevelt's backing he was nominated for vice-president and elected. On Roosevelt's death Truman became president. In 1948 he was elected president.

Truman authorized the first uses of the atomic bomb (Hiroshima and Nagasaki, August 6 and 9, 1945), bringing World War II to a rapid end. He was responsible for creating NATO, the Marshal Plan, and what came to be called the Truman Doctrine (to aid nations such as Greece and Turkey, threatened by Soviet or other communist takeover). He broke a Soviet blockade of West Berlin with a massive airlift, 1948-49. When communist North Korea invaded South Korea, June 1950, he won UN approval for a "police action" and sent in forces under Gen. Douglas MacArthur. When MacArthur opposed his policy of limited objectives, Truman removed him from command.

Truman was responsible for a higher minimum-wage, increased social-security, and aid-for-housing laws.

The More Colorful Facts

Astrological Sign: Taurus

Nicknames: Billie Spunk*, Fair Deal President, Give 'em Hell Harry, Haber-dasher Harry, Man from Independence, Man from Missouri, Pepper Pot Truman.

*So-called by White House staff.

Presidential Notes: "Is there anything I can do for you?" HST asked Mrs. Franklin Roosevelt after she told him the president was dead. Eleanor promptly asked Truman: "Is there anything we can do for *you?* You are the one in trouble now."

On his Oval office desk, HST kept two mottoes: "The Buck Stops Here" and Mark Twain's "Always Do Right." The reverse side of "The Buck Stops Here" read "I'm from Missouri."

HST often wore an American Legion button in his lapel.

Leslie Coffelt, a guard defending Blair House, was killed November 1, 1950, when two Puerto Rican nationalists attempted to break in. HST and his family were in temporary residence at the time, but no member of the family was injured. Coffelt was posthumously awarded the Execptional Civilian Service Honor and the Meritorious Civilian Service Award. Oscar Collazo, one of the two Puerto Rican nationalists, was injured in the shoot-out and was taken to Washington's Gallinger Hospital, while his collegue, Griselio Torresola, was slain. HST commuted Collazo's death sentence to life on July 24, 1951, and Collazo was sent to the federal prison at Leavenworth, Kansas. In a surprise move on September 10, 1979, President Jimmy Carter commuted his life sentence and he was freed.

Truman liked to call White House visitors "customers."

A "Fair Deal," based on the the economic and social health of the nation, was a theme of the Truman presidency.

HST's personal physician, Major General Dr. Wallace H. Graham, started the first White House dispensary.

Daughter Margaret Truman called the White House the "Great White Jail."

Lionel Hampton, who played at HST's inauguration, was the first black musician to play at a presidential inauguration.

"Independence" was the nickname of the presidential airplane. The plane (call numbers 6505) was a DC-6 with a Pratt and Whitney engine and the first to use water injection. The plane is now on display at Wright-Patterson Air Force Base.

Political advisors were nicknamed the "Missouri Gang."

HST sang the "Missouri Waltz" in a duet with actress Lauren Bacall at the Washington Press Club in February 1945. The photograph of Miss Bacall sitting atop the piano with the president playing became quite popular with the press and the public. According to biographers, HST hated the song.

When First Lady Bess Truman attempted to christen the U.S. *Capitol,* a C-54 aircraft, in 1954, the bottle of champagne refused to break against the nose of the aircraft. After several unsuccessful attempts by Mrs. Truman and military leaders, the bottle was broken with a hammer.

HST was the first president to ride in a submerged enemy submarine, the *U2513,* when it was being tested near Key West, Florida.

As former president, HST was issued Medicare Card #1.

HST changed the presidential seal to a "peace" symbol rather than a "war" symbol. Prior to his term, the eagle looked toward the talon with the arrows of war. HST had the head changed so it looked toward the talon holding the olive branches.

Family Notes: HST called his wife Bess "The Boss" and his daughter Margaret "the one who bosses the Boss." He also called Margaret "My Baby." White House staff called HST, Bess, and Margaret the "Three Musketeers" because they enjoyed each other's company so much.

Campaign Notes: *The Chicago Tribune*, on November 3, 1948, erroneously proclaimed Republican Thomas Dewey the winner with the headline "Dewey Beats Truman."

"We Wanna Disaffiliate." A 1948 NEA Service cartoon by Dorman H. Smith.

"I'm Just Wild About Harry," a 1948 campaign song, was written by Noble Sissle and Eubie Blake in 1921.

IGHAT was a 1948 political acronym for "I've Got Hatred Against Truman."

"Loneliest campaign" was the nickname given to HST's 1948 presidential run.

Namesakes: Harry S. Truman Drawbridge, the seventh largest vertical lift drawbridge in North American. Built in 1945, it is located in Kansas City, Missouri, and is 427 feet at its longest span.

Harry S. Truman Reservoir. The Kaysinger Bluff Dam and Reservoir in Southern Missouri was renamed after the 33d president and dedicated on May 27, 1970, by President Richard Nixon.

Stamp: Harry Truman Issue, an eight-cent stamp commemorating HST's death, 1973.

Homes: 219 North Delaware Street, Independence, Missouri. Bess Truman's birthplace and the home she and HST lived in from 1919, the year of their marriage.

Birthplace: At the time of his birth, the population of Lamar, Missouri, was around 800; the house had no number on a street with no name. The address has since been named 1009 Truman Place.

Other Positions: First job was as a sweeper and mopper at $2 per week at Jim Clinton's pharmacy in Independence, Missouri.

HST worked as a mail boy in 1902 for $7 a week for the Kansas City *Star.*

In December 1902, HST was employed for $35 per month by the National Bank of Commerce: the "Zoo." A fellow employee of this Kansas City, Missouri, bank and his roommate for a while was Arthur Eisenhower, eldest brother of Dwight D. Eisenhower.

In 1901, HST took a job as a timekeeper for the Santa Fe Railroad working for contractor L.J. Smith. He was paid $1.50 a day or 15 cents an hour.

Bookkeeper at the Union National Bank, Kansas City, Missouri in 1903 at $60 a month.

Store owner. HST and Eddie Jacobsen opened Truman and Jacobsen, a men's furnishing store located on 12th Street in downtown Kansas City near the Muehlebach Hotel in 1920. The store went bankrupt in 1922.

Health: HST suffered a near fatal case of diphtheria in 1893.

Memberships: HST joined the Ku Klux Klan in 1922 because he needed their backing to be elected judge in Jackson County, Missouri. Within a year, HST resigned and received his $10 entry fee back when he refused to follow their demands that no Jews or Catholics be appointed to public office.

National Old Trails Association elected HST president in 1923.

Shirt size: 15½, with 33″ sleeves

Favorite Sports: Horseshoes. He had horsehoe pits dug on the back lawn of the White House.

Favorite Books: *Great Men and Famous Women,* 4 volumes, by Charles F. Home (a childhood favorite).

Tallulah, Tallulah Bankhead's autobiography, that Truman claimed was the best book he read while in the White House.

Favorite Slang Word: Manure. First Lady Bess Truman was asked why she allowed her husband to use the word, to which she replied that it took her twenty years to get him to use it.

Favorite Cocktail: Old-fashioned, made with 99% bourbon.

Favorite Bourbon: I.W. Harper. He liked it undiluted with no chaser. A supply was kept in his personal bathroom, and it was reported that Bess didn't know anything about this stash.

Political Stands: When former Democratic President HST toured Disneyland he refused to ride on Dumbo the Elephant because the elephant is the symbol of the Republican party.

Quotes: "As useful as a cow's fifth teat"—on the vice-presidency

Musical Notes: In 1900, maestro Ignace Jan Paderewski, on a tour of Kansas City (Missouri), taught a young student of Mrs. E. C. White how to play the turn in his Minuet in G. The student was HST.

At a state dinner at Potsdam, Germany, on July 19, 1945, Truman played Beethoven's Minuet in G. British Prime Minister Winston S. Churchill and Soviet leader Joseph Stalin attended the dinner.

DWIGHT DAVID EISENHOWER

Thirty-fourth president

1953-61

The Straight Facts

Born: October 14, 1890
Birthplace: Denison, Texas
Ancestry: Swiss-German
Physical Characteristics: 5'10", blue eyes, light brown hair
Religion: Presbyterian
Occupation: Army officer
Wife: Mamie Geneva Doud Eisenhower (1896-1979)
Date of Marriage: July 1, 1916
Children: Two sons
College: United States Military Academy at West Point, class of 1916
Military History: General, U.S. Army
Political Party: Republican

Previous Political Offices: None
Vice-President: Richard Milhous Nixon
Died: March 28, 1969, in Washington, D.C.
Burial Place: Eisenhower Center, Abilene, Kansas
Firsts: First president born in Texas
First president of the 50 states
First president to appear on color television
Biography in Brief: Dwight David Eisenhower was the son of David Jacob Eisenhower and Ida Elizabeth Stover. He was graduated from West Point, 1915. He was on the American military mission to the Philippines, 1935-39, and during four of those years on the staff of Gen. Douglas MacArthur. He was made commander of Allied forces landing in North Africa, 1942; full general, 1943. He became supreme Allied commander in Europe, 1943, and as such led the Normandy invasion on June 6, 1944. He was given the rank of general of the army December 20, 1944, made permanent in 1946. On May 7, 1945, he received the surrender of the Germans at Rheims. He returned to the U.S. to serve as chief of staff, 1945-48. From 1948 to 1953, he was president of Columbia University, but took leave of absence in 1950 to command NATO forces.

Eisenhower resigned from the army and was nominated for president by the Republicans, 1952. He defeated Adlai E. Stevenson in the election. He again defeated Stevenson, 1956. He called himself a moderate; favored "free market system" vs. government price and wage controls; kept government out of labor disputes; reorganized defense establishment; promoted missile programs. He continued foreign aid; sped end of Korean fighting; endorsed Taiwan and Southeast Asia defense treaties; backed UN in condemning Anglo-French raid on Egypt; advocated "open skies" policy of mutual inspection to USSR. He sent U.S. troops into Little Rock, Arkansas in September 1957, during the segregation crisis and ordered the Marines into Lebanon July to August 1958.

During his retirement at his farm near Gettysburg, Pennsylvania, Eisenhower took up the role of elder statesman, counseling his three successors in the White House.

The More Colorful Facts

Astrological Sign: Libra
Nicknames: Alarmist Ike*, Gloomy Face†, Great Delegator, Little Ike‡, Red Ike‡, Swede‡.

*So-called as a Lieutenant colonel by fellow officers at Fort Ord in 1939 because he was sure the U.S. would soon be involved in a war.
†As a cadet at West Point.
‡Childhood nickname.

"Who Else?" In a 1956 cartoon, John Fischetti comments on Eisenhower's great popularity (NEA Service).

Original Family Name: Eisenhauer. The family first came to America in 1741 with a party of German Mennonites.

Presidential Notes: *Barbara Anne* (after his granddaughter) was the presidential yacht during DDE's term. This 92-foot cruiser cost the government $60,000 a year to maintain.

Columbine was the name of the presidential plane during DDE's term chosen by First Lady Mamie in honor of the state flower of her home state of Colorado. Two planes actually bore this name. The *Columbine II* (call number 48-610) was scrapped and *Columbine III* (call number 53-7885) is now on display at Wright Paterson Air Force Base.

Actor Robert Montgomery was a favorite who helped DDE prepare for television appearances.

"Nice Old Men and a Plumber" was the sarcastic nickname given to DDE's cabinet. The plumber was Martin Durkin who resigned less than one year after his appointment.

"Pink Palace" was the staff nickname for the White House during the Eisenhower term, because Mamie was particularly partial to the color.

Su Avitar in Modor, Fortiter in Re ("Gently in Manner, Strongly in Deed") was the plaque on DDR's desk in the Oval Office.

DDE was the only president to see action in both World Wars.

DDE was the only president to hold a pilot's license.

Family Notes: "Icky" was the nickname of Eisenhower's first-born son, Doud Dwight Eisenhower, born September 12, 1917. He died of scarlet fever on

January 2, 1921. As a memorial, DDE would send Mamie flowers every year on his birthday.

"Mrs. Ike" is what DDE called Mamie.

Campaign Notes: "I Like Ike" was the campaign slogan used by Republicans in 1952 and 1956; it was coined by Henry D. Spalding. It was also the title of the presidential campaign theme song written by Irving Berlin in 1952 for DDE. In 1956 the slogan was slightly altered to "I Still Like Ike" or "I Like Ike Even Better."

"Communism, Korea, and Corruption" was a 1952 campaign slogan.

"Look Ahead Neighbor Special" was the nickname of DDE's 1952 presidential campaign train.

"Peace and Prosperity" was a 1956 Republican campaign slogan.

"Ben Hogan for President. If we're going to have a golfer, let's have a good one!" was an anti-DDE bumper sticker during the 1956 presidential campaign and FEF ("Forget Eisenhower Forever") was an anti-Eisenhower campaign acronym in the same campaign.

Homes: Gettysburg, Pennsylvania. A brick farmhouse on the southwestern edge of Gettysburg National Military park was the only home DDE ever owned. He lived there from 1955 to 1969.

Namesakes: Eisenhower College, a small liberal arts school located near Seneca Falls, New York. The school closed in 1982 after fourteen years due to inflationary pressure.

"Eisenhower Blues," a song recorded by J.B. Lenoir on Parrot Records. On the flip side was "I'm in Korea."

Mount Eisenhower, mountain in Banff National Park in the Canadian Rockies.

Stamp: Dwight Eisenhower Issue, a six-cent stamp commemorating DDE's death, October 14, 1969.

School Days: DDE starred on the Abilene, Kansas, high school football team and was president of the Athletic Association.

In the *Helianthus,* the Abilene High School yearbook, in 1909, when DDE and brother Edgar graduated from this school, the prediction for their future was that Ike would be a professor of history and Edgar the president of the United States.

West Point Days: Highest rank DDE attained was color sergeant.

His dormitory was Cullum Hall.

Cadet DDE and two friends formed The Misogynist Club while at West Point. They were not true to the club's name as all three were married within one year of graduation from the Academy.

Sports: DDE's football career was ended when, as a cadet at West Point, he tackled Jim Thorpe in an Army vs. Carlisle game and wrenched his knee.

DDE hit a 104-yard hole-in-one on the 13th tee at the Seven Lakes Country Club. He used a 9-iron.

Other positions: Ice lifter, Belle Springs Creamery. In 1910, young DDE worked the night shift at this Abilene creamery for $90 a month. His job was to lift chunks of ice, usually weighing around 300 pounds. His father, David, was also employed at the same plant as a maintenance mechanic.

Football coach, Peacock Military Academy. At the request of his commanding officer, Maj. Gen. Frederick Funston, 2d Lt. DDE served as the coach in 1915 for this San Antonio, Texas, school. He was paid $150.

Football coach, St. Louis College, San Antonio, Texas, 1916

Military career: "Bayonet" was the nickname of DDE's private military parlor car in Great Britain during World War II.

General DDE won five stars:

DATE AWARDED	SERVING AT:
September 29, 1941	Louisiana
March 27, 1942	The Pentagon
July 7, 1942	London
February 15, 1943	Algiers
December 16, 1944	Battle of the Bulge

"Look" was the Allied code name for DDE in World War II.

"Operation Grief" was the code name for a Nazi plot to kill General DDE in 1943.

Memberships: Newspaper Carriers' Hall of Fame

Awards: 1963 Alexander Hamilton Medal, awarded by Columbia University to a distinguished aluminus or faculty member for distinguished service in any field.

Senator Joseph L. Bristow, the Kansas senator (from 1909 to 1915), appointed DDE to West Point. He had taken the exam arranged by Bristow for candidates wishing nomination to either West Point or Annapolis. Paul Heath, editor of the Abilene *Chronicle* recommended DDE to Bristow. DDE preferred Annapolis so he could attend with his friend Everett E. "Swede" Hazlett, Jr. (who would later become an admiral) but was appointed to West Point instead as he had passed Annapolis' maximum admittance age of 20 years.

Distinguished Service Medal.

Culzean Castle. The Scottish people gave General DDE lifetime use of this castle after World War II.

Grand Cross of Legion of Honor, French Military award, presented to Gen. DDE in 1943.

Oak Leaf Cluster, presented to Gen. DDE by President Harry S. Truman in 1945.

Order of Solomon with Placque and Cordon, Ethiopian military award, presented in 1948.

Order of the Elephant, Danish military award, presented in 1947.

Courtship: The Original, a San Antonio, Texas, Mexican restaurant was where Lt. DDE and Miss Mamie Geneva Doud had their first date in October 1915. The menu never changed and standard fare was enchiladas, chili, and tamales. A dinner for two cost $1.25 including tip.

The Orpheum, a vaudeville house also called the Palace of San Antonio, was a spot DDE and Mamie often attended.

Favorite Dessert: Prune whip

Favorite Television Show: "The Fred Waring Show" (1949-54)

Favorite Writers: Zane Grey and Luke Short, American writers of western novels

Favorite Books: *Life of Hannibal* (while in high school). DDE once said the vivid description of the Punic War inspired him to a military career.

Favorite War Film: *The Story of G.I. Joe.*

Favorite Card Games: Bridge. Mrs. Eisenhower's favorite card game was Bolivia.

Books: *Crusade in Europe, 1948.* Became the basis for a 1949 television series, one of two based on books by U.S. presidents.

Epitaph: "A great man passed this way in defense of freedom."—self-written.

JOHN FITZGERALD KENNEDY

Thirty-fifth president

1961-63

The Straight Facts

Born: May 29, 1917
Birthplace: Brookline, Massachusetts
Ancestry: Irish
Physical Characteristics: 6'1" tall, blue eyes, reddish-brown hair, 170 lbs.
Religion: Roman Catholic
Occupation: Newspaperman
Wife: Jacqueline Lee Bouvier Kennedy (1929-)
Date of Marriage: September 12, 1953
Children: One daughter, two sons
College: Harvard University, class of 1940
Military History: Lieutenant, U.S. Navy

Political Party: Democrat

Previous Political Offices: Member, U.S. House of Representatives (1947-53); Member, U.S. Senate (1953-61)

Vice-president: Lyndon Baines Johnson

Died: November 22, 1953, in Dallas, Texas

Burial Place: Arlington National Cemetery, Arlington, Virginia

Firsts: First president born in the twentieth century

First president to be a Roman Catholic

First president to serve in the Navy

First president to win a Pulitzer Prize

First president to have both parents survive him

Biography in Brief: John F. Kennedy was the son of Joseph Patrick Kennedy, a financier, who later became ambassador to Great Britain, and Rose Elizabeth Fitzgerald. He entered Harvard, attended the London School of Economics briefly in 1935, and received a B.S. from Harvard in 1940. He served in the Navy, 1941-45, commanded a PT boat in the Solomons, and won the Navy and Marine Corps Medal. He wrote *Profiles in Courage,* which won a Pulitzer Prize. He served as representative in Congress, 1947-53; was elected to the Senate in 1952, reelected 1958. He nearly won the vice-presidential nomination in 1956.

In 1960, Kennedy won the Democratic nomination for president and defeated Richard M. Nixon, Republican. He was the first Roman Catholic president.

In April 1961, the new Kennedy administration suffered a severe setback when an invasion force of antiCastro Cubans, trained and directed by the U.S. Central Intelligence Agency, failed to establish a beachhead at the Bay of Pigs in Cuba.

Kennedy's most important act was his successful demand October 22, 1962, that the Soviet Union dismantle its missile bases in Cuba. He established a quarantine of arms shipments to Cuba and continued surveillance by air. He defied Soviet attempts to force the Allies out of Berlin. He made the steel industry rescind a price rise. He backed civil rights, a mental health program, arbitration of railroad disputes, and expanded medical care for the aged. Astronaut flights and satellite orbiting were greatly developed during his administration.

On November 22, 1963, Kennedy was assassinated in Dallas, Texas.

The More Colorful Facts

Astrological Sign: Gemini

Nicknames: Jack the Zipper, Man of the 60s, Man of the New Frontier, Suicide Senator.

Presidential Notes: First president to name a relative to a cabinet post (Brother Robert F. Kennedy to attorney general).

In November 1961, JFK granted an exclusive interview, the first for a U.S. president, to Aleksei Adzhubei, the editor of *Izvestia.* Adzhubei's father-in-law was Soviet premier Nikita Khrushchev.

Friends and advisers were called the "Irish Mafia."

JFK called Barbara Tuchman's *The Guns of August* his presidential handbook.

The theme of the Kennedy presidency was "The New Frontier".

"Oh God, thy sea is so great and my boat so small" was the inscription on a plaque which rested on JFK's Oval Office desk. The saying, a Breton fisherman's prayer, was presented to him by Vice Admiral Hiram Rickover.

The Kennedy family donated "Morning on the Seine," a Claude Monet waterscape in lavender, blue, and green, to the White House. The Kennedys led off the dancing at their first White House ball to the tune of "Mr. Wonderful."

First boy scout to become president.

The last phone call JFK made was to Ruth Carter Johnson to thank her for the art works placed in his Fort Worth hotel suite.

Family Notes: Charles Bartlett, news columnist for the Chattanooga *News,* is credited with introducing Congressman JFK to "Inquiring Camera Girl" (for the Washington *Times Herald*) Jacqueline Bouvier at a dinner at his home during June 1951. JFK always said he "reached across the asparagus and asked her for a date." Both Bartlett and his wife served in the wedding party when they were married.

JFK called daughter Caroline "Buttons," and she called him "Silly Daddy." Son John F. Kennedy, Jr. (John-John) called his father "Foo Foo Head." Jacqueline called him "Bunny."

Campaign Notes: 1946 congressional campaign theme was "The New Generation Offers a Leader."

Newly elected Senator JFK fulfilled one of his 1958 campaign promises by singing "Heart of My Heart," a popular barbershop quartet song, to his supporters. On the last night of the campaign, patrons at the G&G Deli in Dorchester, Massachusetts, were treated to the sight and sounds of Jack, Bobby, and Teddy Kennedy singing the song on top of a table.

The theme on JFK's 1960 presidential primary posters was "A Time for Greatness."

The theme song of the 1960 campaign was "High Hopes," written by Sammy Cahn and Jimmy Van Heusen.

Caroline was the name of the Kennedy family two-engine Convair airplane used during the 1960 campaign. The $385,000 plane was owned by one of the family businesses and leased to JFK for $1.75 per mile.

During the 1960 campaign, Jackie wrote "Campaign Wife," a weekly column, which was distributed by the Democratic National Committee.

Namesakes: Mount Kennedy, a previously unnamed 14,000-foot mountain in the Yukon. Robert F. Kennedy climbed the mount, one of the highest in North America, and placed at the summit three PT-109 tie clasps and a copy of JFK's inaugural address. The climb was especially notable because Bobby was afraid of heights.

Kennedy International Airport, formerly Idlewild, in New York, N.Y.

Avenue du President Kennedy, in Paris, France, was formerly the Quai de Passy.

Stamp: Kennedy Birthday Issue: A 13-cent stamp in honor of JFK's 50th birthday, May 29, 1966.

Homes: 3307 N Street NW, Washington, D.C. The three-story Georgetown townhouse the Kennedys bought in late 1957 after Caroline's birth.

Hickory Hill, 4700 Chain Bridge Road, McLean, Virginia. The home of the newlywed senator and his wife. They later sold the home to Robert and Ethel Kennedy. Ethel and her children still live there. The home had been the property of the late Supreme Court Justice Robert Jackson and during the Civil War was used by Gen. George B. McClellan as one of his campaign headquarters.

Florida Little White House, 601 North Country Road, Palm Beach, Florida. Purchased by JFK's father in 1933, it was also used as a retreat during the presidency.

Other Positions: As a war correspondent for International News Service (INS), JFK covered Truman's trip to Potsdam and the founding of the United Nations.

Pets: Bluebell and Marybelle, hamsters at the White House belonging to Caroline and John-John.

Clipper, a German shepherd given to Jackie by Joseph P. Kennedy, Sr., on Thanksgiving Day 1961. When press-shy Jackie was asked what the pup would be fed, she replied, "Reporters."

Pushinka, a dog given to the Kennedys by Nikita Khrushchev. The dog was a pup of Strelka, the first Soviet dog in space. It was examined for electronic bugs.

Shannon, Irish cocker spaniel given to JFK by Irish Prime Minister Eamon de Valera.

Love Affairs: JFK supposedly had a brief affair with Inga Arvad, a European beauty contest winner whom he called Inga-Binga. He was removed from Naval intelligence duty and reassigned to PT boats when it was discovered she had Nazi connections.

Judith Campbell Exner claims she had an affair with JFK while he was in the White House. Judith was introduced to JFK by Frank Sinatra (another beau) at the Sands Hotel in Las Vegas on February 7, 1960. Exner was also associated with Mafia chieftain Sam Giancana. The latest evidence supports her claim of a relationship with JFK.

Syndicated columnist Earl Wilson first reported an affair between JFK and Marilyn Monroe in the spring of 1964. The affair supposedly lasted from the summer of 1961 until her death in August 1962.

Health: JFK suffered from Addison's disease, caused by deficient secretion of the adrenal glands. He frequently received treatments of cortisone injections from Dr. Janet Travell, the first female White House physician.

Hat Size: 7¾ (brother Bobby had the same hat size)

Favorite Foods: Fettucini, fish chowder, noodles and butter, tomato soup (especially when laced with whipped cream).

Favorite Songs: "Bill Bailey Won't You Please Come Home," "Blue Skies."

Favorite Poems: "I Have a Rendezvous with Death" by Alan Seeger; "John Brown's Body" by Stephen Vincent Benét.

Favorite Color: Blue

Favorite Drink: Daiquiri. Both JFK and Jackie liked to drink them while lounging at the White House pool. Jackie had the recipe taped to the wall in the kitchen in order for the staff to make them right.

Favorite After Dinner Drink: Brandy stinger

Favorite Scotch: Ballantine

Favorite Beer: Heineken

Favorite Musical: *Camelot*

Favorite Dessert: Anything as long as it was chocolate.

Favorite Writer: Ian Fleming, author of the James Bond thrillers.

Favorite Christmas Carol: "Silver Bells"

Favorite Books: *The Making of a Statesman,* by Sir Robert Walpole; *Seven Pillars of Wisdom,* by T.E. Lawrence; *Pilgrim's Way,* by John Buchan (Lord Tweedsmuir).

Coincidences: Senator William J. Fulbright told JFK: "Dallas is a very dangerous place. I wouldn't go there—don't you go."

Three hours before the assassination, JFK said: "If anybody really wanted to shoot the president of the United States, it is not a very difficult job—all one has to do is get on a high building some day with a telescopic rifle and there is nothing anyone can do to defend against such an attempt."

Liberace, the pianist known for his flashy tuxedos and candelabras, claimed the death of JFK saved his life. He was napping in a Pittsburgh nightclub dressing room when someone woke him up to tell him that JFK had been killed. He was disturbed at the news and could not go back to sleep. Later in the day, Liberace was taken ill and rushed to the hospital where it was discovered that he had been poisoned by toxic fumes from a solution used to clean a recently returned costume. Had he slept longer, he could have died from overexposure to the fumes.

Awards & Citations: Selected as one of "The Ten Outstanding Men of 1946" by *Future* magazine. Also named that year were Arthur Schlesinger and Joe Louis.

Outstanding Young Man, presented to JFK in 1947 when he was a congressman by the Junior Chamber of Commerce.

Washington's Gay Young Bachelor, 1951.

Memberships: Knights of Columbus, fourth degree.

Muckers, a club founded by JFK, Lem Billings (his lifelong friend), and several others at Choate with the objective of bucking the system. Their antics almost led to their explusion.

Spee Club, the posh Harvard social club that 25 years earlier had refused membership to his father because he was Irish.

Boats: *Honey Fitz,* named after his maternal grandfather, was the name of the presidential yacht during the JFK presidency.

Patrick J, a 45-foot cabin cruiser, less well known than the *Honey Fitz.* It was also known as a cocktail boat.

Marlin, a 52-foot cabin crusier.

Victura, a 24-foot sloop. Ted Kennedy sailed it in a race and finished ninth on the day of the Chappaquiddick accident.

College Thesis: "Appeasement at Munich: The Inevitable Result of the Slowness of the British Democracy to Change from a Disarmament Policy." It won a rating of magna cum laude from Harvard and qualified him to graduate with honors in political science. It was later published as *Why England Slept.*

Sports Feats: In 1937, JFK captained *Flash II* to win the Nantucket Sound Championship Sailing Race.

JFK, along with his brother Joe, Jr., was on the 1939 Harvard team that won the MacMillan Cup, an intercollegiate sailing championship trophy.

Last Words: "My God, I've been hit." However, there is a controversy over whether or not he would have been able to speak after the first shot.

"Stroke." In a 1962 cartoon, Bill Crawford lampoons
Kennedy's relationship with Congress (NEA Service).

LYNDON BAINES JOHNSON
Thirty-sixth president

1963-69

The Straight Facts

Born: August 27, 1908
Birthplace: Stonewall, Texas
Ancestry: English
Physical Characteristics: 6′3″, brown eyes, black hair
Religion: Disciples of Christ
Occupation: Schoolteacher, politician
Wife: Claudia Alta "Lady Bird" Taylor Johnson (1912-)
Date of Marriage: November 17, 1934
Children: Two daughters
College: Southwest Texas State College, class of 1930
Military History: Commander, U.S. Navy
Political Party: Democrat
Previous Political Offices: Texas director, National Youth Administration

(1935-37); Member, U.S. House of Representatives (1937-48); Member, U.S. Senate (1948-61); Senate Democratic whip (1951-53); Senate majority leader (1953-61); Vice-president of the United States (1961-63)

Vice-President: None, first term; Hubert Horatio Humphrey (1911-78), second term

Died: January 22, 1973, in Texas

Burial Place: LBJ Ranch, Johnson City, Texas

Firsts: First president to have oath administered by a woman

First president to take the oath in an airplane

First president to take the oath with his wife holding the Bible

First president to be present at his predecessor's assassination

Biography in Brief: Lyndon B. Johnson was the son of Sam Ealy Johnson and Rebekah Baines. He received a B.S. degree at Southwest Texas State Teachers College, 1930; attended Georgetown University Law School, Washington, 1935. He taught public speaking in Houston, 1930-32; served as secretary to Rep. R. M. Kleberg, 1932-35. In 1937 Johnson won a contest to fill the vacancy caused by the death of a representative and in 1938 was elected to the full term, after which he returned for four more terms. He was elected U.S. senator in 1948 and reelected in 1954. He became Democratic leader, 1953. Johnson was Texas' favorite son for the Democratic presidential nomination in 1956 and had strong support in the 1960 convention, where the nominee, John F. Kennedy, asked him to run for vice president. His campaigning helped overcome religious bias against Kennedy in the South.

Johnson became president on the death of Kennedy. Johnson worked hard for welfare legislation, signed civil rights, antipoverty, and tax reduction laws, and averted strikes on railroads. He was elected to a full term in 1964. The war in Vietnam overshadowed other developments during his administration.

In face of increasing division in the nation and his own party over his handling of the war, Johnson announced that he would not seek another term, March 31, 1968.

Retiring to his ranch near Johnson City, Texas, Johnson wrote his memoirs and oversaw the construction of the Lyndon Baines Johnson Library.

The More Colorful Facts

Astrological Sign: Virgo

Nicknames: Booming Voice*, Dynamic Texan, Great Guided Missile†, Keeper of the Bird House, King Lyndon the First, Light bulb Lyndon, Lochnivar of the Pedernales‡, Riverboat Gambler§, Uncle Cornpone.

*So-called by the White House Staff
†So-called as vice-president by Kennedy aides. He called them the Georgetown Jelly Beans.
‡So-called by the male members of the White House press corps.
§Kennedy often used this nickname for LBJ.

Original Family name: Johnston. The family tree can be traced back to 1662.

First Name: Three months elapsed between the birth of LBJ to his ultimate naming. After three months of no decision from her husband, Sam Ealy Johnson, as to what the name of their first born would be, Rebekah Baines Johnson told her husband that there would be no cooking or cleaning until the child had a name. He suggested Clarence, Dayton, or Linden (after his friend, W.C. Linden) and she choose the latter but changed the spelling to Lyndon.

Presidential Notes: "Now, let's get airborne," was LBJ's first presidential order after being sworn in by Federal Judge Sarah T. Hughes.

Friends and advisors were called the "Texas Mafia."

LBJ's impromptu press conferences were called "Walkie-Talkies" because the press was allowed to keep up with him while he walked the White House grounds.

In 1964, LBJ received 61 percent of the popular vote, the most of any president.

"Come now, let us reason together," quoted from the prophet Isaiah, was a catch phrase of the LBJ administration.

"The Great Society" was the theme of the Johnson presidency.

Peter Hurd painted the official portrait of LBJ. LBJ did not care for

"Would you call 'Be My Valentine—Ho Chi Minh,' a 'sincere' peace feeler?" LBJ by Jim Berry (NEA Service).

any likeness of himself, and claimed this was the ugliest he had ever seen. Hurd began his career as a WPA artist.

LBJ sometimes called the White House "Lonely Acres."

The Lyndon Johnson Birthplace in Stonewall, Texas was declared a national historical park in 1969, the only presidential home so declared.

The first commercial telephone call via satellite was placed by LBJ to British Prime Minister Harold Wilson in June 1965.

On August 3, 1966, LBJ attended a pre-season game between the Washington Redskins and the Baltimore Colts, becoming the first president to attend a pro football game while in office.

Pets: Edgar, a beagle, gift from FBI director J. Edgar Hoover after Him (beagle) was killed.

Him and Her were pet beagles born on June 27, 1964. Him's paw prints are implanted on the cement walkway which leads to the White House press room.

Family Notes: First Lady Claudia Alta Taylor Johnson's nickname "Lady Bird" was given to her by the family maid, Alice Tittle.

Luci Johnson married Patrick John Nugent on August 6, 1966, at the National Shrine of the Immaculate Conception in Washington, D.C. The reception was held at the White House. It was the first marriage of a presidential daughter in a church. The marriage was dissolved by divorce in 1979.

Luci Johnson used the alias Amy Nunn to attend Marquette University's Senior Prom in 1965. She wore a silver wig designed by Jean Louis for the occasion and spent the entire evening unrecognized.

Lady Bird attended her first White House dinner in 1941 at the invitation of the Roosevelts. Lady Bird wrote in her diary that she believed the night would be her first and only trip to the White House.

Lady Bird placed a sign that read "Please don't ask the president to have seconds" over the White House stove.

Lynda Bird Johnson married Charles Spitall Robb, a former U.S.M.C. officer, in the White House on December 9, 1967. In 1980, he was elected Democratic governor of Virginia. His grandfather, Robert W. Wolley, served in the Woodrow Wilson administration.

White House staff called First Lady Lady Bird Johnson the "Gentle Hand." Daughter Luci was called "Luci Watusi" after her energetic dancing style.

Campaign Notes: "All the Way with LBJ" was the Democratic presidential campaign slogan in 1964 coined by Dr. Herman Silvers. It also served as the theme song of the campaign with lyrics by Eli L. Schaff and music by Bee Walker. Laura Lane sang it at the Atlantic City convention.

"Lady Bird Special" was the nickname given to the train used by Lady Bird Johnson during her solo whistlestop campaign in the South during the 1964 presidential campaign. The 16-car train left Alexandria, Virginia, on October 16, 1964.

Homes: The Elms, LBJ's Norman mansion located in the Spring Valley section of Washington, D.C. Previously, the home had been owned by Perle Mesta. LBJ changed the name from the French, "Les Ormes."

Heywood, LBJ's other ranch. He purchased the 4,718-acre ranch from Texas Christian University in 1961 for $500,000.

L.B.J. Ranch, 400-acre ranch located on the Pedernales River, outside Johnson City, Texas, purchased from an aunt in 1951.

Namesakes: Lake Lyndon B. Johnson, originally named The Llano River, manmade waters in Texas.

Stamp: Lyndon Johnson issue, an eight-cent stamp, in commemoration of LBJ's death, 1973.

High School Years: At age 15 LBJ became the youngest graduating senior at Johnson City High School. The class motto was "Give the world the best you have and the best will come back to you." LBJ served as president of the debate team and also class president because no one else in the class of six wanted the job.

College Years: Percy Brigham, a bank officer, approved a $75 student loan for LBJ to attend Southwest Texas State Teachers College, even though he was under age. When Brigham died, LBJ, then president, flew to Texas for his funeral.

Other Positions: Editor-in-chief (and other jobs), *College Star*, the Southwest Texas State Teachers College newspaper.

Owner, Johnson Shoe Shine Shop. The first business enterprise of young LBJ. He took out ads in the local paper advertising his trade which was practiced in Cecil Maddox's barbershop. His father stopped the operation within a few weeks as he felt that, at age nine, LBJ was too young.

State director, National Youth Administration, 1935. At the age of 27, he was the youngest state director in this New Deal agency.

English teacher, Sam Houston High School, 1930-31.

Teacher and principal, Welhausen School, a Mexican-American school in Cotulla, Texas.

Courtship: LBJ had his first date with Claudia "Lady Bird" Taylor at the Hotel Driskill in Austin, Texas. He asked her for a breakfast date and she didn't give him an answer. He showed up anyway and Lady Bird "just happened" to go by on the appointed day.

St. Mark's Episcopal Church was the site of the November 17, 1934, nuptials of LBJ and Claudia Alta Taylor. In postwedding confusion, they forgot to pick up the marriage certificate. Twenty years later, when an old file was found, the Johnsons finally received the certificate.

Shirt size: 17½, 34″ sleeve

Favorite Foods: Rum pie; canned green peas which he loved juice and all; tapioca.

Favorite Cocktail: Cutty Sark and soda

Favorite Beverage: Fresca

Favorite Actress/Singer: Carol Channing. She thrilled LBJ by singing "Hello, Lyndon" at a White House party.

Favorite Christmas Carol: "Silent Night"

Favorite Game: Dominoes

Favorite Song: "The Yellow Rose of Texas"

Favorite Color: Yellow

Awards: Silver Star, for coolness under fire as a lieutenant commander during World War II.

Secret Service Codes: Volunteer for LBJ; Victoria for Lady Bird; Velvet for Lynda Bird; Venus for Luci; Volcano for The LBJ Ranch.

Coincidences: "Wabash Cannonball" was the nickname given to a Navy transport Martin B-26 Marauder aircraft that Commander LBJ was assigned to fly on during World War II. For some reason, LBJ left his seat and when he returned it was taken. Johnson was them reassigned to fly another transport, the "Heckling Hare." Johnson claimed he never knew what made him leave his seat but was glad he did; the "Wabash Cannonball" crashed with no survivors.

Books: *The Vantage Point,* 1970

RICHARD MILHOUS NIXON

Thirty-seventh president

1969-74

The Straight Facts

Born: January 9, 1913
Birthplace: Yorba Linda, California
Ancestry: English, Scots-Irish
Physical Characteristics: 5'11½" tall, brown eyes, brown hair
Religion: Quaker
Occupation: Lawyer
Wife: Thelma Catherine "Pat" Ryan Nixon (1912-)
Date of Marriage: June 21, 1940

Children: Two daughters

College: Whittier College, class of 1934

Military History: Lieutenant, U.S. Navy

Political Party: Republican

Previous Political Offices: Member, U.S. House of Representatives (1947-51); Member, U.S. Senate (1951-53); Vice-president of the United States (1953-61)

Vice-President: Spiro Theodore Agnew (1918-), first term; Gerald Rudolph Ford, second term

Firsts: First president born in California

First president to visit China

First president to appoint a vice-president under the 25th Amendment to the Constitution

First president to resign from office

Biography in Brief: Richard M. Nixon is the son of Francis Anthony Nixon and Hannah Milhous. Nixon was graduated from Whittier College, 1934; Duke University Law School, 1937. After practicing law in Whittier and serving briefly in the Office of Price Administration in 1942, he entered the navy, and served in the South Pacific.

Nixon was elected to the House of Representatives in 1946 and 1948. In 1950 he was elected to the Senate.

He was elected vice-president in the Eisenhower landslides of 1952 and 1956. With Eisenhower's endorsement, Nixon won the Republican nomination in 1960. He was defeated by Democrat John F. Kennedy, returned to California, and was defeated in his race for governor in 1962.

In 1968, he won the presidential nomination and went on to defeat Democrat Hubert H. Humphrey.

Nixon was the first U.S. president to visit China and Russia (1972). He and his foreign affairs advisor, Henry A. Kissinger, achieved a detente with China.

Reelected 1972, Nixon secured a cease-fire agreement in Vietnam and completed the withdrawal of U.S. troops.

Nixon's second term was cut short by a series of scandals beginning with the burglary of Democratic party national headquarters in the Watergate office complex on June 17, 1972. Nixon denied any White House involvement in the Watergate break-in.

On July 24, 1974, the Supreme Court ruled that Nixon's claim of executive privilege must fall before the special prosecutor's subpoenas of tapes relevant to criminal trial proceedings. That same day, the House Judiciary committee opened debate on impeachment. On July 30, the committee recommended House adoption of three articles of impeachment charging Nixon with obstruction of justice, abuse of power, and contempt of Congress.

On Aug. 5, Nixon released transcripts of conversations held six days after the Watergate break-in showing that Nixon had known of, approved, and directed Watergate cover-up activities. Nixon resigned from office Aug. 9.

"...and then there was one ...." During the Watergate crisis, John Lane gives his view of Nixon's situation (NEA Service).

The More Colorful Facts

Astrological Sign: Capricorn

Nicknames: Gloomy Gus*, Iron Butt, Iron Pants, Richard the Chicken-Hearted†, Tricky Dicky.

Origin of Family Name: In Gaelic, Nixon is a derivation of the words "he faileth not."

Toujours Pret is the motto on the Nixon family coat of arms. It means

*School nickname.
†Because he would not debate Hubert Humphrey in the 1968 campaign.

"Always Ready." Also on the coat of arms is a gamecock and shield with five coins from the Byzantine era symbolizing one who is trustworthy.

Presidential Notes: "Forward Together" was the theme of the 1969 inaugural.

"Gemstone" was the cover designation for the Watergate break-in.

RMN was the first president to visit Moscow, May 22, 1972.

One of RMN's first acts was to rename the presidential yachts *Patricia* and *Julie* after his daughters.

It was a Sony 800B tape recorder that was installed to record all of RMN's conversations in the Oval Office.

"Spirit of '76" was the nickname of Air Force One during Nixon's presidency.

Family Notes: Daughters Julie and Tricia were in the audience when the Beatles made their American debut live on "The Ed Sullivan Show" in November 1964.

RMN's mother, Hannah, called her son the "best potato masher a mother could wish for."

First Lady Pat Nixon had bit parts in the films *Ben Hur, Becky Sharp, The Great Ziegfeld,* and *Small Town Girl.*

Nicknames of Pat Nixon include Antiseptic Pat, Pat The Plu-Perfect, Pat the Robot, and Plastic Pat.

Campaign Notes: On election day November 8, 1960, RMN drove himself 150 miles to Tijuana, Mexico, to have lunch with Mayor Xicotencatl Leyva Aleman. They dined on enchiladas, tacos, and German beer.

CREEP was the acronym given to the committee to reelect the president; also known as CRP.

"Dick and Pat Nixon 1960 Campaign Victory Train" was the nickname given to the train the Nixons used during the whistle-stop tour in the 1960 campaign.

"Nixon is the Man for Me" was a song written by J. Maloy Roach for the 1960 Republican campaign.

"Nixon's The One" was a slogan used in 1968 presidential campaign.

"Nixon: Now More Than Ever" was a Republican campaign theme in 1972.

"Richard Nixon is The One" was a song written for RMN in 1972 by Raymond Maurer and Ray Maurer, Jr.

Homes: La Casa Pacifica, San Clemente, California

810 Fifth Avenue, New York, New York. Address of the Nixon apartment in New York City, first rented on June 1, 1963. The apartment overlooks Central Park at 62nd Street and was purchased for $135,000.

Famous Ancestors: General "Mad" Anthony Wayne, through his paternal grandmother.

Famous Relatives: Jessamyn West, a noted American novelist, was a cousin. She also went to Whittier College and when RMN was young, she used to babysit for him. The lead character in her novel *Friendly Persuasion* was modeled after Joshua Vickers Milhous, maternal great grandfather of the president. The novel was later made into a movie starring Gary Cooper, Dorothy McGuire, and Anthony Perkins.

College Days: As a freshman debater, RMN argued the topic "All Nations Should Adopt a Policy of Free Trade" in a debate with the University of Southern California and won his portion, giving Whittier an upset victory.

At Whittier, RMN appeared in the following plays: *The Trysting Place, Bird in Hand, Price of Coal,* and *The Tavern.* He also served as a stage manager for *The Mikado* and *The Pirates of Penzance.*

RMN and Dean Triggs started the Orthogonian Society at Whittier College because the college only had one society at the time—The Franklin Society. Members were called Square Shooters and they were dedicated to the four B's—beans, brawn, brains, and bowls. The motto of the society was *Ecrasons L'infame* (stamp out evil), with its symbol being a boar's head. RMN was the first president of the society.

RMN was graduated third out of 25 in the first graduating class at Duke University Law School, the class of 1937. RMN had won a $200 tuition grant scholarship to attend. In his senior year, RMN was elected president of the Duke Bar Association.

Other positions: Barker at the Wheel of Chance, Slippery Gulch Rodeo, Prescott, Arizona, summers of 1929 and 1930.

Town attorney, La Habra, California, 1938.

Assistant city attorney, Whittier, California, 1938- . City records still show him on the books in this position because he never resigned when he was elected to the U.S. Congress in 1946.

President (first and last), Citra-Frost company, 1940-41.

RMN once applied and was accepted as a trainee for the FBI. The job was never offered, however, as federal funds were withdrawn.

Military Career: In 1944, naval lieutenant RMN operated Nixon's Snack Shack, the only hamburger stand in the South Pacific.

First Political Race: RMN ran against Jerry H. Voorhis, the incumbent Democratic congressman in California's 12th District, in 1946, and won by 16,000 votes. He had become the Republican challenger by answering an ad placed in 26 newspapers by the Committee of One Hundred, a GOP group. They selected RMN after an interview and contributed $300 to his campaign.

Memberships: Chowder and Marching Club. An organization of 15 newly elected Republican congressmen, founded by RMN in 1947. They would meet every Wednesday for lunch to discuss strategy, bills, reports, and amendments. One of the members was Michigan's Gerald R. Ford. Others were Kenneth Keating (New York), Norris Cotton (New Hampshire), Glen Davis and John Byrnes of Wisconsin, Donald Jackson and John J. Allen of California, John Lodge (Connecticut), Thurston B. Morton (Kentucky), Harold Lovre (South Dakota), Walter Norldad (Oregon), J. Caleb Boggs (Delaware), Charles Potter (Michigan), Claude Blackwell (Missouri), and Charles Nelson of Maine.

Columbia Country Club, Bethesda, Maryland, a golf club.

Estrella Country Club, San Clemente, California, golf club.

Iredell Law Club, law society at Duke.

Kiwanis, in La Habra, California, as a young lawyer.

Order of the Coif, Duke Law School honor society, reserved for those in top 10 percent of their law school class, 1936.

Famous Speeches: Checkers, the pet cocker spaniel of the Nixon family, was the subject of a famous speech. During the 1952 presidential campaign, it was discovered that RMN had a secret $18,000 personal fund stashed away under an assumed name. *The New York Post* on September 18, 1952, headlined a story by Leo Katcher, "Secret Rich Man's Trust Fund Keeps Nixon in Style Far Beyond His Salary." RMN was asked to resign from the ticket but chose to stay and defend himself against any charges of wrong-doing. On September 23, 1952, at NBC's El Capitan Studios in Los Angeles, he made public a list of all gifts received, including Checkers, and said "We're going to keep him!" Checkers died in 1964 and is now buried in the Bide-A-Wee Pet Cemetery on Long Island, New York.

Awards: Harvard Club of California Prize, as a senior at Whittier High School for foremost all-around scholar.

Southern California Intercollegiate Extemporaneous Speaking Champion, 1934.

Former president RMN was nominated for a Grammy award in the Best Spoken Word category for the album version of his television interview with David Frost.

Shoe Size: 11D

Shirt Size: 16

Allergies: Wool

Favorite Film: *Patton,* starring George C. Scott

Favorite Song: "Home on the Range." He often played it on the White House piano.

Favorite Fowl: Quail, especially when served with white wine and Madeira sauce.

Favorite Lunchtime Drink: Pineapple malt (as a young lawyer).

Favorite Cigar: Don Diego

Favorite Ice Cream: Macadamia nut

Favorite Drink: Dry martini

Favorite TV Series: "Kojak"

Favorite Baseball Player: Roy E. Sievers, who played for the St. Louis Browns, Washington Senators, Chicago White Sox, and the Philadelphia Phillies. He hit .267 in 1887 career games and was named Rookie of the Year in 1949.

Secret Service Codes: Searchlight for RMN; Starlight for Patricia R. Nixon; Storm King for Nixon home in San Clemente; Strawberry for Nixon secretary Rosemary Woods

Famous Quotes: "Gentlemen, this is my last news conference . . . . You'll not have Dick Nixon to kick around anymore" on November 6, 1962, after losing race for the California governorship to Edmund (Pat) Brown.

Books: *RN*, Nixon's memoirs

Six Crises, 1962, an autobiographical account of his career until then. The crises were: 1) The Alger Hiss Case, 2) The Fund Campaign, 3) The Heart Attack (Eisenhower's), 4) Caracas Trip, 5) Khrushchev (the Kitchen Debate) and 6) the Campaign of 1960. Except for the last crisis, the book was ghost written by Alvin Moscow.

GERALD RUDOLPH FORD, JR.

Thirty-eighth president

1974-77

The Straight Facts

Born: July 14, 1913
Birthplace: Omaha, Nebraska
Ancestry: English
Religion: Episcopalian
Physical Characteristics: 6' tall, blue eyes, blond hair
Occupation: Lawyer, politician
Wife: Elizabeth "Betty" Bloomer Warren Ford (1918-)
Date of Marriage: October 15, 1948
Children: One daughter, three sons
College: University of Michigan, class of 1935
Military History: Lieutenant commander, U.S. Navy
Political Party: Republican

Previous Political Offices: Member, U.S. House of Representatives (1949-73); House minority leader (1965-73); Vice-president of the United States (1973-74)

Vice-President: Nelson Aldrich Rockefeller (1908-79)

Firsts: First to be appointed vice-president under the 25th Amendment of the-Constitution

First president to succeed on the resignation of his predecessor

First to become president without being elected by the people

First president born in Nebraska

Biography in Brief: Gerald R. Ford is the son of Leslie King and Dorothy Gardner, and was named Leslie, Jr. When he was two, his parents were divorced and his mother moved with the boy to Grand Rapids, Michigan. There she met and married Gerald R. Ford, who formally adopted the boy and gave him his own name.

He was graduated from the University of Michigan, 1935, and Yale Law School, 1941.

He began practicing law in Grand Rapids, but in 1942 joined the navy and served in the Pacific, leaving the service in 1946 as a lieutenant commander.

He entered congress in 1948 and spent 25 years in the House, eight of them as Republican leader.

On October 12, 1973, after Vice-president Spiro T. Agnew resigned, Ford was nominated by President Nixon to replace him. It was the first use of the procedures set out in the 25th Amendment.

When Nixon resigned on August 9, 1974, Ford became president, the first to serve without being chosen in a national election. On September 8, he pardoned Nixon for any federal crimes he might have committed as president. Ford vetoed 48 bills in his first 21 months in office, saying most would prove too costly. He visited China. In 1976, he was defeated in the election by Democrat Jimmy Carter.

The More Colorful Facts

Astrological Sign: Cancer

Nicknames: Gentle Tiger*, Jinx of The Links**, Mr. Nice Guy.

Presidential Notes: GRF, born Leslie Lynch King, Jr., has been the only president to have been adopted. When his mother remarried in 1918, her new husband, Gerald Rudolf Ford, adopted her son and gave the boy his name; GRF changed the spelling his middle name to Rudolph. He did not know he was adopted until in high school.

*So-called by congressional colleagues.

†Self-imposed because he claimed that every professional golfer he played with never won the tournament.

"You mean they're all security guards?" John Lane takes a look at Ford during the 1976 presidential campaign which he lost (NEA Service).

GRF appointed Anne Armstrong as the first woman to serve as U.S. Ambassador to the Court of St. James's.

GRF was the first president to appear on the long-running NBC Sunday afternoon show, "Meet The Press."

Family Notes: It is reported that GRF wore one black and one brown shoe to his wedding to Elizabeth Bloomer on October 15, 1948.

"First Mama" is First Lady Betty Ford's CB handle.

First Lady Betty Ford appeared on "The Mary Tyler Moore Show" in 1976. Mrs. Ford, portraying herself, called Mary's boss, Lou Grant (Ed Asner), inquiring if the president had left his pipe at Lou's apartment after a party. Lou let Mary, who didn't believe it really was the First Lady, talk to her: "Hello Mary, this is Betty, Betty Ford" to which Mary replied "Hello Betty, this is Mary, Queen of Scots."

Son Steven stars as Andy Richards in the CBS television soap opera, "The Young and The Restless."

Campaign Notes: "Bozo and the Pineapple" was the uncomplimentary nickname given to the Gerald Ford/Robert Dole ticket in the 1976 presidential campaign.

1976 presidential campaign performance was marred by Ford's statement during the presidential debates that "Poland is not under Soviet domination."

Homes: Rancho Mirage, near Palm Springs, California. This retirement home is built near the 13th green of the Thunderbird golf course.

Fraternity: Delta Kappa Epsilon at University of Michigan; Phi Delta Phi, legal fraternity at Yale Law School.

Sports Career: GRF was a member of the University of Michigan football team (1931-34), and was selected most valuable player in 1934. An outstanding high school athlete, GRF was also wooed by Michigan State and Northwestern, but credited the recruitment efforts of coach Harry Kipke as the key to his selection of Michigan. His football jersey number at the University of Michigan was 48.

As a University of Michigan graduate GRF played in the summer 1935 college football All-Star game against the Chicago Bears. The All-Stars beat the Bears 5-0 and GRF was paid $100 for the win.

GRF played center on the East team in the East-West Shrine Game on January 1, 1935. The East lost 19-13 and GRF played 58 minutes of the 60-minute game.

Former President GRF shot a hole-in-one on the 177-yard 5th hole at the Memphis Classic on June 8, 1977. The tournament is held each year at the Colonial Country Club by entertainer Danny Thomas to help raise money for St. Jude's Children's Hospital.

Both the Detroit Lions and The Green Bay Packers offered GRF a tryout.

As president, GRF hit a golf ball that hit and injured spectator Gene Bartelt at the North Hills Country Club in Milwaukee, Wisconsin.

Military Career: GRF served during WWII, from June 1943 through December 1944, on the U.S.S. *Monterey,* a light aircraft carrier. GRF narrowly escaped death on December 18, 1944, when the *Monterey* was caught in the Great Pacific Typhoon; over 800 servicemen were lost in the storm.

Other Positions: GRF modeled for covers of *Cosmopolitan* and *Look* magazines, both in the late 1930s.

Forest ranger, Yellowstone National Park, summer of 1936. Michigan Senator Arthur H. Vandenberg help GRF get the position. He directed traffic and fed bears.

Awards: Most Popular High School Senior, 1934, in a contest sponsored by the Majestic Theatre.

Meyer Morton Trophy, 1931, a silver football presented to the outstanding freshman football player during spring practice at the University of Michigan.

Selected as one of 25 former football players to *Sports Illustrated's* 25th anniversary All-American Award team.

Father of the Year, May 1974, by the National Father's Day Committee.

Francis Boyer Award, 1977, awarded by American Enterprise Institute to an eminent thinker who has developed notable insights on the relationship between the nation's public and private sectors.

Left-hander of the Year Award, 1977 and 1979.

Clubs: Burning Tree, the prestigious golf club joined by Congressman GRF in

1956. It is also known as the "Club of the Presidents." Other members are Richard Nixon and George Bush.

Favorite Fruit: Strawberries

Favorite Ice Cream: Butter pecan

Favorite Song: "Oklahoma"

Favorite Prayer: Proverbs 3:5-6: "Trust in the Lord with all thine heart and lean not unto thine own understanding. In all thy ways acknowledge Him and He shall direct thy paths." GRF always says this in a time of crisis.

Quips About and By: "He played too much football with his helmet off," Lyndon Johnson once said about Congressman GRF. In 1968, at the annual Gridiron Dinner, GRF put on his old Michigan football helmet and found that it no longer fit. He told the audience that "heads tend to swell in Washington."

Secret Service Codes: Passkey for GRF; Pinafore for Betty Ford

Assassination Attempts: On September 5, 1975, in Sacramento, California, Lynnette "Squeaky" Fromme, a follower of Charles Manson, attempted to assassinate GRF. Dressed in a long red gown, she aimed a .45 caliber semiautomatic pistol at the president. Fromme was sentenced to life imprisonment on December 17, 1975. During the trial, she hit U.S. attorney Dwayne Keyes in the head with an apple. Fromme is now at the Federal Women's Correctional Institution at Alderson, West Virginia.

Sara Jane Moore, a one-time FBI informant, attempted to assassinate GRF on September 22, 1975, at the St. Francis Hotel in San Francisco. She used a .38 caliber pistol. Upon arrest, the police found 13 bullets in her purse and another 100 bullets in her car. A few days before the attempt, the police had taken a .45 caliber gun away from her; Miss Moore claimed that if she had had her .45, she would have gotten GRF. In 1976, she was sentenced to life imprisonment and now is in the Federal Correctional Institute in Pleasanton, California.

Only 17 days passed between the two assassination attempts which were made only 80 miles apart in California.

Books: *A Time to Heal,* 1979, an autobiography ghost written by Trevor Ambrister of *The Reader's Digest.*

Portrait of an Assassin, 1965, co-authored with Jack Stiles. The book was about Lee Harvey Oswald. GRF had served as a member of the Warren Commission.

JAMES EARL (JIMMY) CARTER, JR.
Thirty-ninth president
1977-81

The Straight Facts

Born: October 1, 1924
Birthplace: Plains, Georgia
Ancestry: English
Physical Characteristics: 5'10" tall, blue eyes, sandy hair, 160 lbs.
Religion: Baptist
Occupation: Peanut farmer
Wife: Eleanor Rosalynn Smith Carter (1928-)
Date of Marriage: July 7, 1946
Children: One daughter, three sons
College: U.S. Naval Academy, class of 1946
Military History: Senior-grade lieutenant, U.S. Navy
Political Party: Democrat
Previous Political Offices: Member, Sumter County Board of Education

(1955-62); Member, Georgia state senate (1963-67); Governor, state of Georgia (1971-75)

Vice President: Walter Frederick Mondale (1928-)

Firsts: First president born in Georgia

First president to be graduated from Annapolis

First president to walk the 1½ mile trek from the Capitol to the White House during his inaugural parade

Biography in Brief: Jimmy (James Earl) Carter was the first president from the Deep South since before the Civil War. His parents, James and Lillian Gordy Carter, had a farm and several businesses at Plains, Georgia.

He attended Georgia Tech, and was graduated from the U.S. Naval Academy. He entered the navy's nuclear submarine program as an aide to Adm. Hyman Rickover, and studied nuclear physics at Union College.

His father died in 1953 and Carter left the navy to take over the family businesses—peanut-raising, warehousing, and cotton-ginning. He was elected to the Georgia state senate, was defeated for governor, 1966, but elected in 1970.

Carter won the Democratic nomination and defeated President Gerald R. Ford in the election of 1976. He played a major role in the peace negotiations between Israel and Egypt. In November 1979, Iranian student militants attacked the U.S. embassy in Teheran and held members of the embassy staff hostage.

Carter was widely criticized for the poor state of the economy and high inflation. He was also viewed as weak in his handling of foreign policy. He reacted to the Soviet invasion of Afghanistan by imposing a grain embargo and boycotting the Moscow Olympic games. His failure to obtain the release of the remaining 52 hostages held in Iran plagued Carter to the end of his term. He was defeated by Ronald Reagan in the 1980 election. Carter finally succeeded in obtaining the release of the hostages on Inauguration Day, as the new president was taking the oath of office.

The More Colorful Facts

Astrological Sign: Libra

Nicknames: Hot/Hot Shot*, Baby Dumpling†, Iron-Ass Jimmy‡.

Presidential Notes: The first movie shown in the Carter White House was *All The President's Men.*

The only soft drink served in the Carter White House was Coca-Cola.

Friends and personal advisers were called the "Georgia Mafia," and included Jody Powell, Hamilton Jordan, Bert Lance, and Charles Kirbo.

*From high school.
†Family nickname as a child from the "Blondie" comic strip.
‡So-called by Walter Mondale, but never to his face.

At the White House Jazz Festival on June 18, 1978, JEC sang "Salt Peanuts" with Dizzy Gillespie.

JEC was the first president to be born in a hospital, the Wise clinic in Plains, Georgia.

One of his final presidential acts was to pardon Peter Yarrow of the folk-singing group Peter, Paul and Mary, from his conviction of child molestation.

First Lady Rosalynn Carter used crackers to check the efficiency of the White House cleaning staff by placing one on a table. If it was gone the next day, she knew they had cleaned.

Family Notes: Billy Beer, named after his brother Billy, was launched in Plains Georgia, on October 31, 1977, with balloons, clowns and prizes. Miz Lillian Carter, JEC's mother, wore a yellow and orange "Billy Beer" t-shirt.

Words inscribed on the can:

I had this beer brewed just for me
I think it is the best I ever tasted and I've tasted a lot
I think you will like it too.

Billy Carter

Today an unopened six-pack sells for over $100.

"Billygate" was the media nickname for the scandal over Billy's acceptance of a Libyan loan.

"I guess I never noticed it." John Lane on Carter and the Bert Lance affair (NEA Service).

"Big Inch Connection" was the media nickname given to a real estate scheme is Plains, Georgia, in which Gloria Carter Spann bought an acre of land in the middle of Plains and sold it square inch by square inch, registering the purchase at the Sumter County Court House.

Billy Carter made over $500,000 in 1977 promoting himself as the "Second Man in the First Family."

First Lady Rosalynn Carter was nicknamed "Steel Magnolia" because she is from the South and is tough.

Campaign Notes: "Leadership for a change" was a 1976 campaign slogan.

During the campaign of 1976, Amy Carter and friends John and Sidney Gnann sold lemonade to reporters for five, and then ten, cents. They expanded to sandwiches (peanut butter, pimento and tuna) and even rented out Frisbees® for 25 cents each quarter of an hour. Unfortunately for Amy, the Secret Service closed the business down because it was getting too popular and was a potential security risk.

"Jimmy Who?" was a slogan used during 1976 Democratic primaries because JEC came from almost nowhere to win. A few weeks after the Carters moved into the White House, Rosalynn picked up the phone and asked the White House operator to connect her with "Jimmy" and the operator replied,"Jimmy who?"

"Grits and Fritz" appeared on campaign bumper stickers for southerner JEC ("Grits") and Walter ("Fritz") Mondale.

Peanut was the name of the campaign plane.

Campaign supporters were called the "Peanut Brigade."

ABC was the acronymn for Anybody But Carter that appeared on campaign buttons in the 1980 campaign.

Boyhood: JEC once presented, as a gift, his mother's diamond engagement ring to Mrs. Eleanor Forrest, his first grade teacher at Plains Elementary School, saying that "My Daddy can always buy Momma another one." Miz Lillian had received the ring from the senior Carter in the mail as she was serving as a nurse at Grady Hospital and away from Plains when she accepted his proposal.

Naval Career: JEC's appointment to Annapolis was arranged by Georgia congressman Stephen Pace in 1942. He entered in 1943 and graduated in 1946 with a ranking of 59th out of 820. JEC's first assignment after graduation from Annapolis was at Pensacola, Florida, flying blimps.

Awards: Plains High School Class of 1941 Salutatorian. He was graduated second out of 23, missing valedictorian because he played hookey one spring day just before graduation.

Plains High School Class of 1941 "Boy Most Likely to Succeed."

Most Outstanding Senator (1963) as Georgia state senator.

Doublespeak Award (1980) from National Council of Teachers of English for outstanding examples of misuse of public language.

Previous Offices: Scout troop master in Plains, Georgia.

President, Georgia chapter of the Certified Seed Organization.

Favorite Food: Mixed nuts as a snack, peach (Georgia, of course) ice cream, licorice candy.

Favorite Beverage: Buttermilk

Favorite Sports: Fly-fishing and tennis

Favorite Book: *Let Us Now Praise Famous Men* by James Agee

Favorite Novel: *War and Peace* by Leo Tolstoy. He claims to have read it first at the age of 12.

Favorite Songwriter: Bob Dylan

Favorite Composer: Sergei Rachmaninov

Favorite Musical Group: The Glenn Miller Orchestra (as a boy)

Favorite Hobby: Woodworking, arrowhead hunting

Favorite Song: "Amazing Grace"

Favorite Sleeping Attire: Jockey shorts

Famous Interview: As the Democratic presidential candidate, JEC admitted to *Playboy's* Robert Scheer that he had "lusted in his heart" over other women.

Curses: Haitian leader Jean Claude Duvalier reportedly had a voodoo curse placed on JEC because he felt he was unfriendly to his reign. The voodoo priests were said to have buried a live bull and pictures of JEC in a pit in a secret midnight ceremony. Duvalier claimed the curse had worked as soon as JEC's popularity declined, the Iranian situation occurred, inflation soared, and he lost the presidency.

Coincidences: The American Airlines pilot who was captain of JEC's 1976 campaign plane was Jimmy (James Kenneth) Carter. No relation. The name of the plane was *Peanut One.*

Secret Service Codes: Deacon (for JEC); Driftwood (for home in Plains, Georgia); Dynamo (for daughter Amy); Dancer (for Rosalynn).

Social Security Number: 259-20-7368

Autobiography: *Why Not the Best?* (1974)

RONALD WILSON REAGAN

Fortieth president
1981-

The Straight Facts

Born: February 6, 1911
Birthplace: Tampico, Illinois
Ancestry: English, Irish
Physical Characteristics: 6'1", blue eyes, brown hair
Religion: Presbyterian
Occupation: Actor
Wife: (1) Sara Jane "Wyman" Fulks Reagan (1914-); (2) Anne Frances
    "Nancy" Davis Reagan, (1921-)
Date of Marriage: (1) January 26, 1940-1948; (2) March 4, 1952
Children: Two daughters, two sons
College: Eureka College, class of 1932
Military History: Captain, U.S. Army Air Corps
Political Party: Republican
Previous Political Offices: Governor, state of California (1967-75)
Vice-President: George Herbert Walker Bush (1924-)

Firsts: First president born in Illinois
First president to have been divorced
First president to have been wounded by, and survive, an assassination attempt
First movie actor to have become president

Biography in Brief: Ronald Wilson Reagan is the son of John Edward Reagan and Nellie Wilson. Reagan was graduated from Eureka (Illinois) College in 1932. Following his graduation, he worked for five years as a sports announcer in Des Moines, Iowa.

Reagan began a successful career as a film actor in 1937, and starred in numerous movies, and later television, until the 1960s. He served as president of the Screen Actors Guild from 1947 to 1952, and in 1959.

He was elected governor of California in 1966, and reelected in 1970.

In 1980, he gained the Republican nomination and won over Jimmy Carter. He was easily reelected in 1984. Reagan, at 73, was the oldest man ever elected president.

Reagan successfully forged a bipartisan coalition in Congress which led to enactment of an economic program which included the largest budget and tax cuts in U.S. history, and a Social Security reform bill designed to insure the long-term solvency of the system. He was shot in an assassination attempt in 1981, and had major surgery in 1985.

In 1983, Reagan sent a task force to lead the invasion of Grenada, and joined three European nations in maintaining a peacekeeping force in Beirut, Lebanon. His opposition to international terrorism led to the U.S. bombing of Libyan military installations in 1986. He has strongly supported El Salvador and other anticommunist governments and forces in Central America.

By his second term, Reagan was considered one of the most popular presidents in history because of the strong economy and low unemployment, spurred by lower interest rates, energy costs, and inflation. He remained unable to control the high budget deficits while resisting all calls for additional taxes or smaller increases in military spending.

He faced a major crisis in 1986-1987, when it was revealed that the U.S. had sold weapons to Iran in exchange for the release of U.S. hostages being held in Lebanon; and that subsequently some of the money was diverted to the Nicaraguan contras.

The More Colorful Facts

Astrological Sign: Aquarius
Blood Type: O positive
Nicknames: Bowl Number 5*, Dutch†, Erroll Flynn of B Movies, Great Communicator, Prince of Persuasion, Ronald The Right.

*By Warner Bros. in the 1930s because of his haircut.
†By his father at birth because he looked like a "fat little Dutchman."

Original Family Name: Regan, changed by RWR's great grandfather Michael in the mid-nineteenth century. The family tree can be traced to Raigin, who was killed fighting Viking invaders in 1014 A.D.

Reagan Family Motto: Mullach Abu which means "The Hills Forever."

Presidential Notes: Friends and personal advisers are called the "California Mafia."

RWR has hung portraits of Coolidge, Lincoln, and Eisenhower in the Cabinet Room in The White House's West Wing.

"Debategate" was the nickname given to the controversy arising from the discovery that aides to candidate RWR had obtained copies of Jimmy Carter's briefing notes before their 1980 televised debates.

Mottos on RWR's desk in the Oval Office are: "It Can Be Done" and "There is No Limit to What a Man Can Do or Where He Can Go If He Doesn't Mind Who Gets the Credit."

The only president to be inaugurated after reaching his seventieth birthday.

RWR's second inaugural, with temperatures at 0° F, was the coldest on record. All activities had to be moved indoors. The parade was cancelled for the first time since its inception as the windchill reached -50° F, but the Brunswick (Ohio) Band marched anyway as they claimed they hadn't come all that way to stand indoors. The parade was later restaged in the summer of 1985 at DisneyWorld in Orlando, Florida; all groups scheduled to perform in January, including Brunswick, were invited. The temperature at Reagan's first inaugural was 56° F.

Family Notes: RWR called his first wife Jane Wyman "Button Nose Number One" and their daughter Maureen "Button Nose Number Two."

RWR took the former Nancy Davis to La Rue's, a restaurant in Los Angeles, on their first date. After dinner they went to Ciro's to hear Sophie Tucker sing.

RWR and Nancy were married at The Little Brown Church in Los Angeles. William Holden and his wife, Ardis (who acted under the name of Brenda Marshall), were the attendants.

The only perfume Nancy Reagan wears is Ruberos.

As First Lady, Nancy Reagan chose drug abuse as her special cause. She appeared on the NBC sitcom "Diff'rent Strokes" to discuss the subject (March 19, 1983), and was featured in "The Chemical People," a two-part PBS Special on drug abuse (November 2 and 9, 1983).

Son Ronald P. Reagan danced with the Joffrey Ballet in New York for several years.

Campaign Notes: "Let's Make America Great Again" was the theme of the 1980 presidential campaign.

"Leadership That's Working" was the theme of the 1984 reelection campaign.

Namesakes: Ronald Reagan Let Them Eat Cake Day, a national satirical bake sale held on October 3, 1983 in hopes of raising $500,000 for community

Reagan as seen through the eyes of political cartoonist John Lane (NEA Service).

groups. Offerings included Breadline Pudding, Misfortune Cookies, and Surplus Cheesecake.

Ronnie Runners, tennis shoes manufactured by CVS International and named after the 40th president. The red, white, and blue shoe says RR84 on the sides. One heel says "Ronnie" and the other says "84."

Superstitions: RWR believes in knocking on wood for good luck.

Suit Size: 42 Long

Shoe Size: 10½

Social Security Number: 480-07-7456

Homes: 1669 San Onofre Drive, Pacific Palisades, California. Designed by architect Bill Stephenson.

Yearling Row, 80-acre ranch in California's Northridge Mountains. RWR traded it when he bought his current ranch, Rancho del Cielo.

Rancho del Cielo (Ranch in the Sky), near Santa Barbara, California. The 688-acre ranch, originally called the Tip Top Ranch, was purchased in 1974 for $574,000 and is located in the Santa Ynez Mountains. Ironically, in 1848, a hunter named John Hinckley shot one of the last (now extinct) California grizzly bears near this location.

Military Career: "Fort Wacky" was the nickname given to the Hal Roach Studios under the jurisdiction of the U.S. Army during World War II, because of the large number of movie talent stationed there, including 2nd Lt. RWR, who was unable to serve on the frontlines because of poor eyesight. The main purpose of the unit was to make documentaries, training films, and newsreels. His three biggest films while there were *Mr. Gardenia Jones, Rear Gunman,* and *For God and Country.*

As a captain, RWR signed the discharge papers for Maj. Clark Gable on June 12, 1944, while at this base.

Acting Notes: First dramatic television appearance was "Disappearance of Mrs. Gordon" on "Airflyte Theater" (CBS) on Dec. 7, 1950.

RWR got his first film role, Andy McLeod, in *Love Is On The Air* after Alexander Ross, whom he resembled, committed suicide.

Bedtime for Bonzo (1951), starring RWR and Diana Lynn, was the subject of much satirical ridicule because the co-star, Bonzo, was a chimpanzee.

RWR was considered for the role of Rick Blaine in *Casablanca* (which means white house in Spanish) and Ann Sheridan as his Ilsa Laszlo.

From 1962 to 1965, RWR hosted "Death Valley Days," a television series sponsored by 20 Mule Team Borax, whose advertising agency was McCann Erickson. RWR's brother Neil Reagan was an executive at the agency and recommended him for the role.

From 1954 to 1962, RWR hosted "The General Electric Theatre." In 1958, he appeared with his wife, Nancy Davis, in a production titled "A Turkey for President."

In *Knute Rockne—All American* (1940), RWR immortalized George Gipp, the legendary Notre Dame University football player.

For his Warner Bros. screentest, then sportscaster RWR ("Dutch") read two pages from Philip Barry's play *Holiday*.

Memberships: Alpha Epsilon Sigma, Eureka College dramatic society, 1929.

Booster's Club, Eureka College. RWR was president.

Emil Verban Society, association of diehard Chicago Cub fans. Club is named for Emil M. Verban who hit .272 in seven seasons and was nicknamed "Dutch" or the "Antelope".

Republican Governor's Association, elected chairman in 1969.

Awards: Acting award for his role in *Aria da Capo* by Edna St. Vincent Millay at Eureka College.

Most Nearly Perfect Male Figure, by Division of Fine Arts at the University of Southern California, 1940.

Hollywood Citizenship Award, presented by *Golden Globe* Magazine in 1957.

Horatio Alger Award, 1969, presented to those who succeed from humble beginnings.

George Spelvin Award, (presented by The Masquers) for outstanding dedication to the field of acting, 1972.

West Coast Father of the Year, 1976. The same year daughter Patti was not allowed to bring rock star boy friend Bernie Lendon into the Reagan home because they had been living together.

Order of The Golden Eagle, Tau Kappa Epsilon's (TKE) most distinguished honor award, presented to Brother RWR, 1984.

Other Positions: Golf caddy, Dixon Country Club, Dixon, Illinois, in his pre-teens in the 1920s.

Sportscaster, WOC (World of Chiropractic), in Davenport, Iowa,

1932. His first professional job, $5 a week and bus fare.

Sportscaster, WHO, in Des Moines, Iowa, 1932-37. He would simulate broadcasts of Chicago Cubs games using wire service ticker tapes and earned $75 a week.

Actor (see Acting Notes for some highlights)

President, Screen Actors Guild, 1947-1952 and 1959-60.

Sports: RWR played guard for the Dixon (Illinois) Dukes in 1927.

Eureka College football uniform number was 33.

RWR played for the Leading Men, a Hollywood baseball team made up of actors. In a 1949 charity game against The Comedians, he hit a grounder toward the shortstop, comedian Donald O'Connor. Seeing that the play would be close, RWR slid in feet first. He was out in more ways than one. Reagan suffered a multiple fracture of the right thigh and it took more than a year to heal.

RWR enjoys horseback riding as one of his favorite forms of exercise.

Health: RWR suffers from Dupuytren's Contracture, a condition that causes the fourth finger of his left hand to curl from time to time into his palm.

RR wears a hearing aid in his right ear to correct a 20-year-old problem caused by being too close to a prop gun being fired during the filming of a movie. He wears an "intra model" which contains a microphone, a battery and an amplifier. The device is less than one-half inch long, fits in his ear canal and is manufactured by Starkey Labs.

Secret Service Codes: Rawhide (for RWR)

Rainbow (for Nancy)

Favorite Comic Strip: Peanuts® by Charles E. Schulz

Favorite Drink: Screwdriver

Favorite Foods: Lasagna, macaroni and cheese, meatball soup

Favorite Snack: Jelly beans. The habit goes back to 1969 when RWR, after his good friend and fellow actor Robert Taylor died of lung cancer, vowed, along with Nancy, to give up smoking. They did this with the aid of jelly benas.

Favorite Book: *The Printer of Udells,* novel by Harold Bell Wright (as a young man)

Favorite TV Shows: "Mission Impossible," "Mannix," "Carol Burnett"

Favorite Snack: Bee pollen

Favorite Desserts: Chocolate brownies, coconut cake

Favorite Flower: Eastern lilac

Favorite Jelly Beans: Jelly Bellies—his favorite flavor is coconut.

Favorite Tailor: Frank Mariani of Beverly Hills, California, makes the majority of Ronald Reagan's clothes.

Songs: "Ballad of President Reagan," "Reagan for Shah," "Reagan Rag," "Reagonomic Blues," "The Reagan Fast Shuffle," "Reaganomics Might Be Working But I'm Not," and "Reaganomics of Love."

Quotes (or Quips): "Honey, I forgot to duck," to wife Nancy after being shot.

"I hope you're all Republicans," to the surgeons who would operate after he was shot.

THE FILMS OF RONALD REAGAN:

Love Is On The Air 1937 Andy McLeod

Submarine D-1 1937 bit deleted from final print

Hollywood Hotel 1937 unbilled bit as a member of Louella Parson's staff

Sergeant Murphy 1938 Sgt. Dennis Murphy

Swing Your Lady 1938 Jack Miller

Accidents Will Happen 1938 Eric Gregg

Cowboy From Brooklyn 1939 Pat Dunn

Boy Meets Girl 1938 as announcer

The Amazing Dr. Clitterhouse 1938 voice can be heard as a radio announcer describing a jewel robbery

Girls On Probation 1938 Neil Dillon

Brother Rat 1938 Dan Crawford

Going Places 1938 Jack Withering

Secret Service Of The Air 1939 Lt. Brass Bancroft

Dark Victory 1939 Alec Hamm

Code Of The Secret Service 1939 Lt. Brass Bancroft

Naughty But Nice 1939 Ed Clark

Hell's Kitchen 1939 Jim

Smashing The Money Ring 1939 Lt. Brass Bancroft

Brother Rate And A Baby 1940 Dan Crawford

An Angel From Texas 1940 Marty Allen

Knute Rockne—All American 1940 George Gipp

Tugboat Annie Sails Again 1940 Eddie Kent

Santa Fe Trail 1940 George Armstrong Custer

The Bad Man 1941 Gil Jones

Million Dollar Baby 1941 Peter Rowan

Nine Lives Are Not Enough 1941 Matt Sawyer

International Squadron 1941 Jimmy Grant

King's Row 1941 Drake McHugh

Juke Girl 1942 Steve Talbot

Desperate Journey 1942 Flying Officer Johnny Hammond

This Is The Army 1943 Johnny Jones

Stallion Road 1947 Larry Hanrahan

That Hagan Girl 1947 Tom Bates

The Voice Of The Turtle 1947 Sgt. Bill Page

John Loves Mary 1949 John Lawrence

Night Unto Night 1949 John

The Girl From Jones Beach 1949 Bob Randolph

It's A Great Feeling 1949 cameo

The Hasty Heart 1950 Yank

Louisa 1950 Hal Norton

Storm Warning 1951 Burt Rainey

Bedtime For Bonzo 1951 Professor Peter Boyd

The Last Outpost 1951 Vance Britten
Hong Kong 1952 Jeff Williams
The Winning Team 1952 Grover Cleveland Alexander
She's Working Her Way Through College 1952 John Palmer
Tropic Zone 1953 Dan McCloud
Law and Order 1953 Frame Johnson
Prisoner Of War 1954 Captain Web Sloane
Cattle Queen of Montana 1954 Farrell
Tennessee's Partner 1955 Cowpoke
Hellcats Of The Navy 1957 Commander Casey Abbott
The Young Doctors 1961 narrated opening sequence
The Killers 1964 Jack Browning

THE FILMS OF NANCY DAVIS* (REAGAN):
The Doctor and the Girl 1949 Marlette
East Side, West Side 1949 Helen Lee
Shadow on the Wall 1950 Dr. Caroline Canford
The Next Voice You Hear 1950 Mrs. Joe Smith
Night Into Morning 1951 Katherine Mead
It's A Big Country 1952 Miss Coleman
Shadow In the Sky 1952 Betty
Talk About A Stranger 1952 Marge Fontaine
Donovan's Brain 1953 Janice Corey
Hellcats Of The Navy 1957 Helen Blair
Crash Landing 1958 Helen Williams

Assassination Attempt: Shot by John W. Hinckley, Jr., on March 30, 1981, at the Washington, D.C., Hilton after addressing the American Enterprise Institute. Hinckley was found not guilty by reason of insanity.

Books: *Where's The Best of Me,* 1965 autobiography written with Richard G. Hubler. The title came from a line he spoke in the 1941 movie *King's Row.*

---

*Nancy Davis is the favorite actress of Ronald Reagan. They appeared in only one film together, *Hellcats Of The Navy.*

INTRIGUING MISCELLANEOUS FACTS

Presidents Who Graduated from U.S. Military Academies
Ulysses S. Grant, U.S. Military Academy, 1834; 21st out of 39
Dwight D. Eisenhower, U.S. Military Academy, 1915*; 61st out of 164
Jimmy Carter, U.S. Naval Academy, 1946; 59th out of 820

Aircraft Carriers Named After Presidents
Theodore Roosevelt (CVA-N)
Franklin D. Roosevelt (CV 42)
Dwight D. Eisenhower (CVA-N-69)
John F. Kennedy (CV 67)

Victims of Unsuccessful Assassination Attempts
Andrew Jackson
Theodore Roosevelt (as an ex-president)
Franklin D. Roosevelt (as president-elect)
Harry S. Truman
Gerald R. Ford (twice)
Ronald Reagan

Presidents Who Were Bald
John Quincy Adams
Martin Van Buren
Dwight D. Eisenhower

*The class of 1915 produced 2 generals of the army, 24 major generals, 2 generals, 7 lieutenant generals, 24 brigadier generals.

Baseball and the Presidents

Benjamin Harrison was the first president to watch a professional baseball game when, on June 6, 1892, he saw Cincinnati beat Washington, 7-4, in 11 innings.

The first president to throw the ceremonial first pitch was William Howard Taft who, on April 14, 1910, was asked by umpire Billy Evans to do the honors. Taft saw the Washington Senators beat the Philadelphia Athletics, 3-0, as Walter Johnson threw a one-hitter.

Since Taft, only President Jimmy Carter has not carried through with the tradition of throwing out the first pitch.

Ronald Reagan considers himself to be a jinx to the Baltimore Orioles as in the four years he has thrown out the first pitch (1982-86) the Birds have lost all four games.

Presidents Who Wore Beards

Abraham Lincoln
Ulysses S. Grant
Rutherford B. Hayes
James A. Garfield
Benjamin Harrison

Presidents Who Were British Subjects at Birth

George Washington
John Adams
Thomas Jefferson
James Madison
James Monroe
John Quincy Adams
Andrew Jackson
William Henry Harrison

Camp David: The Presidential Retreat

Originally called Hi Catoctin (Shangri-La to Franklin D. Roosevelt), Camp David, which is located in Maryland's Catoctin Mountains, was named for presidential grandson David (Dwight David II) Eisenhower. The lands were cleared in 1939, and it was built by the Civilian Conservation Corps (CCC) and the Works Progress Administration (WPA). The retreat includes 10 cabins, a lodge, a conference room for 50, a presidential office, a projection theater, a skeet range, basketball courts, and a trampoline.

Presidents Who Had No Children of Their Own

George Washington
James Madison
Andrew Jackson

James K. Polk
James Buchanan

Christmas Trees in the White House

Franklin Pierce was the first president to erect a Christmas tree in the White House, in 1856.

Grover Cleveland was the first to trim a tree with electric lights, in 1895. Calvin Coolidge was the first to light the national Christmas tree, in 1923. Theodore Roosevelt, a conservationist, banned Christmas trees in his household because he opposed the cutting down of evergreen trees. His children would smuggle small trees into their bedroom, out of his sight.

Five Presidents Who Served as Generals in the Civil War

Ulysses S. Grant
Rutherford B. Hayes
James A. Garfield
Chester A. Arthur
Benjamin Harrison

Presidents Before Congress

Only three presidents have testified before congressional committees: George Washington to deliver his opinion of the Jay Treaty, Abraham Lincoln to defend his wife against spying charges, and Gerald Ford on the Watergate affair.

Presidential Dark Horses

In politics, a dark horse candidate is one who is not well known or favored at the time of the nomination or election. The term originated as British race track slang, referring to the practices of dyeing the coat of a well known horse another color, usually black, and entering him in a race under a false name. Only the jockeys and their friends would know enough to bet on a "dark horse." The first dark horse president was James K. Polk, then Speaker of the House; he was nominated on the ninth ballot. Others were Franklin Pierce (49th ballot), Rutherford B. Hayes (17th ballot), James A. Garfield (36th ballot), and Warren G. Harding (10th ballot). Calvin Coolidge was a surprise dark horse nominee for vice-president in 1920.

Incumbents Who Were Defeated for Reelection

John Adams by Thomas Jefferson
Martin Van Buren by William Henry Harrison
Grover Cleveland by Benjamin Harrison
Benjamin Harrison by Grover Cleveland
William Howard Taft by Woodrow Wilson
Herbert Hoover by Franklin D. Roosevelt
Gerald R. Ford by Jimmy Carter
Jimmy Carter by Ronald Reagan

Presidents Who Married Divorced Women
Andrew Jackson to Rachel Donelson Robards
Warren G. Harding to Florence Kling DeWolfe
Gerald R. Ford to Elizabeth Bloomer Warren

Presidents Who Played Football for Their College Teams
Dwight D. Eisenhower for the U.S. Military Academy
Richard M. Nixon for Whittier College
Gerald R. Ford for the University of Michigan
Ronald Reagan for Eureka College

Presidents Who Attained the Rank of General
George Washington
Andrew Jackson
William Henry Harrison
Zachary Taylor
Franklin Pierce
Andrew Johnson
Ulysses S. Grant
Rutherford B. Hayes
James A. Garfield
Chester A. Arthur
Benjamin Harrison
Dwight D. Eisenhower

Presidents Who Served as Governor
California: Ronald Reagan
Georgia: Jimmy Carter
Massachusetts: Calvin Coolidge
New Jersey: Woodrow Wilson
New York: Martin Van Buren, Grover Cleveland, Theodore Roosevelt,
    Franklin D. Roosevelt
Ohio: Rutherford B. Hayes, William McKinley
Tennessee: James K. Polk, Andrew Johnson
Virginia: Thomas Jefferson, James Monroe, John Tyler

Presidents Who Served as Indentured Servants
Millard Fillmore as a clothmaker
Andrew Johnson as a tailor

No President Has Lost Reelection in Wartime
1812	War of 1812	James Madison
1864	Civil War	Abraham Lincoln
1900	Spanish-American War	William McKinley
1916	World War I	Woodrow Wilson

1944	World War II	Franklin D. Roosevelt
1948	Korean War	Harry S. Truman
1972	Vietnam War	Richard M. Nixon

Presidents Who Studied Law or Were Admitted to the Bar

John Adams
Thomas Jefferson
James Madison
James Monroe
John Quincy Adams
Andrew Jackson
Martin Van Buren
John Tyler
James K. Polk
Millard Fillmore
Franklin Pierce
James Buchanan
Abraham Lincoln
Andrew Johnson
Rutherford B. Hayes
James A. Garfield
Chester A. Arthur
Grover Cleveland
Benjamin Harrison
William McKinley
Theodore Roosevelt
William H. Taft
Calvin Coolidge
Franklin D. Roosevelt
Harry S. Truman
Richard M. Nixon
Gerald R. Ford

Presidents Who Were Born in a Log Cabin

Andrew Jackson
Zachary Taylor
Millard Fillmore
James Buchanan
Abraham Lincoln
James A. Garfield

Presidents Who Were Masons

Name	Lodge	Initiation Date
George Washington	Lodge #4	Fredericksburg, Virginia 08/04/1753
James Monroe	Lodge #6	Williamsburg, Virginia 1775

Andrew Jackson*	Lodge #1	Harmony - Nashville, Tennessee 1800
James K. Polk	Lodge #1	Columbia, Tennessee 09/14/1820
James Buchanan	Lodge #43	Lancaster, Pennsylvania 01/24/1817
Andrew Johnson	Lodge #119	Greenville, Tennessee 1851
James A. Garfield	Lodge #20	Magnolia - Columbus, Ohio 11/22/1864
William McKinley†	Lodge #21	Hiram - Winchester, Virginia 05/03/1865
Theodore Roosevelt	Lodge #806	Matineck - Oyster Bay, New York 04/24/1901
William Howard Taft	Lodge #356	Kilwinning - Columbus, Ohio 02/18/1909
Warren G. Harding	Lodge #70	Marion, Ohio 08/27/1920
Franklin D. Roosevelt	Lodge #8	Holland - Hyde Park, New York 11/28/1911
Harry S. Truman*	Lodge #450	Belton, Missouri 03/09/1909
Lyndon B. Johnson	Lodge #561	Johnson City, Texas 10/30/1937

Presidents Who Served as Mayors

Andrew Johnson	Greeneville, Tennessee	1830-34
Grover Cleveland	Buffalo, New York	1882
Calvin Coolidge	Northampton, Massachusetts	1919-11

Presidents Who Served as Minister to Foreign Countries

Colombia: William Henry Harrison, 1828-29
France: Thomas Jefferson, 1784-87; James Monroe, 1794-96 and 1803
Great Britain: John Adams, 1785-88; James Monroe, 1803; John Quincy Adams, 1815-17; Martin Van Buren, 1831-55; James Buchanan, 1853-55
Netherlands: John Adams, 1780; John Quincy Adams, 1794-95
Portugal: John Quincy Adams, 1796
Prussia: John Quincy Adams, 1797
Russia: John Quincy Adams, 1814-17; James Buchanan, 1832-33

Presidents Who Were Elected with Less Than 50 Percent of the Popular Vote

John Quincy Adams	1824	30.54%‡
James K. Polk	1844	49.56%
Zachary Taylor	1848	47.35%
James Buchanan	1856	45.63%
Abraham Lincoln	1860	39.76%

*Grand Master
†Knight Templar
‡Andrew Jackson had 43.1% of the vote but Adams won when the election was decided by the House of Representatives.

Rutherford B. Hayes	1876	48.04%*
James A. Garfield	1880	48.32%
Grover Cleveland	1884	48.53%
Benjamin Harrison	1888	47.86%†
Grover Cleveland	1892	46.04%
Woodrow Wilson	1912	41.85%
Woodrow Wilson	1916	49.26%
Harry S. Truman	1948	49.51%
John F. Kennedy	1960	49.71%
Richard M. Nixon	1968	43.36%

Presidents Who Had Moustaches
Chester A. Arthur
Grover Cleveland
Theodore Roosevelt
William Howard Taft

Presidential National Historic Sites
These locations have been declared national historical sites and are administered by the National Park Service.

Peterson House (where Lincoln died)	Washington, D.C.	1894
Abraham Lincoln Birthplace	Hodgenville, Kentucky	1916
Andrew Jackson Home, "The Hermitage"	Nashville, Tennessee	1935
Franklin D. Roosevelt Birthplace	Hyde Park, New York	1944
John Adams Home, "Peacefield"	Quincy, Massachusetts	1946
Theodore Roosevelt Home, "Sagamore Hill"	Oyster Bay, New York	1962
Theodore Roosevelt Birthplace	New York, New York	1965
Herbert Hoover Birthplace	West Branch, Iowa	1965
Ford's Theatre	Washington, D.C.	1966
Theodore Roosevelt Inauguration Site, "Wilcox Home"	Buffalo, New York	1966
John F. Kennedy Birthplace	Brookline, Massachusetts	1967
Dwight D. Eisenhower Home	Gettysburg, Pennsylvania	1967
William Howard Taft Home	Cincinnati, Ohio	1969
Abraham Lincoln Home	Springfield, Illinois	1971
Martin Van Buren Home, "Lindenwald"	Kinderhook, New York	1974
Eleanor Roosevelt Home	Hyde Park, New York	1977

*Samuel J. Tilden had 51% but Hayes won by a single electoral vote.
†Grover Cleveland had 48.6% but Harrison had more electoral votes.

| James A. Garfield Home, "Lawnfield" | Mentor, Ohio | 1980 |
| Harry S. Truman Home | Independence, Missouri | 1982 |

National Memorials

These sites have been declared national memorials and are administered by the government.

Washington Monument	Washington, D.C.	1848
Lincoln Memorial	Washington, D.C.	1922
Mt. Rushmore	South Dakota	1925
Thomas Jefferson Memorial	Washington, D.C.	1943
Theodore Roosevelt Island	Washington, D.C.	1947

Presidents Who Did Not Attend College
George Washington
Andrew Jackson
Martin Van Buren
Zachary Taylor
Millard Fillmore
Abraham Lincoln
Andrew Johnson
Grover Cleveland
Harry S. Truman

Presidents Who Were Only Children
None

Presidents Who Were Awarded Phi Beta Kappas
John Quincy Adams
Martin Van Buren*
Franklin Pierce*
Rutherford B. Hayes*
James A. Garfield*
Chester A. Arthur
Grover Cleveland*
Theodore Roosevelt
William H. Taft
Woodrow Wilson*
Calvin Coolidge*
Franklin D. Roosevelt*
Harry S. Truman*
Dwight D. Eisenhower*

*Honorary

Presidents Who Were Stamp Collectors
Franklin D. Roosevelt
Dwight D. Eisenhower
Richard M. Nixon
Gerald R. Ford

Where to Find the Presidential Libraries

Jimmy Carter Library	Atlanta, Georgia
Dwight D. Eisenhower Center	Abilene, Kansas
Gerald R. Ford Library	Ann Arbor, Michigan
Rutherford B. Hayes Library	Fremont, Ohio
Herbert C. Hoover Library	West Branch, Iowa
Lyndon B. Johnson Library	Austin, Texas
John F. Kennedy Library	Boston, Massachusetts
Richard M. Nixon Library (proposed)	San Clemente, California
Franklin D. Roosevelt Library	Hyde Park, New York
Harry S. Truman Library	Independence, Missouri

Presidents Who Were Reelected While in Office
George Washington
Thomas Jefferson
James Madison
James Monroe
Andrew Jackson
Abraham Lincoln
Ulysses S. Grant
William McKinley
Theodore Roosevelt
Woodrow Wilson
Calvin Coolidge
Franklin D. Roosevelt
Harry S. Truman
Dwight D. Eisenhower
Lyndon B. Johnson
Richard M. Nixon
Ronald Reagan

How Much Money Did the Presidents Make?
The salary paid to the president has changed five times:

George Washington to Ulysses S. Grant (first term)	$25,000 per year
Ulysses S. Grant (second term) to Theodore Roosevelt	$50,000 per year

William Howard Taft to Franklin D. Roosevelt	$75,000 per year (taxable)*
Harry S. Truman to Lyndon B. Johnson	$100,000 per year (taxable)
Richard M. Nixon to the present	$200,000 per year (taxable)†

Both Herbert Hoover and John F. Kennedy donated their presidential salaries to charity. Kennedy also donated his salary while a congressman and a senator.

Split Party Ticket

Only twice have a president and vice-president been elected from two different parties. In 1840, William Henry Harrison was a Whig and John Tyler a Democrat. In the election of 1864, Abraham Lincoln was a Republican and Andrew Johnson a Democrat; they joined under the National Union ticket. John Adams, a Federalist, and Thomas Jefferson, a Democratic-Republican, were also from two different parties but they were elected separately, not together.

Presidents Who Owned Slaves

George Washington
Thomas Jefferson
James Madison
Andrew Jackson
John Tyler
James K. Polk
Zachary Taylor
Andrew Johnson
Ulysses S. Grant

Who Succeeds the President?

1. Vice-President
2. Speaker of the House of Representatives
3. President Pro Tempore of the Senate
4. Secretary of State
5. Secretary of the Treasury
6. Secretary of Defense
7. The Attorney General
8. Secretary of the Interior
9. Secretary of Agriculture
10. Secretary of Commerce
11. Secretary of Labor
12. Secretary of Health and Human Services

*Includes $25,000 per year (non-taxable) travel expense; paid 1909-49.
†Includes $40,000 per year (non-taxable) travel expense and $50,000 living expenses (taxable); paid 1949-present.

13. Secretary of Housing and Urban Development
14. Secretary of Transportation
15. Secretary of Energy
16. Secretary of Education

Presidents Who Were Employed as School Teachers
John Adams
Millard Fillmore
Franklin Pierce
James A. Garfield
Chester A. Arthur
Grover Cleveland
William McKinley
Woodrow Wilson

Presidents on Time Covers
Richard M. Nixon	64 times
Jimmy Carter	33 times
Ronald Reagan	43 times
Lyndon B. Johnson	23 times
Gerald R. Ford	22 times
Dwight D. Eisenhower	21 times
John F. Kennedy	11 times

Presidents Selected as Time's Man of the Year
1932	Franklin D. Roosevelt
1934	Franklin D. Roosevelt
1941	Franklin D. Roosevelt
1944	Dwight D. Eisenhower
1945	Harry S. Truman
1948	Harry S. Truman
1959	Dwight D. Eisenhower
1961	John F. Kennedy
1964	Lyndon B. Johnson
1967	Lyndon B. Johnson
1971	Richard M. Nixon
1972	Richard M. Nixon (shared with Henry A. Kissinger)
1976	Jimmy Carter
1980	Ronald Reagan
1984	Ronald Reagan (shared with Soviet President Yuri Andropov)

Presidents Pictured on Treasury Notes
$1,000	Abraham Lincoln
$5,000	James Monroe

$10,000 Grover Cleveland
$100,000 Ulysses S. Grant
$1,000,000 Theodore Roosevelt
$100,000,000 James Madison
$500,000,000 William McKinley

Presidents Portrayed on U.S. Paper Currency

$1 George Washington
$2 Thomas Jefferson
$5 Abraham Lincoln
$20 Andrew Jackson
$50 Ulyssess S. Grant
$500 William McKinley
$1,000 Grover Cleveland
$5,000 James Madison
$100,000 Woodrow Wilson

Presidents Portrayed on U.S. Coins

$ .01 Abraham Lincoln
$ .05 Thomas Jefferson
$ .10 Franklin D. Roosevelt
$ .25 George Washington
$ .50 John F. Kennedy
$1.00 Dwight D. Eisenhower

Presidents Who Served in the House of Representatives

California: Richard M. Nixon
Illinois: Abraham Lincoln
Massachusetts: John Quincy Adams, John F. Kennedy
Michigan: Gerald R. Ford
New Hampshire: Franklin Pierce
New York: Millard Fillmore
Ohio: William Henry Harrison, Rutherford B. Hayes, James A. Garfield, William McKinley
Pennsylvania: James Buchanan
Tennessee: Andrew Jackson, James K. Polk (speaker), Andrew Johnson
Texas: Lyndon B. Johnson
Virginia: James Madison, John Tyler

Presidents Portrayed on U.S. Savings Bonds

$25 George Washington
$50 Franklin D. Roosevelt
$75 Harry S. Truman
$100 Dwight D. Eisenhower
$200 John F. Kennedy

$500	Woodrow Wilson
$1,000	Theodore Roosevelt
$5,000	William McKinley
$10,000	Grover Cleveland

Presidents Who Were Elected to the Senate
California: Richard M. Nixon
Indiana: Benjamin Harrison
Massachusetts: John Quincy Adams, John F. Kennedy
Missouri: Harry S. Truman
New Hampshire: Franklin Pierce
New York: Martin Van Buren
Ohio: William Henry Harrison, James A. Garfield*, Warren G. Harding
Pennsylvania: James Buchanan
Tennessee: Andrew Jackson, Andrew Johnson
Texas: Lyndon B. Johnson
Virginia: James Monroe, John Tyler

Presidents Pictured on Treasury Bonds
$50	Thomas Jefferson
$100	Andrew Jackson
$500	George Washington
$1,000	Abraham Lincoln
$5,000	James Monroe
$10,000	Grover Cleveland
$100,000	Ulysses S. Grant
$1,000,000	Theodore Roosevelt

Presidents Who Never Vetoed a Bill Passed by Congress
John Adams
Thomas Jefferson
John Quincy Adams
Martin Van Buren
William H. Harrison
Zachary Taylor
Millard Fillmore
James A. Garfield

Only Presidents Elected from Vice-Presidency to Presidency
John Adams
Thomas Jefferson
Martin Van Buren

*Elected but did not serve, as he was simultaneously elected president.

Women Who Ran For President

Victoria Claflin Woodhull	1872	Equal Rights Party
Belva Ann Lockwood	1884	National Equal Rights Party
Belva Ann Lockwood	1888	Woman Suffrage & Humanitarian Party
Ann Milburn	1940	National Greenback party
Ellen L. Jensen	1952	Washington Peace Party
Yette Bronstein	1964	Best Party
Charlene Mitchell	1968	Communist Party
Linda Jenness—Evelyn Reed*	1972	Socialist Workers Party
Margaret Wright	1975	People's Party
Deirdre Griswold	1980	Worker's World Party
Margaret Smith	1980	Peace and Freedom Party
Ellen McCormack	1980	Right to Life Party

Presidents Who Saw Military Action in WWI

Harry S. Truman
Dwight D. Eisenhower

Presidents Who Served in the Military in WWII

Dwight D. Eisenhower
John F. Kennedy
Lyndon B. Johnson
Richard M. Nixon
Gerald R. Ford
Ronald Reagan

Anti-FDR Slogans

The Republicans used many different slogans on their campaign buttons and ribbons in 1940 and 1944 to end President Franklin Roosevelt's "reign" in the White House, including:

ADAM WAS THE ONLY INDISPENSABLE MAN

ALL I HAVE LEFT IS A VOTE FOR WILLKIE

BOY! DA WE NEED A CHANGE!

CLIP DAD'S WINGS WITH YOUR VOTE

CONFUCIOUS SAY MAN WHO STAND UP TWICE, NO GOOD THIRD TIME

CONFUCIOUS SAY WILLKIE OK

CONFIDENTIALLY I'M VOTING FOR WILLKIE

DE-THRONEMENT DAY NOV. 5th

DICTATOR? NOT FOR US

DON'T BE A JACKASS, FOLLOW THE EAGLE

*Reed ran in states where it was required that candidates must meet the constitutional provision of being 35 years old.

DR. JEKYLL OF HYDE PARK

EDITH WILLKIE FOR FIRST LADY

8 YEARS IS ENOUGH

ELEANOR? NO SOAP!

ELEANOR START PACKING, THE WILLKIES ARE COMING

ELECTION RETURNS WILLKIE 1st ROOSEVELT 2nd

F.D.R. A COSTLY LESSON

FINANCIAL DEBAUCHERY RUN RIOT

FLASH! DEEDS MADE AMERICA, NOT FIRESIDE CHATS

FLASH! DO NOT DISTURB I AM HERE FOR LIFE

FLASH! JOBS WE WANT, NOT RELIEF

FLASH! YOU CAN'T HAVE ROOSEVELT AND PROSPERITY TOO

FLASH! WE WANT WORK NOT RELIEF

FORCE FRANKLIN OUT AT THIRD

F. RANKLIN D. EFICIT R. OOSEVELT

GIVE MA PERKINS THE GATE

GOOD BYE ROOSEVELT HELLO WILLKIE

GUARD OUR PEACE

HELP ROOSEVELT OUT!

HERE'S YOUR HAT FRANK WHAT'S YOUR HURRY?

HI-YO WENDELL—FRANKLIN AWAY

I AM A DEMOCRAT FOR WILLKIE

I AM A WILLKIE DEMOCRAT

I DON'T WANT ELLIOT AS MY CAPTAIN!

I DON'T WANT ELEANOR EITHER

IF I WERE 21 I'D VOTE FOR WILLKIE

INDEPENDENT WILLKIE VOLUNTEER

I TOLD YOU SO

I TOLD YOU SO IT'S WILLKIE

I TOLD YOU SO THAT MAN IS HERE AGAIN NOV. 6

IT'S TIME FOR A CHANGE

I WANT TO BE A CAPTAIN

I WANT TO BE A CAPTAIN TOO

I WON'T MAKE THE SAME MISTAKE AGAIN

JOBS, NOT RELIEF WITH WILLKIE

LEARN TO SAY "WENDELL WILLKIE"

LET'S GIVE FRANKLIN UNEMPLOYMENT INSURANCE

LET'S START WITH A CLEAN STATE

LET'S SWAP RIDERS NOT HORSES

LIFE AND PROSPERITY IN A DEMOCRACY WITH WILLKIE

LINCOLN DIDN'T, WASHINGTON WOULDN'T, ROOSEVELT SHOULDN'T

LUCKY WILLKIE

MAH FRIENDS GOOD BYE

"MY DAY" WHEN I VOTE FOR WILLKIE

MY FRIENDS BUT NOT MY SUBJECTS

MY FRIENDS—GOOD BYE!

MY FRIENDS, I'M INDISPENSABLE

NAPOLEON MET HIS WATERLOO, FRANK YOU WILL TOO

NEW DEAL A MIS-DEAL!

NEW DEAL CONSOLATION: 9,000,000 UNEMPLOYED

99 OUT OF 100 WANT WILLKIE, WHY NOT ME TOO?

NO CROWN FOR FRANKLIN

NO DICTATOR LATER!

NO MORE FISHING TRIPS ON BATTLESHIPS

NO FRANKLIN THE FIRST

NO MAN IS GOOD THREE TIMES

NO MORE FIRESIDE CHATS

NO NEW DEAL, WE WANT A SQUARE DEAL

NO ROOSEVELT DYNASTY

NO ROYAL FAMILY

NO THIRD INTERNATIONALE THIRD REICH THIRD TERM

NO THIRD TERM AND INDISPENSABLE MAN

NO 3RD TERM DICTATOR

NO THIRD TERM-ITES

NOV. 5TH FRANKLIN GETS HIS WALKING PAPERS

ODDER THAN FICTION—ROOSEVELT SAYS "I MADE A MISTAKE"

ONE PARTY NATION? NOTHING DOING, FRANKLIN!

OUT! STEALING THIRD

PAPA:—"I WANT TO BE A CAPTAIN TOO"

PEACE! WILLKIE SAYS IT'S WONDERFUL

PERHAPS ROOSEVELT IS ALL YOU DESERVE

PRESERVE YOUR BILL OF RIGHTS—ELECT WILLKIE

PUT BUCK PRIVATE WILLKIE IN THE WHITE HOUSE

ROOSEVELT FOR EX PRESIDENT

ROOSEVELT GETS HIS WALKING PAPERS

ROOSEVELT GONE WITH THE WIND

ROOSEVELT GOODBYE, HELLO WILLKIE

ROOSEVELT NO MORE JUST FORGET IT

ROOSEVELT? NO! NO! 1000 TIMES NO!

ROTTEN EGGS WITH ROOSEVELT, OMELETTES WITH WILLKIE

RUSSIA, 3RD INTERNATIONAL GERMANY, 3RD REICH U.S.A., 3RD TERM???

SAVE THE SHIP—TO HELL WITH THE CAPTAIN

SCORE A TOUCHDOWN WITH WILLKIE

60 BILLION BUCKS WHEE!

SURE I'LL VOTE FOR ROOSEVELT, HA HA HA HA HA

THANKSGIVING DAY NOV. 5TH

THERE IS NO INDISPENSABLE MAN

THE WHITE HOUSE IS UNDER NEW MANAGEMENT

THINK! WALLACE MIGHT BE PRESIDENT

THIRD INTERNATIONAL, THIRD REICH, THIRD TERM???

THIRD TERM GRAB? IT CAN'T HAPPEN HERE!

THIRD TERM TABOO 23 SKIDOO

TWO GOOD TERMS DESERVE A REST

TWO GOOD TIMES IS ENOUGH FOR ANY MAN

VOTE FOR WILLKIE AND GET OUT OF THE DOG HOUSE

WASHINGTON SWEEPSTAKES 1ST WENDELL, 2ND FRANKLIN, 3RD ELEANOR

WE DON'T WANT ELEANOR EITHER

WE MILLIONAIRES WANT WILLKIE

WE WANT EDITH NOT ELEANOR

WE WANT ROOSEVELT TO ABDICATE

WE WANT WILLKIE

WENDELL PITCHING FRANKLIN OUT!

WHO SMOKED OUT WHO

WILLKIE: 48 ROOSEVELT: 0

WILLKIE NOW OR THE ROOSEVELTS FOREVER

WILLKIE NOT ROYAL BUT LOYAL

WILLKIE OR BUST

WILLKIE SAYS SPINACH IS SPINACH IT SURE IS FRANKLIN

WITH WILLKIE WE WON'T NEED RELIEF

WORST PUBLIC ADMINISTRATION

YEHUDI IS FOR WILLKIE TOO!

Who Played The Presidents In The Movies?

John Adams

"Omnibus"	1955	(TV)	Robert Preston
John Paul Jones	1959		William Daniels
"Profiles In Courage"	1965	(TV)	David McCallum
1776	1972		Pat Hingle
"Land of the Free"	1974	(TV)	Burgess Meredith
Independence (short)	1976		Pat Hingle
"The American Woman: Portraits In Courage"	1976	(TV)	Frank Langella
"George Washington" (Mrs. Abigail Adams)	1984	(TV)	Hal Holbrook Christine Estabrook
"Family Ties" (episode)	1985	(TV)	Ben Piazza
"George Washington II"	1986	(TV)	Paul Collins

John Quincy Adams

"Profiles In Courage"	1965	(TV)	Douglas Campbell
"The Adams Chronicles" (PBS Mini-series)	1976	(TV)	David Birney, George Grizzard, William Daniels

Chester Alan Arthur

Silver Dollar	1932		Emmett Corrigan
Cattle King	1963		Larry Gates

Jimmy Carter

The Cayman Triangle	1977		Ed Beheler
Black Sunday	1977		Ed Beheler
"Saturday Night Live"	1978	(TV)	Dan Akroyd
(Mrs. Rosalynn Carter)			Laraine Newman
"The Jeffersons (episode)"	1979	(TV)	Walt Hanna
"Voyagers (episode)"	1983	(TV)	Walt Hanna
"Sadat"	1983	(TV)	Walt Hanna

Grover Cleveland

Lillian Russell	1940		William B. Davidson
"Profiles In Courage"	1965	(TV)	Carroll O'Connor
Buffalo Bill and the Indians	1976		Pat McCormick
(Mrs. Frances Cleveland)			Shelley Duvall
"The Wild Wild West Revisited"	1979	(TV)	Wilford A. Brimley

Calvin Coolidge

The Court Martial of Billy Mitchell	1955		Ian Wolfe
"Backstairs at the White House"	1979	(TV)	Ed Flanders
(Mrs. Grace Coolidge)			Lee Grant

Dwight D. Eisenhower

The Long Gray Line	1958		Harry Carey, Jr.
The Longest Day	1962		Henry Grace*
"The Francis Gary Powers Story"	1976	(TV)	James Flavin†
"Tail Gunner Joe"	1977	(TV)	Andrew Duggan
"Ike"	1979	(TV)	Robert Duval
(Mrs. Mamie Eisenhower)			Bonnie Bartlett
"Backstairs at the White House"	1979	(TV)	Andrew Duggan
(Mrs. Mamie Eisenhower)			Barbara Barrie
"Churchill and the Generals"	1981	(TV)	Richard Dysart
The Right Stuff	1983		Robert Beer
"Kennedy"	1983	(TV)	
(Mrs. Mamie Eisenhower)			Carmen Matthews
"The Last Days of Patton"	1986	(TV)	Richard Dysart
"Ike"	1986	(PBS)	E. G. Marshall

Gerald R. Ford

"Saturday Night Live"	1975	(TV)	Chevy Chase
The Pink Panther Strikes Again	1976		Dick Crockett
The Bees	1978		Walter Hanna
"The Betty Ford Story"	1987	(TV)	Josef Sommers
(Mrs. Betty Ford)			Gena Rowlands
Mike Ford			Daniel McDonald

*Grace, an art director, not an actor was chosen for his resemblence to Ike.
†Flavin's last movie role; he died April 23, 1976.

Jack Ford			Bradley Whitford
Steve Ford			Brian McNamara
Susan Ford			Nan Woods
Gayle Ford			Laura Leigh Hughes

James A. Garfield

Night Riders	1939		Lawrence Wolf
No More Excuses	1968		Van Johnson
"Captains and the Kings"	1979	(TV)	Richard Matheson

Ulysses S. Grant

The Birth of a Nation	1915		Donald Crisp
Flaming Frontier	1926		Walter Rodgers
Abraham Lincoln	1930		E. Allyn Warren
Only the Brave	1930		Guy Oliver
Union Pacific	1939		Joseph Crehen
The Adventures of Mark Twain	1941		Joseph Crehen
They Died With Their Boots On	1942		Joseph Crehen
Silver River	1948		Joseph Crehen
"Omnibus"	1950's	(TV)	James Whitmore
The Iron Mistress	1952		Hayden Rourke
Sitting Bull	1954		John Hamilton
From the Earth to the Moon	1958		Morris Ankrum
The Horse Soldiers	1959		Stan Jones
How The West Was Won	1962		Harry Morgan
"The Court Martial of General George Custer"	1977	(TV)	Richard Dysart
"Freedom Road"	1979	(TV)	John McLiam
The Legend of the Lone Ranger	1980		Jason Robards
"The Blue and the Gray"	1982	(TV)	Rip Torn
"Wild Wild West"	TV Series		James Gregory, Roy Engel
"North and South, Book II"	1986	(TV)	Anthony Zerbe
"Liberty"	1986	(TV)	Alan North

Warren G. Harding

"Backstairs at the White House" (Mrs. Florence Harding)	1979	(TV)	George Kennedy Celeste Holm

Benjamin Harrison

Stars and Stripes Forever	1952	Roy Gordon

William Henry Harrison

Two Gentlemen From West Point	1942	Douglass Dumbrille

Rutherford B. Hayes

Buffalo Bill	1944	John Dilson

Herbert C. Hoover

Fires of Youth	1931		Tom Jensen
"Backstairs at the White House"	1979	(TV)	Larry Gates
(Mrs. Lou Hoover)			Jan Sterling

Andrew Jackson

The Eagle of the Sea	1926		George Irving
The Frontiersman	1927		Russell Simpson
The Gorgeous Hussy	1936		Lionel Barrymore
(Mrs. Rachel Jackson)			Beulah Bondi
The Buccaneer	1938		Hugh Sothern
Man of Conquest	1939		Edward Ellis
The Remarkable Andrew	1942		Brian Donlevy
Lone Star	1952		Lionel Barrymore
The President's Lady	1953		Charlton Heston
(Mrs. Rachel Jackson)			Susan Hayward
Davy Crockett, King of the Wild Frontier	1955		Basil Ruysdael
The First Texan	1956		Carl Brenton Reid
The Buccaneer	1958		Charlton Heston
"First Ladies' Diaries"	1965	(TV)	Gerald Gordon
"Bridger"	1976	(TV)	John Anderson
"The Adams Chronicles"	1976	(TV)	Wesley Addy

Thomas Jefferson

Janice Meredith	1924		Lionel Adams
America	1924		Frank Walsh
The Man Without A Country	1925		Albert Hart
Alexander Hamilton	1931		Montogu Love
Old Louisiana	1937		Allan Cavan
The Howards of Virginia	1940		Richard Carlson
(at age 11)			Buster Phelps
The Remarkable Andrew	1942		Gilbert Emery
Magnificent Doll	1946		Grandon Rhodes
The Far Horizons	1955		Herbert Heyes
"Our American Heritage"	1960	(TV)	Ralph Bellamy
1776	1972		Ken Howard
(Mrs. Martha Jefferson)			Blythe Danner
Independence (short)	1976		Ken Howard
"The Adams Chronicles"	1976	(TV)	Albert Stratton
"The Rebels"	1979	(TV)	Kevin Tighe
"Brothers To Dragons"	1975	(PBS)	James Eichelberger
"Family Ties (episode)"	1985	(TV)	Michael Gross
(Mrs. Martha Jefferson)			Meredith Baxter Birney
"George Washington, Part II"	1986	(TV)	Jeffrey Jones

Andrew Johnson

Tennessee Johnson	1942		Van Heflin
"Profiles In Courage"	1965	(TV)	Walter Matthau
"The Case Against Mulligan"	1975	(TV)	Walter Klauun
"The Ordeal of Dr. Mudd"	1980	(TV)	William Hindman

Lyndon B. Johnson

How To Succeed In Business Without Really Trying	1967		Ivan Triesault
"The Private Files of J. Edgar Hoover"	1977	(TV)	Andrew Duggan
"King"	1978	(TV)	Warren Kemmerling
"Blood Feud"	1983	(TV)	Forrest Tucker
The Right Stuff	1983		Donald Moffit
"Kennedy"	1983	(TV)	Nesbitt Blaisdell
(Mrs. Lady Bird Johnson)			Tanny McDonald
"Robert Kennedy and His Times"	1985	(TV)	G. D. Spradlin
(Mrs. Lady Bird Johnson)			Danna Hansen
"Twilight Zone" (episode)	1986	(TV)	Jeff Hardin
"LBJ"	1987	(TV)	Randy Quaid
(Mrs. Lady Bird Johnson)			Patti Lupone
"Lyndon Johnson"	1987	(PBS)	Laurence Luckinbill

John F. Kennedy

PT 109	1963		Cliff Robertson
"Missiles of October"	1974	(TV)	William Devane
"Johnny, We Hardly Knew Ye"	1977	(TV)	Paul Rudd
"Young Joe, The Forgotten Kennedy"	1977	(TV)	Sam Chew, Jr.*
(as a boy)			Lance Kerwin
"The Private Files of J. Edgar Hoover"	1978	(TV)	William Jordan
"King"	1978	(TV)	William Jordon
"Jacqueline Bouvier Kennedy"	1981	(TV)	James Franciscas
(Mrs. Jacqueline Kennedy)			Jaclyn Smith
(as a child)			Heather Hobbs
"Blood Feud"	1983	(TV)	Sam Groom
"Kennedy"	1983	(TV)	Martin Sheen*
(Mrs. Jacqueline Kennedy)			Blair Brown
(Caroline Kennedy)			Hanna Fallon
"JFK - A One Man Show"	1984	(PBS)	Mike Farrell
"Robert Kennedy and His Times"	1984	(TV)	Cliff DeYoung*
(Mrs. Jacqueline Kennedy)			Juanin Clay

*Only three actors have portrayed both John and Robert Kennedy. Chew played Bobby in *Tail Gunner Joe*, Sheen in "The Missiles of October," and DeYoung in "King."

"Twilight Zone"(episode)	1986	(TV)	Andrew Robinson
"LBJ"	1987	(TV)	Charles Frank
(Mrs. Jacqueline Kennedy)			Robin Curtis

Abraham Lincoln

Under One Flag	1911	Ralph Ince
The Seventh Son	1911	Ralph Ince
The Fall of Black Hawk	1912	H.G. Lonsdale
Lincoln's Gettysburg Address	1912	Ralph Ince
Songbird of the North	1913	Ralph Ince
The Battle of Gettysburg	1913	Willard Mack
Lincoln the Lover	1914	Ralph Ince
The Man Who Knew Lincoln	1914	Ralph Ince
The Birth of a Nation	1915	Joseph Henabery
The Heart of Lincoln	1915	Francis Ford
The Battlecry of Peace	1915	William Ferguson
The Life of Abraham Lincoln	1915	Frank McGlynn
The Crisis	1916	Samuel Drane
The Lincoln Cycle	1917	Benjamin Chapin
Battle Hymn of the Republic	1917	Ralph Ince
Victory and Peace	1918	Rolf Leslie
Lincoln's Thanksgiving Story	1918	Benjamin Chapin
Child of Democracy	1918	Benjamin Chapin
Son of Democracy	1918	Benjamin Chapin
The Copperhead	1919	Meyer F. Stroell
The Land of Opportunity	1920	Ralph Ince
The Highest Law	1921	Ralph Ince
Lincoln's Gettysburg Address	1922	Ellery Paine
The Days of Buffalo Bill	1922	Joel Day
Barbara Freitchie	1924	George A. Billings
The Dramatic Life of Abraham Lincoln	1924	George A. Billings
(Mrs. Mary Lincoln)		Nell Craig
Abraham Lincoln	1924	George A. Billings
(at age 7)		Danny Hoy
The Iron Horse	1924	Charles E. Bull
The Man Without A Country	1925	George A. Billings
Hands Up	1926	George A. Billings
The Heart of Maryland	1927	Charles E. Bull
Lincoln's Gettysburg Address	1927	Rev. Lincoln Caswell
Court Martial	1928	Frank Austin
Two Americans	1929	Walter Huston
Lincoln's Gettysburg Address	1930	George A. Billings
Only the Brave	1930	Walter Huston
Abraham Lincoln	1930	Walter Huston

(Mrs. Mary Lincoln)			Kay Hammond
The Littlest Rebel	1935		Frank McGlynne
Roaring West	1935		Frank McGlynn
The Prisoner of Shark Island	1936		Frank McGlynn
(Mrs. Mary Lincoln)			Leila McIntyre
Hearts in Bondage	1936		Frank McGlynn
Cavalry	1936		Bud Buster
The Plainsman	1936		Frank McGlynn
(Mrs. Mary Lincoln)			Leila McIntyre
Western Gold	1937		Frank McGlynn
Wells Fargo	1937		Frank McGlynn
The Man Without A Country	1937		Frank McGlynn
Courage of the West	1937		Albert Russell
Victoria the Great	1937		Percy Parsons
The Lone Ranger	1937		Frank McGlynn
The Mad Empress	1939		Frank McGlynn
Lincoln in the White House	1939		Frank McGlynn
Of Human Hearts	1939		John Carradine
Young Mr. Lincoln	1939		Henry Fonda
(Mrs. Mary Lincoln)			Marjorie Weaver
Abe Lincoln in Illinois	1939		Raymond Massey
(Mrs. Mary Lincoln)			Ruth Gordon
Land of Liberty	1939		Frank McGlynn
Custer's Last Stand	1939		Frank McGlynn
Virginia City	1940		Victor Killain
Abraham Lincoln	1940		Raymond Massey
(Mrs. Mary Lincoln)			Ruth Gordon
Santa Fe Trail	1940		Charles Middleton
They Died With Their Boots On	1941		Charles Middleton
"Omnibus"	1950's	(TV)	Royal Dano
Rock Island Trail	1950		Jeff Corey
Transcontinent Express	1950		Jeff Corey
New Mexico	1951		Hans Conreid
The Tall Target	1951		Leslie Kimmell
Prince of Players	1955		Stanley Hall
(Mrs. Mary Lincoln)			Sarah Padden
Springfield Incident	1955		Tom Tyron
The Day Lincoln Was Shot	1956	(TV)	Raymond Massey
The Story of Mankind	1957		Austin Green
"Lincoln: The Young Years"	1959	(TV)	Royal Dano
"The Passerby" ("Twilight Zone" episode)	1961	(TV)	Austin Green
How The West Was Won	1962		Raymond Massey
"Abe Lincoln In Illinois"	1964	(TV)	Jason Robards
"Star Trek" (episode)	1967	(TV)	Lee Bergere

"The Great Man's Whiskers"	1971	(TV)	Dennis Weaver
Lincoln's Gettysburg Address	1973		Charlton Heston
"Sandburg's Lincoln"	1974	(TV)	Hal Holbrook
(Mrs. Mary Lincoln)			Sada Thompson
"The Case Against Mulligan"	1975	(TV)	Fred Stuthman
"The Rivalry"	1975	(TV)	Arthur Hill
The Last of Mrs. Lincoln	1976		
(Mrs. Mary Lincoln)			Julie Harris
(Robert Lincoln)			Michael Cristofer
(Tad Lincoln)			Robby Benson
The Faking of the President	1976		William Deprato
"The Adams Chronicles"	1976	(TV)	Stephen D. Newman
"Captains and the Kings"	1976	(TV)	Ford Rainey
The Lincoln Conspiracy	1977		John Anderson
Guardian of the Wilderness	1977		Ford Rainey
"The Blue and the Gray"	1982	(TV)	Gregory Peck
(Mrs. Mary Lincoln)			Janice Carroll
"Voyagers"(episode)	1983	(TV)	John Anderson
(Mrs. Mary Lincoln)			Rachel Bond
"Dream West"	1986	(TV)	F. Murray Abraham
"North and South, Book II"	1986	(TV)	Hal Holbrook

James Madison

The Buccaneer	1938		
(Mrs. Dolley Madison)			Spring Byington
Magnificent Doll	1946		Burgess Meredith
(Mrs. Dolley Madison)			Ginger Rogers
"George Washington II"	1986	(TV)	Guy Paul

William McKinley

Message to Garcia	1936		John Carradine
			(voice only)
This Is My Affair	1937		Frank Conroy
"Captains and the Kings"	1976	(TV)	Stephen Coit

James Monroe

The Man Without A Country	1925		Emmett King
"George Washington II"	1986	(TV)	Robert Kelly

Richard M. Nixon

Is There Sex After Death?	1971		Jim Dixon
"The Watergate Cover-up Trial"	1975	(PBS)	Harry Spillman
The Faking of the President	1976		Richard M. Dixon
"The Private Files of J. Edgar Hoover"	1977	(TV)	Richard M. Dixon
The Cayman Triangle	1977		Anderson Humphreys
"Tail Gunner Joe"	1977	(TV)	Richard M. Dixon

Born Again	1978		Harry Spillman
"Blind Ambition"	1979	(TV)	Rip Torn
(Mrs. Pat Nixon)			Cathleen Cordell
Hopscotch	1980		Richard M. Dixon
Where The Buffalo Roam	1980		Brian Cummings
			(voice only)
"Concealed Enemies"	1984	(PBS)	Peter Riegert
Secret Honor	1984		Philip Baker Hall

Franklin Pierce

The Great Moment	1944		Porter Hall

James K. Polk

Can't Help Singing	1944		Edward Earle
The Oregon Trail	1959		Addison Richards
"Dream West"	1986	(TV)	Noble Willingham

Ronald W. Reagan

"Rapmaster Ronnie"	1984	(MTV)	Bob Schmidt
"Saturday Night Live"	1986	(TV)	Randy Quaid
(Mrs. Nancy Reagan)			Terry Sweeney
"Spies Like Us"	1985	(MTV)	himself
"Humor and the Presidency"	1986	(HBO)	Jim Morris

Franklin D. Roosevelt

I'd Rather Be Rich		Play	George M. Cohan
Yankee Doodle Dandy	1942		Capt. Jack Young
This Is The Army	1943		Capt. Jack Young
The Beginning or the End	1947		Sir Godfrey Tearle
Sunrise at Campobello	1960		Ralph Bellamy
(Mrs. Eleanor Roosevelt)			Greer Garson
The Pigeon That Took Rome	1962		Richard Nelson
First to Fight	1967		Stephen Roberts
"Eleanor and Franklin"	1976	(TV)	Edward Herrmann
(Franklin at age 16)			Ted Eccles
(Mrs. Eleanor Roosevelt)			Jane Alexander
(Eleanor at age 14)			Mackenzie Phillips
MacArthur	1977		Dan O'Heriby
"Ring of Passion"	1977	(TV)	Stephen Roberts
"The Private Files of J. Edgar Hoover"	1978	(TV)	Howard DeSilva
"Ike"	1979	(TV)	Stephen Roberts
"Backstairs at the White House"	1979	(TV)	John Anderson
(Mrs. Eleanor Roosevelt)			Eileen Heckert
"The Long Days of Summer"	1980	(TV)	Stephen Roberts
"FDR: The Last Year"	1981	(TV)	Jason Robards
"Churchill and the Generals"	1981	(TV)	Arthur Hill

Annie	1982		Edward Herrmann
(Mrs. Eleanor Roosevelt)			Lois de Banzie
"The Winds of War"	1983	(TV)	Ralph Bellamy
"Voyagers" (Episode)	1983	(TV)	Nicholas Pryor
"Murrow"	1986	(TV)	Robert Vaughn
"Crossings"	1986	(TV)	Jack Denton
"Hoover"	1986	(TV)	David Ogden Stiers

Theodore Roosevelt

Womanhood, the Glory of a Nation	1917		Himself
General Pershing	1919		W.E. Whittle
Sundown	1924		E.J. Radcliffe
Lights of Old Broadway	1925		Buck Black
The Rough Riders	1927		Frank Hopper
I Loved A Woman	1933		E.J. Radcliffe
This Is My Affair	1937		Sidney Blackmer
Yankee Doodle Dandy	1942		Wallis Clark
In Old Oklahoma	1943		Sidney Blackmer
Buffalo Bill	1944		Sidney Blackmer
I Wonder Who's Kissing Her Now	1947		John Morton
My Girl Tisa	1948		Sidney Blackmer
Take Me Out to the Ballgame	1949		Edward Cassidy
Fancy Pants	1950		John Alexander
The First Traveling Saleslady	1956		Edward Cassidy
Brighty of the Grand Canyon	1960		Karl Swenson
"Profiles In Courage"	1965	(TV)	Whit Bissell
The Wind and the Lion	1975		Brian Keith
"Eleanor and Franklin"	1976	(TV)	William Phipps
"Captains and the Kings"	1976	(TV)	Lee Jones De Broux
"Eleanor and Franklin: The White House Years"	1977	(TV)	David Healy
Bully	1978		James Whitmore
"Wild and Wooly"	1978	(TV)	David Doyle
Ragtime	1981		Robert Boyd
"Voyagers"(episode)	1982	(TV)	Gregg Henry
The Indomitable Teddy Roosevelt	1985		Bob Boyd
(as a child)			Harold Mark Kingsley
(Mrs. Edith Roosevelt)			Philippa Roosevelt

William Howard Taft

"The Winds of Kitty Hawk"	1978	(TV)	Ross Durfee
"Backstairs at the White House"	1979	(TV)	Victor Buono
(Mrs. Helen "Nellie" Taft)			Julie Harris

Zachary Taylor

The Yankee Clipper	1927		Harry Holden

Distant Drums	1951		Robert Barrat
Seminole	1953		Fay Roope

Harry S. Truman

The Beginning of the End	1946		Art Baker
"Portrait: The Man from Independence"	1974	(TV)	Robert Vaughn
Give 'Em Hell Harry	1976		James Whitmore
Collision Course	1976		E.G. Marshall
"Truman at Potsdam" (Hallmark Hall of Fame)	1976	(TV)	Ed Flanders
MacArthur	1977		Ed Flanders
"Tail Gunner Joe"	1977	(TV)	Robert Symonds
"Harry S. Truman: Plain Speaking"	1977	(TV)	Ed Flanders
"Backstairs at the White House" (Mrs. Bess Truman)	1979	(TV)	Harry Morgan Estelle Parsons
"Enola Gay"	1980	(TV)	Ed Nelson
"Eleanor, First Lady of the World"	1982	(TV)	Richard McKenzie

Martin Van Buren

The Gorgeous Hussy	1932		Charles Trowbridge

George Washington

A Heroine of '76	1911		Phillips Smalley
Molly, the Drummer Boy	1914		Charles Ogle
The Battlecry of Peace	1915		Joseph Kilgour
Betsy Ross	1917		Frank Mayo
The Spirit of '76	1917		Noah Beery
America	1924		Arthur Dewey
Janice Meredith	1924		Joseph Kilgour
The Flag	1927		Francis X. Bushman
The Winners of the Wilderness	1927		Edward Hern
Alexander Hamilton	1931		Alan Mowbray
The Phantom President	1931		Alan Mowbray
The Howards of Virginia	1940		George Houston
Remarkable Andrew	1942		Montague Love
Where Do We Go From Here?	1945		Alan Mowbray
Monsieur Beaucaire	1946		Douglass Dumbrille
The Time of Their Lives	1946		Robert Barrat
Unconquered	1947		Richard Gaines
John Paul Jones	1959		John Crawford
"Our American Heritage"	1960	(TV)	Howard St. John
Lafayette	1962		Howard St. John
"From Sea to Shining Sea" (episode)	1974	(TV)	Fritz Weaver
Washington - The Man	1975		Lorne Greene

"Valley Forge"	1975	(TV)	Richard Basehart
Independence	1976		Patrick O'Neal
"The Adams Chronicles"	1976	(TV)	David Brooks
"First Ladies' Diaries"	1976	(TV)	James Luisi
"The Rebels"	1979	(TV)	Peter Graves
"George Washington"	1984	(TV)	Barry Bostwick
(Mrs. Martha Washington)			Patty Duke Astin
Revolution	1985		Frank Windsor
"George Washington, Part II"	1986	(TV)	Barry Bostwick
(Mrs. Martha Washington)			Patty Duke

Woodrow Wilson

The Battle Cry of Peace	1915		Himself
Womanhood, the Glory of a Nation	1917		Himself
General Pershing	1919		R. A. Faulkner
Wilson	1944		Alexander Knox
(Mrs. Ellen Wilson)			Ruth Nelson
(Mrs. Edith Wilson)			Geraldine Fitzgerald
The Story of Will Rogers	1952		Earl Lee
The Unforgettable Year 1919	1952	(USSR)	L. Kovsakov
Oh! What A Lovely War	1969		Frank Forsyth
"First Ladies' Diaries"	1976	(TV)	Michael Kane
"Backstairs at the White House"	1979	(TV)	Robert Vaughn
(Mrs. Ellen Wilson)			Kim Hunter
(Mrs. Edith Wilson)			Claire Bloom
"You Are There—Ordeal of a President"	Episode (TV)		G. Wood

Fictional Presidents

Gabriel Over the White House	1933	The President	Walter Huston
The President Vanishes	1934	The President	Arthur Byron
Grand Old Guard	1935	The President	Gavin Gordon
Joe and Ethel Turp Call on the President	1940	The President	Lewis Stone
Yankee Doodle Dandy	1942	voice only	Paul Frees
Princess O'Rourke	1943	The President	F. D. Roosevelt*
The Long Gray Line	1955	voice only	Paul Frees
A Man Called Peter	1955	The President	William Forrest
The Absent-Minded Professor	1961	Rufus Daggett	Leon Ames

Advise and Consent	1962	The President	Franchot Tone
Son of Flubber	1963	Rufus Daggett	Leon Ames
"I Dream of Genie"("Twilight Zone" episode)	1963	George P. Hanley	Howard Morse
Dr. Strangelove	1964	Merklin Muffley	Peter Sellers
Fail Safe	1964	The President	Henry Fonda
Kisses For My President	1964	Leslie McCloud	Polly Bergen
Of Thee I Sing	play	John Wintergreen	William Gaxton
Let Them Eat Cake	play	Alexander Throttlebottom	Victor Moore
Seven Days In May	1964	Jordan Lyman	Frederic March
You Only Live Twice	1967	The President	Alexander Knox
In Like Flint	1967	The President	Andrew Duggan
The Virgin President	1968	Fillard Millmore future 43rd pres.	Severn Darden
Wild In the Streets	1968	Max Frost	Chris Jones
The Monitors	1969	The President	Ed Begley
Colussus: The Forbin Project	1970	The President	Gordon Pinsent
Escape From the Planet of the Apes	1971	The President	William Windsor
City Beneath the Sea	1971	The President	Richard Basehart
Vanished	1971	Paul Roudebush	Richard Widmark
The Man	1972	Douglas Dilman	James Earl Jones
Black Jack	1973	The President	James Daly
Hail to the Chief	1973	The President	Dan Resin
The President's Plane Is Missing	1973	Jeremy Haines	Tod Andrews
Werewolf in Washington	1973	The President	Biff MCGuire
The Pink Panther Strikes Again	1976	The President	Dick Crockett
Twilight's Last Gleaming	1977	David T. Stevens	Charles Durning
Winter Kills	1977	The President	Jack Warner
Washington Behind			

*Cameo role.

Closed Doors	1977	Richard Monckton	Jason Robards
The Greek Tycoon	1978	James Cassidy	James Franciscus
Superman I	1978	The President	E.G. Marshall
Grandpa Goes To			
Washington	1978	The President	Richard Eastham
A Fire in the Sky	1978	The President	Andrew Duggan
*Americathon**	1979	Chet Roosevelt	John Ritter
Meteor	1979	The President	Henry Fonda
First Family	1980	Manfred Link	Bob Newhart
(the alcoholic			
First Lady)		Mrs. Link	Madeline Kahn
(the nymphomanic			
First Daughter)		Gloria Link	Gilda Radner
"Scout's Honor"	1980 (TV)	The President	Peter Hobbs
The Man Who Saw			
Tomorrow	1980	The President	Ross Evans
The Kidnapping of			
the President	1980	Adam Scott	Hal Holbrook
Escape From New			
York	1981	The President	Donald Pleasance
Superman II	1981	The President	E.G. Marshall
World War III	1982	Gerald Brown	Rock Hudson
The Crisis Game	1983	The President	Edmund S. Muskie
Dead Zone	1983	The President	Martin Sheen†
Dreamscape	1984	The President	Eddie Albert
"America Under			
Siege"	1986 (TV)	Maxwell Monroe	Hal Holbrook

Vice-Presidents (Fictional):

Of Thee I Sing	1931	Alexander Throttlebottom	Victor Moore
Advise and Consent	1962	The Vice President	Lew Ayres
The Man	1972	The Vice President	Lew Ayres
The President's Plane			
Is Missing	1973	Kermit Madigan	Buddy Ebsen
Billy Jack Goes to			
Washington	1978	The Vice President	Pat O'Brien
The Kidnapping of the			
President	1980	Ethan Richards	Van Johnson
Protocol	1985	The Vice President	Richard Mereck

*Presidential grandson David Eisenhower had a cameo role.
†He was a future president as seen in a premonition but it never came to pass.

Similarities between Presidents Theodore and Franklin D. Roosevelt

1. Distant cousins.
2. Both had eight letters in their first names.
3. Both were of Dutch descent.
4. Both were from New York.
5. The fathers of both presidents died while they were in their teens.
6. Both suffered from physical handicaps: Theodore had asthma and Franklin had polio.
7. Both wore glasses; Theodore was blind in the left eye.
8. Both were graduated from Harvard.
9. Both attended Columbia Law School.
10. Both were elected to Phi Beta Kappa: Theodore as an undergraduate and Franklin as an alumni.
11. Both were married while in their twenties.
12. Both had six children.
13. Both served in the New York state assembly.
14. Both served as governor of New York.
15. Both served as assistant secretary of the navy.
16. Both were Masons.
17. Both had books published in their lifetimes.
18. Both ran for vice-president.
19. Both were nominated for national office in Chicago.
20. Both defeated presidential opponents from the same state.
21. Both exercised pocket vetoes.
22. Both were shot at by maniacs.
23. Both died suddenly.
24. Both died in their sixties.
25. Both were buried in New York.
26. Both were survived by their wives.
27. The wives of both presidents lived more than 75 years.
28. The wives of both presidents died in New York.

THE
PRESIDENTIAL
CURSE

It's been called the Indian Curse. It's been called the Zero Year Mystery. It's been called the 20-Year Jinx. It's been called a Presidential Mystery. No matter what it is called, this phenomenon has been fatal for seven American presidents. Every president elected in a "0" year, since 1840, has died in office—in an odd year.

The most popular story of the legend attributes the death cycle to an Indian curse made during the War of 1812. Tenskawatawa, also known as Elskwatawa, Lalawethika, or The Prophet, was a Shawnee medicine man who with his brother Tecumseh led the British and Indian troops against the Americans during part of the war. Tecumseh was killed on October 5, 1813, in the Battle of the Thames, supposedly by Richard Mentor Johnson, who later served as vice-president under Martin Van Buren, but there appears to be no truth to this story. Reportedly, the Prophet was so distraught at his brother's death that he cursed the commander of the United States forces and "all who follow him."

Twenty seven years later, the commander of the forces was now Pres. William Henry Harrison. When he died of pneumonia 31 days after ascending to the presidency in 1841, the curse was remembered and the legend was born. For 140 years the curse has held, alternating between elected and reelected presidents:

1840	William Henry Harrison	Died 1841 of Pneumonia	Elected
1860	Abraham Lincoln	Died 1865 of Assassination	Reelected
1880	James A. Garfield	Died 1881 of Assassination	Elected
1900	William McKinley	Died 1901 of Assassination	Reelected
1920	Warren G. Harding	Died 1923 of Cerebral Hemmorhage	Elected
1940	Franklin D. Roosevelt	Died 1945 of Cerebral Hemmorhage	Reelected
1960	John F. Kennedy	Died 1963 of Assassination	Elected
1980	Ronald W. Reagan	?	Reelected

In addition to the deaths and alternating election patterns, there are many other similarities that seem to defy just mere coincidence, including:

- All seven were born east of the Mississippi River.
- Three (Lincoln, Harding, Kennedy) had seven letters in their last names.
- Three (Harrison, Garfield, McKinley) had eight letters in their last names.
- Roosevelt had nine letters in his last name.
- Four (Lincoln, Garfield, McKinley, Kennedy) died by assassination.
  Two (Harding, Roosevelt) died of cerebral hemorrhage.
  Harrison died of pneumonia.
- Two were born in January (McKinley and Roosevelt).
  Two were born in February (Harrison and Lincoln, and also Reagan).
  Two were born in November (Garfield and Harding).
  Kennedy was born in May.
- Of the two born in January, one died of assassination (McKinley) and one of illness (Roosevelt).
  Of the two born in February, one died of assassination (Lincoln) and one of illness (Harrison).
  Of the two born in November, one died of assassination (Garfield) and one of illness (Harding).
- By birth, two were the first born child (Harding and Roosevelt).
  Two were the second child (Lincoln and Kennedy, as is Reagan).
  Two were the seventh child (Harrison and McKinley).
  Garfield was the fifth child.
- By length of office, two served less than six months (Harrison and Garfield).
  Two served more than two years, but less than three years (Harding and Kennedy).
  Two served one full term, but less than one year of their second term (McKinley and Lincoln).
  Roosevelt served three full terms and less than one year of his fourth term.
- The astrological conjuncture of Jupiter-Saturn appeared in the sky at some time during the "0" year.

Will the incumbent president become the next victim? He has had two very close calls.

On March 30, 1981, Ronald Reagan was wounded in an unsuccessful assassination attempt. The bullet entered near the heart and lungs, causing him to lose over four pints of blood; Reagan's heart rhythm had to be reestablished by electronic means. True believers in the curse say it was right that Reagan did not die at that time.

In the election of 1984, Ronald Reagan was overwhelmingly reelected to a second term in office. On July 13, 1985, President Reagan was operated on for colon cancer. In an unprecedented move, he authorized Vice-president George Bush to serve as "Acting President" during the time he was under anesthesia.

President Reagan has already broken part of the curse. Of the three reelected presidents, Lincoln, McKinley and Roosevelt, all three died in the first year of their reelected term. Ronald Reagan has already survived into 1988, although some could argue that since he authorized Vice-president George Bush to serve as "Acting President" on July 13, 1985, he fulfilled the curse.

True believers in the curse envision two possible conclusions to the Ronald Reagan presidency. He will serve his term and break the pattern or he will die in 1987 and continue the curse.

We'll just have to wait and see what happens.

Similarities between Presidents James A. Garfield and William McKinley

1. Both were from Ohio.
2. Both had eight letters in their last names.
3. Both were of English descent.
4. Both had siblings who died in infancy.
5. Both taught school.
6. Both were lawyers.
7. Both were married in Ohio.
8. The firstborn child of each president was a girl.
9. Both had two children who died in infancy.
10. Both served in the Civil War.
11. Both were decorated for bravery.
12. Both were Masons.
13. Both were Republicans.
14. Both served as congressmen from Ohio.
15. Both served as senators from Ohio.
16. Both served as members of the Senate Ways and Means Committee.
17. The mothers of both presidents attended their sons' inauguration.
18. Both were firm believers in Christ.
19. Both were shot twice, at close range, and only one hit was fatal.
20. Both locations of the fatal bullet were mysteries to the doctors.
21. Both probably died of inept medical care.
22. Both died in September.
23. Both died in office.
24. Garfield lived 80 days after being shot; McKinley lived 8 days.
25. The wives of both presidents were with them when they died.
26. Both died away from the White House
27. Both were succeeded by vice-presidents from the state of New York.
28. Both were buried in Ohio.
29. Both were survived by their wives.

Similarities between Presidents Abraham Lincoln and John Kennedy

Life:

1. Both presidents had seven letters in their last names.
2. Both were over six feet tall.
3. Both were athletic men.
4. Both enjoyed sitting in rocking chairs.
5. Both were known for their quick wit.
6. Both liked to quote the Bible.
7. Both liked to quote Shakespeare.
8. Both could express themselves well. Kennedy won the Pulitzer Prize, and many of Lincoln's works are considered classics.
9. Both seemed to have lazy eye muscles which would sometimes cause one to deviate.
10. Both suffered from genetic diseases. It is suspected that Lincoln had Marfan's disease and Kennedy suffered from Addison's disease.
11. Both served in the military. Lincoln was a scout captain in the Black Hawk War and Kennedy served as a naval lieutenant in World War II.
12. Both were boat captains. Lincoln was skipper of the *Talisman*, a Mississippi River boat, and Kennedy was skipper of PT 109.
13. Neither president was known to carry money and constantly borrowed funds from friends.
14. Both had no fear of their mortality and disdained bodyguards.
15. Both often stated how easy it would be to shoot a president.
16. Both received many letters threatening their lives. In the year of his death, Lincoln received over 80 letters. In the year of his death, Kennedy received over 800 letters.

Death:

17. Both presidents were shot in the head.
18. Both were shot on a Friday.
19. In each case, that Friday was one before a holiday. Lincoln was shot on Good Friday and Kennedy was shot on the Friday before Thanksgiving.
20. Both were seated beside their wives when shot.
21. Neither Mrs. Lincoln nor Mrs. Kennedy were injured.
22. Both wives held the bullet-torn heads of their husbands.
23. Both presidents were in the company of another couple when shot.
24. In each case, the man was injured but not fatally. Major Rathbone was slashed by a knife and Governor Connolly was shot.
25. Lincoln was shot at Ford's Theatre. Kennedy was shot in a Ford product, a Lincoln limousine.
26. Lincoln sat in Box 7 at Ford's Theatre. Kennedy rode in car 7 in the Dallas motorcade.
27. Both presidents received the best medical attention available.

28. Both received closed chest massage.
29. Both presidents died in a place with the initials P and H. Lincoln died in the Peterson House and Kennedy died in Parkland Hospital.
30. The wives of both presidents were with them when they died.
31. Autopsies were performed on both presidents.
32. Both autopsies were performed by military personnel.
33. Both Lincoln and Kennedy were buried in mahogany caskets.
34. The bodies of both presidents rested on the same catafalque and caisson.
35. Mrs. Kennedy insisted that her husband's funeral mirror Lincoln's as closely as possible.

The Assassins:
36. Both assassins had three names: John Wilkes Booth and Lee Harvey Oswald.
37. There are 15 letters in each assassin's name.
38. Both assassins struck when in their mid-twenties. Booth was born in 1838 and Oswald was born in 1939.
39. Each assassin lacked a strong father figure in his life. Booth's father died when he was 13 years old and Oswald's died before he was born.
40. Each assassin had two brothers whose careers he coveted. Booth's two brothers were more successful actors and Oswald envied his brothers' military lives.
41. Both assassins were privates in the military. Booth was a private in Virginia militia and Oswald was a private in the Marine Corps.
42. Both assassins were born in the South.
43. Both assassins were known sympathizers to enemies of the United States. Booth supported the Confederacy and Oswald was a Marxist.
44. Both assassins were fond of writing down their thoughts; Booth kept a diary and Oswald kept a journal.
45. Both assassins often used aliases. Booth frequently used "J. Wilkes" and Oswald used the name "Alek J. Hidell."
46. Both assassins knew of their victims' whereabouts by reading of it in the newspapers.
47. Both assassins planned their deed well.
48. Booth shot Lincoln at a theatre and was cornered in a warehouse. Oswald shot Kennedy from a warehouse and was cornered in a theatre.
49. The handyman, bill distributor, and part-time concession operator at Ford's Theatre was Joseph "Peanuts John" Burroughs. The concession stand operator at the Texas Theatre was Butch Burroughs.
50. Booth was aided in his escape from Washington by Oswald (Oswell) Swan and Lewis Paine (also known as Payne). Oswald got his job at the Schoolbook Depository through the aid of Mrs. Ruth Paine, his landlady.
51. Each assassin was detained by an officer named Baker. Lt. Luther B.

Baker was the leader of the cavalry patrol which trapped Booth at Garrett's barn. Officer Marion L. Baker, a Dallas motorcycle patrolman, briefly detained Oswald on the second floor of the School Depository until he learned that he worked there.

52. Both assassins envisioned their deeds as a way to glory and fame.
53. Both assassins received their fame posthumously since they were shot down before they achieved it.
54. Both assassins were killed with a single shot from a Colt revolver.
55. Both assassins were shot in a blaze of light—Booth after the barn was set afire and Oswald in front of television cameras.
56. Both assassins were shot before their version of the presidential assassination could be learned.
57. Both assassins were shot by religious men; Booth was killed by Boston Corbett and Oswald was killed by Jack Ruby.
58. Both of these assassins had changed their names. Corbett's real first name was Thomas and Ruby changed his from Jacob Rubenstein.
59. Both Corbett and Ruby were known as unstable men prone to violence.

Family and Friends:
60. Both presidents were named for their grandfathers.
61. Both were born second children.
62. Before each was elected to the presidency, each lost a sister to death.
63. Both married while in their thirties.
64. Both married dark-haired, twenty-four-year-old women.
65. Each wife had been previously engaged to someone else.
66. Both wives were from socially prominent families.
67. Both wives were fluent in French.
68. Both wives were known for their high fashion in clothes.
69. Both wives were criticized by their husbands for spending money.
70. Both wives renovated the White House after many years of neglect.
71. Each couple had four children, two of whom died before becoming a teen.
72. Each couple lost a son while in the White House.
73. Both the Lincoln and Kennedy children rode ponies on the White House lawn.
74. Lincoln had sons named Robert and Edward. Kennedy had brothers named Robert and Edward.
75. Both presidents were related to U.S. Senators. Lincoln's cousin, General Isaac Barnard of Pennsylvania, was first elected in 1827. Kennedy's brother Edward was first elected in 1962 from Massachusetts and brother Robert was elected from New York in 1964.
76. Shortly after his father was assassinated, Robert T. Lincoln (with mother and brother) moved to a home located at 3014 N Street, N.W., in Georgetown. Shortly after his father was assassinated, John

F. Kennedy, Jr. (with mother and sister), moved to a home located at 3017 N Street, N.W., in Georgetown.

77. Both presidents were related to Democratic U.S. attorney generals who graduated from Harvard University: Levi Lincoln, Sr. (Jefferson) and Robert F. Kennedy (Kennedy).

78. Both presidents were related to ambassadors to the Court of St. James's (Great Britain): Robert T. Lincoln (B. Harrison) and Joseph P. Kennedy, Sr. (F. Roosevelt).

79. Both presidents were friends with Illinois Democrats named Adlai E. Stevenson; Lincoln's friend would become Grover Cleveland's vice president and Kennedy's friend would twice be the Democratic presidential nominee.

80. Both knew a Doctor Charles Taft. Lincoln was treated by Dr. Charles Sabin Taft, M.D., who was the half-brother of son Tad's playmates and chief surgeon at the Judiciary Square Hospital. Kennedy knew Dr. Charles Phelps Taft, LLD, who was mayor of Cincinnati (Ohio) and son of President William Howard Taft.

81. Both presidents had friends and advisors named Billy Graham. Lincoln's friend was William Mentor Graham, a New Salem (Illinois) schoolteacher, and Kennedy knew the evangelist, Rev. Billy Graham.

82. Kennedy had a secretary named Evelyn Lincoln (whose husband Harold's nickname was Abe); she warned him not to go to Dallas. Legend says Lincoln had a secretary named John Kennedy who told him not to go to the theatre, although no actual record of this person can be found.

Politics:

83. Both presidents were first elected to the U.S. House of Representatives in '46.

84. Both were runners-up for their party's nomination for vice-president in '56.

85. Both were elected to the presidency in '60.

86. Both had the legality of their elections contested.

87. Both were involved in political debates. The Lincoln-Douglas debates were in 1858 and the Kennedy-Nixon debates in 1960.

88. Both were concerned with the problems of American blacks and made their views known in '63. Lincoln told of his in the Emancipation Proclamation and Kennedy in his report to Congress on Civil Rights.

89. In 1964, William O. Douglas and Harry Goldin published books entitled *Mr. Lincoln and the Negroes* and *Mr. Kennedy and the Negroes*.

Vice-Presidents:

90. Both Lincoln and Kennedy were succeeded by Southern Democrats named Johnson.

91. Andrew Johnson was born in 1808; Lyndon Johnson was born in 1908.

92. There are six letters in each Johnson's first name.

93. Both Johnsons were large men.
94. Both Johnsons were the fathers of two daughters.
95. Both Johnsons served in the military. Andrew was a brigadier general in the Civil War and Lyndon was a commander in the navy during World War II.
96. Both Johnsons were former southern senators.
97. Both Johnsons entered the presidency in their mid-fifties.
98. Both Johnsons had urethral stones, the only presidents to have them.
99. Both Johnsons faced reelection opponents whose names began with G; Andrew Johnson could have run against Ulysses S. Grant and Lyndon Johnson faced Barry Goldwater in the election of 1964.
100. Both Johnsons chose not to run for reelection in '68.

Conspiracies:
101. Investigations for conspiracy were conducted for both presidential assassinations.
102. Autopsies were done on both assassins to clarify identity.
103. Formal investigations were conducted after each presidential death.
104. In each case, after a number of years, the investigation was reopened without really resolving who was involved in the assassination.

PRESIDENTIAL
ELECTION
RETURNS
1789-1984

The Constitution of the United States of America provides that the president and vice-president shall be elected by presidential electors who are chosen in a manner prescribed by individual state legislatures (Article II, Section 1). The number of electors is equal to the whole number of senators and representatives to which the state may be entitled in the Congress. Some states choose their electors by popular vote, while in others they are chosen directly by the legislature.

The names of electors are identified with specific party affiliation and are designated by political groups. They are, morally, committed to vote for the candidate endorsed by their party. The honor to serve as an elector is available to all citizens except those excluded by the Constitution: senators, representatives and other persons "holding an office of Trust or Profit under the United States."

Prior to 1804, no disctinction was made between the candidates for president and vice-president. The candidate who received the greatest number of electoral votes became president and the next highest recipient became vice-president. In 1796, this resulted in the election of a Federalist president (John Adams) and a Democratic-Republican vice-president (Thomas Jefferson). To prevent this from happening in the future, the 12th Amendment to the Constitution was passed in 1804. It required that the presidential and vice-presidential candidates be listed on separate ballots. The 12th Amendment also provided that the candidates should not be inhabitants of the same state.

On February 27, 1951, the 22nd Amendment to the Constitution was passed and dictated that no person shall be elected to the office of president of the United States more than twice. In the case of someone succeeding to the office on the death of a president, if there were less than two years to go in the original term, that person could be reelected twice. If there were more than two years left in the original term, that person could only be elected once.

There were no conventions, platforms or nominations in the elections of 1789, 1792, and 1796. During the election of 1800, the practice of nominating candidates in Congressional caucuses began. These caucuses were usually held in secret. In September 1812, the Federalists held a convention in New York at which they nominated candidates. However, no platform was formulated.

The practice of nominating candidates by state legislatures instead of Congressional caucuses began in 1828. Opponents of the caucus system argued that it defeated the purpose of the Constitution. When the election was held in November, only South Carolina chose her electors by legislative ballot. The other 23 states did so by popular vote.

The first nominating convention was held in 1830 by the Anti-Masonic party in Philadelphia. However, they did not nominate a presidential candidate until 1831 at their second convention. In 1831, the first convention that featured national nominating was held in Baltimore by the National Republican Party which nominated Henry Clay of Kentucky. By 1832, both the major parties, the National Republicans and the Democrats, were holding their own nominating conventions. The Democrats adopted the two-thirds majority rule at their convention.

Originally, there was no uniform date for national elections. Each state could affix its own date, but the election was required to be held at least 34 days before the first Wednesday in December, which was the day presidential electors met (1 Stat. L. 239). In 1887, the meeting day of electors was changed to the second Wednesday in February (24 Stat. L. 373). The Act of 1934 (48 Stat. L. 879) fixed the date as the sixth of January, at which time the votes are counted in the presence of both houses of Congress. In most states, the electors meet on the first Monday after the second Wednesday in December at their capitals to formally place their votes.

The Act of 1845 (5 Stat. L. 721) set the first Tuesday after the first Monday in November as Election Day. Congress has approved a measure in 1986 that will call for all polls to close at the same time (9:00 E.S.T.) across the country in 1988 so that no candidate will be declared a winner before the polls close on the west coasts.

Three other Constitutional Amendments which affect presidential voting are the 20th, 23rd and the 26th. The "Lame Duck" or 20th Amendment to the Constitution was passed on March 4, 1932; it provided that "the terms of the president and vice-president shall end at noon of the 20th day of January." It was ratified on January 23, 1933, and took effect on October 15, 1933. Franklin Roosevelt became the first president to take the oath on January 20th in 1937. The 23rd, passed on April 3, 1961, granted the right to vote in presidential elections to residents of the District of Columbia. The 26th Amendment, enacted on June 20, 1971, extended the right to vote to all American citizens eighteen years or older.

POPULAR AND ELECTORAL VOTE
FOR PRESIDENT FOR MAJOR PARTIES

The elected president is listed first for each year below. (F) Federalist; (D) Democrat; (R) Republican; (DR) Democrat Republican; (NR) National Republican; (W) Whig; (P) Progressive; (SR) States' Rights; (LR) Liberal Republican; Asterisk (*)—See notes.

Year	Candidate	Popular	Elec.*
1789	George Washington (F)	Unknown	69
	No opposition	—	—
1792	George Washington (F)	Unknown	132
	No opposition	—	—
1796	John Adams (F)	Unknown	71
	Thomas Jefferson (DR)	Unknown	68
1800*	Thomas Jefferson (DR)	Unknown	73
	Aaron Burr (DR)	Unknown	73
1804	Thomas Jefferson (DR)	Unknown	162
	Charles Pinckney (F)	Unknown	14
1808	James Madison (DR)	Unknown	122
	Charles Pinckney (F)	Unknown	47
1812	James Monroe (DR)	Unknown	128
	DeWitt Clinton (F)	Unknown	89
1816	James Monroe (DR)	Unknown	183
	Rufus King (F)	Unknown	34
1820	James Monroe (DR)	Unknown	231
	John Quincy Adams (DR)	Unknown	1
1824*	John Quincy Adams (DR)	105,321	84
	Andrew Jackson (DR)	155,872	99
	Henry Clay (DR)	46,587	37
	William H. Crawford (DR)	44,282	41
1828	Andrew Jackson (D)	647,231	178
	John Quincy Adams (NR)	509,097	83
1832	Andrew Jackson (D)	687,502	219
	Henry Clay (NR)	530,189	49
1836	Martin Van Buren (D)	762,678	170
	William H. Harrison (W)	548,007	73
1840	William H. Harrison (W)	1,275,017	234
	Martin Van Buren (D)	1,128,702	60
1844	James K. Polk (D)	1,337,243	170

1800—Elected by House of Representatives because of tied electoral vote.
1824—Elected by House of Representative. No candidate polled a majority. In 1824, the Democrat Republicans had become a loose coalition of competing political groups. By 1828, the supporters of Jackson were known as Democrats, and the J.Q. Adams and Henry Clay supporters as National Republicans.

Year	Candidate	Popular	Elec.*
	Henry Clay (W)	1,299,068	105
1848	Zachary Taylor (W)	1,360,101	163
	Lewis Cass (D)	1,220,544	127
1852	Franklin Pierce (D)	1,601,474	254
	Winfield Scott (W)	1,386,578	42
1856	James C. Buchanan (D)	1,927,995	174
	John C. Fremont (R)	1,391,555	114
1860	Abraham Lincoln (R)	1,866,352	180
	Stephen A. Douglas (D)	1,375,157	12
	John C. Breckinridge (D)	845,763	72
	John Bell (Const. Union)	589,581	39
1864	Abraham Lincoln (R)	2,216,067	212
	George McClellan (D)	1,808,725	21
1868	Ulysses G. Grant (R)	3,015,071	214
	Horatio Seymour (D)	2,709,615	80
1872*	Ulysses S. Grant (R)	3,597,070	286
	Horace Greeley (D-LR)	2,834,079	—
1876*	Rutherford B. Hayes (R)	4,033,950	185
	Samuel J. Tilden (D)	4,284,757	184
1880	James A. Garfield (R)	4,449,053	214
	Winfield S. Hancock (D)	4,442,030	155
1884	Grover Cleveland (D)	4,911,017	219
	James G. Blaine (R)	4,848,334	182
1888*	Benjamin Harrison (R)	5,444,337	233
	Grover Cleveland (D)	5,540,050	168
1892	Grover Cleveland (D)	5,554,414	277
	Benjamin Harrison (R)	5,190,802	145
	James Weaver (P)	1,027,329	22
1896	William McKinley (R)	7,035,638	271
	William J. Bryan (D-P)	6,467,946	176
1900	William McKinley (R)	7,219,530	292
	William J. Bryan (D)	6,358,071	155
1904	Theodore Roosevelt (R)	7,628,834	336
	Alton B. Parker (D)	5,084,491	140
1908	William H. Taft (R)	7,679,006	321
	William J. Bryan (D)	6,409,106	162

1872—Greeley died Nov. 29, 1872. His electoral votes were split among four individuals.
1876—Fla., La., Ore., and S.C. election returns were disputed. Congress in joint session (Mar. 2, 1877) declared Hayes and Wheeler elected president and vice-president.
1888—Cleveland had more votes than Harrison but the 233 electoral votes cast for Harrison against the 168 for Cleveland elected Harrison president.

Year	Candidate	Popular	Elec.*
1912	Woodrow Wilson (D)	6,286,214	435
	Theodore Roosevelt (PR)	4,216,020	88
	William H. Taft (R)	3,483,922	8
1916	Woodrow Wilson (D)	9,129,606	277
	Charles E. Hughes (R)	8,538,221	254
1920	Warren G. Harding (R)	16,152,200	404
	James M. Cox (D)	9,147,353	127
1924	Calvin Coolidge (R)	15,725,016	382
	John W. Davis (D)	8,385,586	136
	Robert M. La Follette (PR)	4,822,856	13
1928	Herbert Hoover (R)	21,392,190	444
	Alfred E. Smith (D)	15,016,443	87
1932	Franklin D. Roosevelt (D)	22,821,857	472
	Herbert Hoover (R)	15,761,841	59
	Norman Thomas (Socialist)	884,781	—
1936	Franklin D. Roosevelt (D)	27,751,597	523
	Alfred Landon (R)	16,679,583	8
1940	Franklin D. Roosevelt (D)	27,243,466	449
	Wendell Willkie (R)	22,304,75	82
1944	Franklin D. Roosevelt (D)	25,602,505	432
	Thomas E. Dewey (R)	22,006,278	99
1948	Harry S. Truman (D)	24,105,812	303
	Thomas E. Dewey (R)	21,970,065	189
	J. Strom Thurmond (SR)	1,169,021	39
	Henry A. Wallace (PR)	1,157,172	—
1952	Dwight D. Eisenhower (R)	33,936,252	442
	Adlai E. Stevenson (D)	27,314,992	89
1956*	Dwight D. Eisenhower (R)	35,585,316	457
	Adlai E. Stevenson (D)	26,031,322	73
1960*	John F. Kennedy (D)	34,227,096	303
	Richard M. Nixon (R)	34,108,546	219
1964	Lyndon B. Johnson (D)	43,126,506	486
	Barry M. Goldwater (R)	27,176,799	52
1968	Richard M. Nixon (R)	31,785,480	301
	Hubert H. Humphey (D)	31,275,166	191
	George C. Wallace (3d party)	9,906,473	46

1956—Democrats elected 74 electors but one from Alabama refused to vote for Stevenson.
1960—Sen. Harry F. Byrd (D-Va.) received 15 electoral votes.
1972—John Hospers of Cal. and Theodora Nathan of Ore. received one vote from an elector of Virginia.

Year	Candidate	Popular	Elec.*
1972*	Richard M. Nixon (R)	47,165,234	520
	George S. McGovern (D)	29,170,774	17
1976*	Jimmy Carter (D)	40,828,929	297
	Gerald R. Ford (R)	39,148,940	240
1980	Ronald Reagan (R)	43,899,248	489
	Jimmy Carter (D)	35,481,435	49
	John B. Anderson (independent)	5,719,437	—
1984	Ronald Reagan (R)	54,281,858	525
	Walter F. Mondale (D)	37,457,215	13

1976—Ronald Reagan of Cal. received one vote from an elector of Washington.

1976—Ronald Reagan of Cal. received one vote from an elector of Washington.

INDEX

NOTE ON USING THIS INDEX: Page references appear in regular and italic type. The italic numbers indicate pages on which illustrations are located.

202, 207, 209, 216, 248
Cass, Lewis, 246
Childless presidents, 200-201
Christmas trees in the White House, 201
Churchill, Winston, 142, 143, 153
Civil War, 73, 83
    presidents who were generals in, 201
Clark, James "Champ," 124
Clay, Henry, 56, 57, 245
Cleveland, Frances Folsom, 99, 101, 102
Cleveland, (Stephen) Grover, 99-103, *99,*
    100, 105, 201, 202, 203, 204, 205, 206,
    209, 210, 211, 216, 239, 246
Clinton, DeWitt, 245
Clinton, George, 27, 31
Colfax, Schuyler, 83
College, presidents who did not attend, 206
Congress, presidents before, 201
Constitutional Convention, 18, 31
Constitution of the U.S., 18, 31, 34
Continental Congress, 31
    First, 18, 22
    Second, 18, 22, 27
Coolidge, John Calvin, 129, 133-136, *133,*
    135, 191, 201, 202, 203, 204, 206, 207,
    216, 247
Coolidge, Grace Anna Goodhue, 133
Cox, James M., 129, 247
Crawford, William H., 245
Cuban missile crisis, 161
Currency, U.S., presidents on, 210
Curtis, Charles, 138
Cypress Grove, 59

D

Dallas, George Mifflin, 56
"Dark horse" presidents, 201
Davis, Jefferson, 50, 60
Davis, John W., 247
Dawes, Charles Gates, 134
Declaration of Independence, 22, 27, 105
Dewey, Thomas, 151, 247
Divorced women, presidents who married,
    202
Douglas, Stephen A., 66, 73, 246
Dred Scott decision, 69

E

Edward VII of England, 70
Eisenhower, Dwight David, 152, 154-158,
    154, 156, 173, 178, 191, 199, 202, 205,
    206, 207, 209, 210, 212, 216, 247
Eisenhower, Mamie Geneva Doud, 154,
    156, 157, 158, 159
Election statistics, 204-205, 208, 245-248
Elms, The, 169
Emancipation Proclamation, 73, 74

F

Fairbanks, Charles Warren, 112
Female presidential candidates, 212
Fictional presidents portrayed in movies,
    226-228
Fictional vice-presidents portrayed in mov-
    ies, 228-229
Fillmore, Abigail, 62
Fillmore, Caroline, 62
Fillmore, Millard, 59, 60, 61-63, *61, 63,* 69,
    102, 202, 203, 206, 209, 210, 211
Football-playing presidents, 202
Ford, Elizabeth "Betty" Bloomer Warren,
    179, 181, 183, 202
Ford, Gerald Rudolph, Jr., 173, 176, 179-
    183, *179, 181,* 185, 199, 201, 202, 203,
    207, 209, 210, 212, 216-217, 248
Foreign countries, presidents who were
    ministers to, 204
Franklin, Benjamin, 22, 27
Fremont, John C., *63,* 69, 73, 246

G

Garfield, James Abram, 74, 91-94, *91, 93,*
    97, 98, 200, 201, 202, 203, 204, 205, 206,
    209, 210, 211, 217, 233, 234, 235, 246
Garfield, Lucretia Randolph, 91, 93
Garner, John Nance, 142
Generals, presidents who were, 202
Gerry, Elbridge, 31
Gettysburg, 157
Gettysburg Address, 73

PICTURE CREDITS

Pharos Books are available at special discounts on bulk purchases for sales promotions, premiums, fundraising or educational use. For details, contact the Special Sales Department, Pharos Books, 200 Park Avenue, New York, NY 10166.